Life In Our Villages

George Francis Millin, Special commissioner of the "Daily News."

LIFE IN OUR VILLAGES.

LIFE

IN

OUR VILLAGES.

BY

THE SPECIAL COMMISSIONER OF THE "DAILY NEWS."

BEING

A Series of Letters written to that Paper in the Autumn of 1891.

————— ❊ —————

CASSELL & COMPANY, LIMITED:

LONDON, PARIS & MELBOURNE.

1891.

T.

𝕿𝖔

THE RIGHT HON. W. E. GLADSTONE, M.P.,

TO WHOM THE AGRICULTURAL POPULATION

OF GREAT BRITAIN AND IRELAND

LOOK

WITH PROFOUND GRATITUDE AND CONFIDENT HOPE,

THESE LETTERS

ARE, BY PERMISSION,

MOST RESPECTFULLY DEDICATED BY

THE WRITER.

CONTENTS.

LIFE IN OUR VILLAGES.

———•◦•———

LETTER I.

THE STAMPEDE INTO THE TOWNS.

August 14.

BEYOND all dispute, the agricultural labourer is abandoning the land he was born on and is making his way into the towns. I have to-day driven and walked a good many miles through parts of the county of Essex, which have from time to time impressed me with a conviction that Hodge must not merely be going into the towns, but be actually gone. "Whom have you left then?" asked one Nonconformist minister of another who had for many years been the pastor of a village congregation that had dwindled and dwindled in the district I have been jogging through to-day. "Old people and fools," was the bitter reply. "You see very few young men about these parts nowadays," said the landlady of a little inn into which I turned for some bread and cheese to-day. "It's only the old folks as be left. As soon as the young 'uns be able to do for theirselves, they be off to better theirselves as they think. They go into the towns and get into the police or the army, or on the line. A good many go on the line." "You can't get men of any sort," said an Essex farmer. "I've done all I can to keep mine, and except the old men that I have had twenty or thirty years—and one of 'em I've had five-and-thirty years —I've got none. I began in the year forty-one, and I've brought up over forty lads to the farming, and they no sooner get to be eighteen, or from that to five-and-twenty,

than they're off. You can't keep them." "And your land no
doubt is suffering for want of labour?" "Of course it is.
It isn't producing half what it might. How can it? Why,
things are choked up with squitch and thistles, and I can't
clear them."

Yes, there is no doubt that Hodge is giving up farming
in these parts, but if you think you are going to get Hodge
himself to tell you why, you will very likely be greatly
mistaken. While to-day sitting over my bread and cheese
at the cross-legged table within the settee of the brick-floored
little public-house, a little old patriarch came in for his
mid-day glass of beer to drink with his bread and bacon.
He peeped, I thought, bashfully round the screen, and seeing
a stranger within, squatted down upon the seat outside close
to the door. "You needn't be afraid to come in, my lad," I
said, wishing to have a little chat with the old man. Perhaps
there was just a touch of the patronising in my tone. If there
was, my priggishness was promptly rebuked. "Oh, I ain't
afeerd o' you, mate," said the old man. "No, no, of course
not." "It ain't the fust time I ha' set 'ere." "No, I expect
not." "Nor you ain't the fust man I ha' seen with a good
coat on his back." Clearly, the old man was troubled
with no bashfulness at the presence of a stranger, and I
went on trying as cunningly as I could to inveigle him
into some little self-revelation; but it was a total failure.
He parried all my questions, assumed an air of the blankest
ignorance on matters with which he must have been per-
fectly familiar, and steadfastly refused to be pumped. But
when presently the landlady joined in with the observations
I have just recorded, he put in, I thought, very acutely.
" You see, sir," said the landlady, " if they settle on the land
they just make a living, and I think as, on the whole, they
be more happy and contented than a good many 'd think
for; but you see there's nothing afore 'em. They never get
on. They don't get no higher wages. They get just enough

to keep 'em ; but since prices ha' gone down so, the farmers can't afford to give 'em more." "What prices ha' gone down ?" demanded the old man. "Why, corn." "Well," was the retort, " and ain't the price o' stock gone up ? Don't a bullock fetch twice as much as it used to since I can remember ? And don't a calf fetch twice as much, and ain't the price o' 'osses double what they used to be ? They talks about their wheat and their barley, but they never says nothing about the price o' bullocks." Clearly, the old man wasn't so utterly incapable of observation as he would have had me think. But the landlord, who now came to the front, said he was of a contented mind, and had always been satisfied with his lot, though to look at the old fellow, and by the tone of his remarks, I should hardly have judged so. "That's what they gets," he growled at one point, as he sliced off a lump of fat bacon on his hunch of bread. "What they earns is another thing." The old fellow was between seventy and eighty years of age—seventy-seven, I think they said ; and his day's work was eleven hours of hoeing, or nine hours with allowances for meals. And every winter the old man spends in the workhouse. "And does he find any fault with the workhouse ? " I asked of the landlord, as we presently jogged along in his light cart. "No ; he don't find no fault. He takes it all quiet enough." At threescore years and fifteen or thereabout, I suppose nine hours of hoeing leaves a man little spirit even for grumbling ; but here is an object-lesson for all the sturdy young fellows from eighteen to twenty-five —11s. a week—on piecework—and nine hours' of hoeing and the much-dreaded workhouse, and a pauper's grave at the end of it all. What wonder if, as the landlady says, they go into the town to " better themselves ? "

And it is the same with the young women. "We get no women to work now," said the farmer I have already quoted. " Some of the old ones 'll do a day now and again, but we get no young women in the field now. They all go into the

town to service. While ladies 'll give thirty or five-and-thirty
pounds for a cook, and sixteen and eighteen pounds for a
housemaid, of course we can't keep 'em here." "And no
doubt when the lasses go, the lads soon begin to follow ? "
" Of course they do." A Baptist minister gave me a striking
illustration of the influence of the young women in assisting
the draining of the country of its labourers. Before he came
into his present ministry, he was in charge of a church in a
village, where pillow-lace-making was a staple industry of the
people, and while it lasted they were thriving, and the church
was prosperous. But foreign competition, or something else,
ruined the lace-making. Things grew worse and worse, till
twelve hours of close working wouldn't pay twopence. Every
girl in the place who was good for anything at all—eighty
or ninety per cent.—flitted into the towns, and all the young
men followed.

" I don't think it's altogether wages," said a very able
observer, another Congregational minister of eight years'
standing in an Essex village. " The country, you see, is very
dull, and it is difficult to see how it can be made otherwise.
The people have to be up at five in the morning, and they
require to be in bed by seven or eight o'clock." This
gentleman's opinion was that their long day's work was too
exhausting to permit of any kind of social life in the evening.
He had tried to get up evening entertainments, and had
tried to start a library ; indeed, he did start one with two or
three hundred volumes, and for a short time it seemed to be
appreciated. But he couldn't keep up an interest in it, and
it had to be dropped. " The hours of labour are so long,
and the work is so heavy, that it leaves the people fit for
nothing in the way of mental improvement at the end of the
day ? " " It leaves them fit for nothing but bed." " Then,
apparently, if social life in the village is to be made brighter
and more attractive, some shortening of the hours of work
seems to be indispensable ? " " Yes ; but then, I confess, I

see a great difficulty. There has been some talk of the union here, and I suppose it is coming." "Yes; they say in London that the great difficulty in the way of effective union there is the disorganised agricultural labourer always ready to pour in from the country to defeat gas-workers and others in their efforts to improve their condition. And Tillett and the rest of them say that the labourers must be organised, and they are preparing to do it." "Well, when the movement reaches here I shall find myself in a great difficulty. There are one or two large farmers—men farming on a large scale and with ample capital—who are doing well. But the great majority of them round here have hardly a pound in their pockets, and to give shorter hours and better pay at their expense means just knocking them over. Even as it is their land is not half cultivated, and they simply cannot stand any further drain upon them. What is to be done it is very difficult to say." "Your observation convinces you that the large farmers have an advantage over the small ones?" " A very decided advantage. They can keep horses and men regularly employed by shifting them about from place to place, and they can buy to greater advantage and sell too. I'll give you an instance. I know two men at this moment who buy oilcake of precisely the same kind. One buys in large quantities for cash, and gets it £3 a ton cheaper than the other, who cannot afford to do so. I know two other men who had hay to sell when the price was low. One was obliged to sell, and got £2 a load for it. The other kept it for a time, and got £4. I know one farmer who buys oats, when he wants them, first-hand. He goes down to the docks, buys direct from the importer in considerable quantities, and entirely saves the profit of the middleman." " The small farmer, then, seems likely to go to the wall?" " He is bound to go to the wall," and it seems, moreover, that the large farmer can do, in proportion, with fewer men, can afford better machinery, and more of it,

than the small man. According to all the testimony I have
met with down here, thus far, things are moving in something of a circle. The want of money and the scarcity of
labour are evolving the system of large farms, and the system
of large farming is tending to dispense more and more with
the need of labour. " Well, what is to be done?" I inquired.
"I cannot undertake to suggest. What we seem to want
is a great statesman to come forward and take the matter
in hand."

LETTER II.

THE COTTAGE HOMES OF ENGLAND.

August 15.

STARTING from Chelmsford this morning, I have driven
some fifteen or twenty miles through the county of Essex.
If I had done merely this I should have brought back with
me the pleasantest possible impression of prosperous
villages and charming little homes, embowered in orchards
and flower-gardens, and tenanted by a comfortable and
contented peasantry, healthy, thriving, happy, and beyond
all comparison better off than the corresponding class in
our great towns. Knowing what I know of life in lower
London, I might well have regarded the constant draining
away of this population thither as due to the infatuation of
mere ignorance, doomed to speedy enlightenment by a
bitter experience, and certain to be followed by repentance.
Life here as we drive along looks so placid, so pleasant, so
easy, that, by comparison, the life of those who are crowding
our dock gates, or are pent up in gas factories, or slaving at
our great railway stations, conducting omnibuses, tramping
the dull streets at night as policemen, or going through the
drudgery of a city warehouse—such life seems a sort of
nightmare.

Here is a little place, just a few yards back from the

highway, a semi-detached cottage. The windows full of
flowers look out across fields of waving corn, and pleasant
meadows, and dark-green woods. Its doorway is sheltered
by a porch that has been a mass of sweet-smelling honeysuckle. Its forecourt garden is full of cloves and fuchsias,
geraniums, and sweet-peas, and under a canopy of old trees
and shrubs is a rustic seat where, when the labourer's work
is done, he may sit and smoke his pipe and watch the sunset, and see the evening primroses unfold, and enjoy

> " The gleam—
> The shadow—and the peace supreme."

It is a house that would have inspired a Cowper or a
Wordsworth to break out in song, or a George Leslie to sit
down before it and paint. Here is another. A pebbled
pathway edged by mossy stones leads up to it through beds
of roses and petunias, nasturtiums and phloxes, interspersed
with currant-bushes and raspberry-canes. Its red-tiled roof
and crumbling chimney stack stand picturesquely out
against a background of plum and walnut, apple and pear
trees, and its latticed windows peep cosily out of a cluster of
vines. " Delightful little houses !" you exclaim as you
rattle past them. Photograph one of these places with the
weather-beaten old rustic smoking his pipe in the arbour,
and the old dame with her knitting at the door, and perhaps
a buxom lass feeding a coop of chickens, and you will have
the picture of a lowly home that it seems madness for the
young people to run away from for life in grimy Spital-
fields, or dreary Shadwell. Show such a picture as
this, and say that Ben Tillett and Tom Mann are coming
down here to commence an agitation among such people,
and Ben Tillett and Tom Mann will strike you at once as
demons of discord who richly deserve to be flung into the
nearest horsepond. Reform in the villages, indeed ! Let
the people alone. God made the country, and man made
the town. These Essex villagers have fresh air, and flowers

and fruit in their season. They have all the delights of the
open country—green fields and shady woods, waving cornfields and laden orchards, and peace and quiet and Sunday
rest. If their wages are low, so are their expenses, and
though they get none of the excitements and stir of town
life, they know nothing of its struggle and strain either.
Let them alone. That is how it would naturally strike the
stranger who should spin along behind a good horse, as I
have been spinning to-day, through Writtle, Cooksmill
Green, Highwood, and the neighbourhood.

I have been doing a little more than this, however.
The Chelmsford and Maldon guardians, to their infinite
credit, and unlike many other Boards in Essex, have taken
an enlightened and thoroughly progressive view of their
duties as the sanitary authorities of their district. Instead
of appointing at a salary of fifteen or twenty pounds a year
a medical officer who is in practice for himself, and who is
expected to attend merely to such matters of health, or
rather of sickness, as the sanitary officer may call his attention to, they have taken the far more sensible and public-
spirited course of engaging the whole time and strength of
a thoroughly competent man. Dr. Thresh, a D.Sc., an
M.B., I suppose one of the youngest, and certainly one of
the ablest medical officers in the kingdom, devotes himself
entirely to travelling about the district, looking after matters
of water supply, drainage, the general sanitary condition of
house property, and all other matters bearing on the public
health. It was in company with Dr. Thresh that I made
my round to-day, and I was able thus to see not only the
outsides of these attractive little houses, but the insides
also and the people who live in them.

The first thing which struck me was the fact that
"absenteeism" and its evils are by no means peculiar
to Ireland. "In that row of houses," I was informed,
"some of the people have lived twenty or thirty years, and

they have none of them ever seen their landlord." We step down and look at one or two cottages. I cannot pretend to say that I was greatly shocked at what I saw. But I certainly ought to have been, and if I had peeped into the same rooms up a court in Lambeth or Poplar I should have been. But it was a delightful summer morning. The cottage doors opened into thriving little garden plots, and it was all so breezy and pleasant without that it really seemed to matter very little what was within. But the cottages were in a scandalous condition, and evidently the agent could not have spent a penny piece upon them for many years. Tumble-down, ramshackle, damp and draughty, any landlord ought to have been heartily ashamed of drawing rent for them. "This is how I manage to keep out the damp, sir," said one woman cheerily from the interior of her little low-raftered den, the floor of which was sunk below the level of the yard. And as she spoke she turned up two or three thicknesses of old rugs and carpets from the brick floor beneath them. "The place is wretchedly damp," observes the doctor as he makes a note or two, and we move on. "The people suffer a good deal from rheumatism and pleurisy, and that sort of thing, what with their brick floors and their broken plaster walls and clay soil." We rattle on past a village school with a score or two of youngsters out in the playground in front. "Some of those children," says my cicerone, "have to come three miles to school, and in the winter time the cross roads are swamps of mud. This road here," he continued, as he pulled up at the end of a lane and dismounted, "was last winter a foot or a foot and a half of liquid slush, and the children had to get along here to school. No wonder they got bronchitis and influenza. I want to go and see whether the landlord has finished a well at one of these cottages down here." No, the well was not finished, and the landlord would have to be touched up again ; but progress had

B

been made, and soon these cottages would have a fair supply of wholesome water. "Come and see where they used to get their water for drinking and cooking," said the doctor, leading the way down an unusually large garden plot. I stepped down a bank, pulled the boughs aside, and found a little stinking pond, into which the surface water drained from the land around. It was all the water they had had for drinking till the authorities insisted on a well being sunk—a mere stagnant ditch. Another cottage —indeed a whole row of cottages—were still drawing supplies from a similar source—just a stagnant puddle under some trees at the bottom of the garden. The woman in whose garden was this water supply for herself and her neighbours, complained bitterly of what they had to put up with at times. The continuous rains of late had freshened up the ditch and rendered the water comparatively wholesome, but at times it was almost black and the stench was dreadful. It made her sick.

The want of good water is one of the great troubles of these villagers, but in the case of some of them it is only one of many evils that make life a misery and a burden. I mentioned just now a cottage whose latticed windows peered out from a luxuriant grape-vine, beneath a roof of picturesque red tiles. "I could get along for water," said the tenant. "I can fetch that from the well over yonder," he said, indicating a supply at some distance across the fields, "and I wouldn't mind if he'd jest put the windows in. I like th' ole place, and I don't want to leave it." Outside and from the road the cottage looked the picture of cosy comfort, but go up to it and peep inside, and go round the back, and you will find it is a filthy, dilapidated pig-sty sort of place, in a condition utterly unfit for habitation. The latticed windows are actually tumbling out, and some of them at the back are really gone, and the holes are stopped up with sacking or pieces of board, while the reeking walls are all mouldy and crumbling. But a place worse than this by far stood a little way off on the same road. It was not one of the most attractive of the cottages about there, but it stood in an open and sunny position; the luxuriant garden plot at the back showed prettily through the open passage leading from the front door, and the children playing about it gave a homely, cheerful aspect to it. But such a house inside I never saw in my life, though I think I have seen a good many of the worst rooms in London. The poor woman begged we would go up-stairs and look at the front bedroom. She had had to move out of it, she said, for she was afraid her bedstead would have tumbled through into the room below. This was not in the least an exaggeration. I really felt it unsafe to stand upon the floor. The walls were cracked and broken. Throughout the house they were patched with tarred sacking or bits of sheet-iron, the roof was leaky, and rain was free to come in from above, and all the winds of heaven had free course through broken floors and ramshackle windows. And that unfortunate family had had to shiver in that miserable ruin—condemned twelve months ago—all through the last dreadful winter. "I was nearly perished to death, sir," said the poor woman, "and they've been threatenin' to put the brokers in for the rates. Can they do it, sir, for a place like this?" Why did they stay there? it will be asked. Well, the simple answer is that they couldn't help it. Why they couldn't help it is a question which I must leave to a future letter. "In a locality where you can find somebody who will sell suitable plots of ground for erecting cottages, and at a reasonable price," says Dr. Thresh, as we drive along, "guardians can erect cottages; but where you have to put compulsory powers into operation, the legal expenses become so heavy that you can't do it." "That is to say in the only cases where the Act is required you find it is of no use?"

"Precisely so. It breaks down just where it is most needed."
Some further comments on our house-to-house visitation I
must leave for another letter.

LETTER III.

WHY THEY GO TO TOWN.

August 18.

"*Cherchez la femme,*" said the Oriental philosopher whenever mischief arose. Inquiry into the causes of the influx of
agricultural labourers into the towns strongly supports the
wisdom of that Eastern potentate. I am fast arriving at a
conviction that the main source of the trouble is to be found in
the influence of the young women. In one of the cottages
we went into in the course of the round of visits I partly
described in my last letter, there were three bonny lasses
who seemed to have completely outgrown the parental
wigwam, which, notwithstanding its flowery picturesque
exterior, was a low-raftered, pokey little place with a general
air of sordid poverty. They had all three been out to
service, but were temporarily at "home." "You wouldn't
like to come back and settle down here?" they were asked.
"No," was the emphatic reply. "You wouldn't catch us
settling down here." They flit out of the old nest into the
towns, these pretty decoy birds, and very likely with at least
three young swains looking wistfully after them. They
become familiar with quite a different world, get new ideas
of home life, acquire quite a different standard for men and
their wages. Presently they come home for a holiday, full
of tales of this higher life and the wonderful earnings of
smart young men of their acquaintance. There is the milk
man—who sees all the life of the busy streets, and spends
his pleasant days in serving pretty girls with milk and eggs,
and gets a pound a week for it. The groom was a villager

once, and not a bit smarter than young Hodge, and when he came to town knew no more about horses. He now gets what is equivalent to five-and-twenty or thirty shillings a week, and has to drive out his master and see all the sights. Dull work turnip-hoeing in the middle of a ten-acre field at a maximum of eleven shillings a week after this. "One of my servants is going to marry a labourer," said a gentleman. "They have been waiting till he got his eleven shillings— full man's wages that is. He has got that now, and he is thinking of getting married. But the girl wants him to come into the town, and it is certainly only natural. She sees that my groom and gardener is getting twice a labourer's wage, though he is no sharper or smarter than the other. She doesn't care to go and settle down for life on eleven shillings a week and no prospect of any rise. She doesn't see why he shouldn't come into the town and get on a bit."

That, no doubt, is a very common case. "When they begin to think about getting married," said this gentleman, "is the time when they begin to be restless and begin to think about getting away from the land"—from about eighteen to five-and-twenty, that is, just the period of life mentioned by the experienced farmer whose pessimistic view of things I gave in my first letter. "It's the young 'uns as can go," said an old labourer in the rather doleful tone of a man who had missed his opportunity. "It's the young 'uns as can go ; it's o' no use for the old 'uns to think about it." Many and many a long year's work had the old man done.

> " Oft did the harvest to his sickle yield,
>   His furrow oft the stubborn glebe had broke :
>   How jocund did he drive his team afield !
>   How bowed the woods beneath his sturdy stroke !"

But it was all over; he could work no more, and now had, I suppose, to depend upon the parish. He sat there quite alone in the world. His sons had gone from him, and his wife had died two years ago. His breezy little room, with the sunbeams pouring in upon its red-brick floor, looked decidedly pleasant, and I couldn't help thinking how different it might have been with the old fellow if one or two of his sons could have been working on the land around, much of which was so manifestly in need of their labour. It is evidently a great grief to many of the old people that their boys will run off to the towns. " I grieved more over my boy as went away to London than I did over the four I'd lost," said a pleasant-faced woman ; " I didn't eat a ha'porth o' food for a fortnight." " But I daresay he likes to come back and see the old home sometimes ? " " Ah, that he do, sir," replied the woman, looking delighted at the thought. " He comes down for a day or two whenever he can, and he says 'There's no place like home after all, mother.' Bless you, when he was at home he'd ha' thought it shame to kiss his mother, but ——" " Ah, and now when he comes back he'll do it, eh ? " " I should jest think he would," laughed the rosy little woman. " But it do improve 'em to go to London," said another comely little matron, as she stood at her cottage door and told us how her boys had got on, evidently divided between her sentiment of pride in the lads and her grief at parting with them. " Somehow they seem quite different when they come home," she said. " And have all your boys gone to London ? " " No, I got two at 'ome now." " And why haven't they gone too ? " " One of 'em had a bad attack of rheumatic fever, and can't go out, and the other has fits." " That," it was remarked as we moved down the garden, " gives you some idea of the sort of people who are being left in many of these villages—just those who can't get away."

To a great extent this exodus from the fields to the towns is an exodus of the spirited and ambitious young man in quest of a more promising sphere. But it is by no means entirely so. In a great many cottages we looked into, the question was put as to why the sons had migrated, and the

answers elicited seemed to show unmistakably that it was a
case of Hobson's choice. "Your son has left the neighbourhood?" was put again and again, and in a great many
instances the answer was in effect, "Yes, sir; he had to go."
"How was that?" "Well, where was he to find work?"
"But aren't the farmers employing so many hands as they
used to do?" "No, that they ain't, nothing like." "How
is it?" "Because they ain't got the money, sir." With the
exception of a few large farmers, everybody who is cultivating
land at all seems to be doing it in the most economical
style possible, and it seems to be the rule now with the
greater number to turn their men adrift as soon as they have
got in their harvest. "We had at least a dozen men out of
work in my parish last winter," said a clergyman whom we
met on the road to-day. "I have not been sufficiently long
in the neighbourhood to be very familiar with affairs, but
with half an eye I could see as soon as I came here that all
the usual winter work of the farms was entirely untouched—
such as the clearing out of ditches and the trimming of
hedges. The men are discharged and the work is not done."

So far as I have seen the county of Essex, I should say
that with the average farmer this is almost the invariable
rule. Men are being turned off after harvest, and are compelled to drift into the towns or the workhouse. They go
away in the winter, and when autumn comes round again
it is not surprising that farmers don't find them at their
beck and call. A large farmer whom I talked with to-day
apparently regarded this as the secret of the whole difficulty.
He himself kept his staff of men on steadily through the
winter, and had lost none of his hands. He is, I should say,
a man of ample means, and can afford to farm well, and
though, like most other people about here, he did a little
grumble at the low price of corn, he evidently considered
himself fairly thriving. There were, he frankly admitted,
considerable advantages in farming on a large scale, and some

of these advantages seemed to accrue to the village adjacent, which was one of the few places I have been through from which the labourers are not migrating, and which seems to be in a fairly thriving state. Here, however, as in so many other parts of the county of Essex, the water supply is a source of difficulty. The villagers have wells, but unfortunately they have also cesspools which often drain into them, and typhoid fever is a frequent scourge here as a consequence. They had formerly one good well to which they could resort if they would, and be safe. The new railway line, however, came along and cut off their supply and appropriated the water, which the railway company now pump up for their own purposes, and sell it to the villagers through a public pump at a shilling a thousand gallons. They have of course to pay this in the form of a rate, and then they have to pay for its being brought to them or fetch it themselves, often from a long distance. In their difficulty the people, or their representatives, approached the owner of a neighbouring estate for permission to make use of a spring of good water bubbling up and running to waste. Nobody ever heard of the spring being of a ha'porth of use to anybody till it was wanted for villagers who were dying with typhoid—I saw to-day a man who had just lost his wife from typhoid for want of it—and who proposed to bring it down to their homes in a pipe, and then the prohibitive charge of fifty pounds a year was made.

LETTER IV.

AN ESSEX DESERT.

August 20.

It ought not to be, though apparently it is, necessary to point out to the readers and correspondents of the *Daily News* that when I quote a man's words I do not necessarily

endorse his opinions or vouch for his statements. I am, I
see, supposed to have been misled with regard to the advantages of large farming. I have certainly expressed no
opinion in favour of large farms. I have merely recorded
the opinions of intelligent local observers who take that view.
Without for the moment expressing an opinion one way or
the other, I may say as a mere matter of fact that I have met
with several people more or less competent to speak on the
point who have unhesitatingly asserted the advantages of
large farming. The last man I questioned on the point was
himself a large farmer, and he seemed to be in no doubt
about it. " It is worth your while to get the best machinery,"
he said. " You can always find work for your horses and a
regular staff of men." That is the opinion of a practical
farmer of long experience. It is for the readers of the *Daily
News* to say what the opinion may be worth. I have heard
none to the contrary of this except in the case of those who
have insisted on the necessity for getting back to the good
old times, when the farmer turned up his shirtsleeves and
worked with his men in the fields, while his daughters milked
the cows and his wife made the butter and cheese. If I
thought that any word of mine could assist in bringing about
this, I can only declare that I should be delighted to say it. A
prosperous farmer among his men, pitchfork in hand, leading,
directing, stimulating those who will share his prosperity
with him, is a king among men. His lot is among the
brightest and the happiest on earth. By all means let his
daughters milk the cows—in a shed constructed on sanitary
principles, of course. The lasses will have the wholesome,
dignifying sense of a useful life, and when they have done
their dairy work, I hope they will dress themselves as prettily
as they know how, and have an evening at the piano, or help
in the village choral society, or manage the village library, or
attend a lecture. Hoorah ! for the good old times plus the
culture and education that we are nowadays coming to

regard as quite consistent with solid work in the world, and which we may rest assured must somehow work in with any general scheme of things if that scheme is to be expected to fall in with the march of human progress, and be permanent. The old style of farmer—sordid, ignorant, opinionated, contemptuous of science and new-fangled notions, did for the old times. But let it be laid down as an axiom that the future has no place for him. He has to go the way of blunderbuses and sedan chairs, and anything tending to reproduce him is a tendency against all the forces of the times.

I repeat that I have again and again heard opinions to the effect that, at all events in this part of the world, the small farmers are going down ; and unquestionably the appearance of the country I travelled through yesterday, say from Wickford to Althorne and Southminster and thence back by road to Chelmsford, bears out this view. A more dreary and depressing stretch of badly farmed crops and land out of cultivation, dilapidated cottages and deserted fields, it would be difficult to find. "That field," said a worthy rector—a downright good old Tory, who had nothing but scathing denunciation for technical education, and who believed that nothing could save us all from the dogs but getting back with all speed to a tax on corn—"that field I have known to grow five and six quarters of wheat to the acre. Now look at it." Certainly such an expanse of seeding docks I never saw. "Afore now," said a working-man later in the day, "I have thrashed out corn as didn't yield more than five or six sacks to the acre." I saw yesterday hundreds upon hundreds of acres of wheat and barley that could hardly yield much more. Thousands of acres I saw yielding nothing at all, but just such vegetation as grows upon land when it is abandoned. Such an expanse of thistledown as stretched out before me at one point on my drive from Althorne to Chelmsford I never saw in my life. A good night's wind, I should think, might sow three or four counties from that field, while everywhere the hedges and ditches and roadside were choked with weeds. Yet there is no work for the villagers of Essex, and they are streaming into the big towns because miles and mile of land—inferior, no doubt, but which nevertheless might comfortably support a large population if they could be got to work upon it under such conditions as science could prescribe and capital secure —cannot be made to yield first three or four profits for other people. The land would support the actual workers on it, but that is nothing at all. It must give the clergyman his tithes, and the farmer his income, and the landowner his rent, and the Lord of the Manor his dues. It will not do that, however; therefore let it go out of cultivation, and let the people stream into the towns. Oh, the pity of it! As one flits along past their lowly homes, how near the people seem to an ideal life of simplicity and purity, comfort and contentment! How near they seem, and yet, alas! how far. I have seen few more pitiable objects than an old woman in a little hovel of a place—in a garden full of flowers —without kith or kin in the village, only a friendly old neighbour to look after her for charity occasionally, the worries of a lifetime gathered in her wrinkled face, and on her lips a desolate cry that it might soon please the good God to take her rather than let her go into the workhouse. But old people are left alone to grow decrepit in towns as well as villages. Well, yes, they are, no doubt; but here it looks as though it would be so natural and easy for some of the young ones to settle around, and they all seem to go away—all but "the old people and fools." If there was a sadder sight confronted me yesterday, it was that of another old woman who looked comfortably off, and who, I was informed, had actually furnished a cottage for her married daughter—whose husband had left her—that she might live next door to a semi-imbecile village ruffian who had under-taken to support her. There are dark depths in some of

these villages. I was driven through one in which I was
assured that till a few years ago marriage was quite the
exception ; and we called at one two-roomed cottage, in
which lived father and mother and a family of six, including
two grown-up sons. It was a case of overcrowding, and
pressure had been put upon them to reduce the number.
One of the sons had been turned out. "But," whispered a
neighbour, "they've took in a lodger." "It ain't a lodger,"
said a nice-looking child of twelve or thereabouts, on inquiry
at the cottage; "It's Lizzie So-and-So." "And who is
Lizzie So-and-So ?" The child's face dropped significantly.
Evidently she was ashamed of it. "It's my brother's young
woman," she said. But how pretty some of the places
look ! The philosopher who should leave out as of no
account in considering the condition of the people, the
subtle charms of the poorest of these cottages, nestling amid
flowers and trees and gardens and green fields, would prove
himself as shallow as he who overlooks the benefits that
come of the friction and stir and stimulus of great populations
and life in cities. Shall we never be able to secure for the
benefit of the whole people some such combination of the
two—the peace and beauty of the country with the moral
and intellectual stimulus of the town, as at present is practicable only for the privileged few ?

"But the land," exclaims my Tory friend the rector,
"won't support the people, and it can't support the people
even if they had it for nothing." "Didn't you tell me it
had yielded five and six quarters of wheat to the acre ?"
"That was when it had been fifty or sixty years under
cultivation, and was in splendid condition. Look at it now.
What can anybody do with that? It would take years to
get that into paying condition again. Where's the capital
to come from ?" "Have you no allotments about here ?"
"My dear sir !" exclaims the rector, with all the emphasis
he could command, "it's the greatest humbug in the world

to believe that prosperity is going to be brought back by giving these people allotments and small holdings." "Well, but haven't you tried them here?" "Yes, we have, and what good have they done, I should like to know!" "But what is the reason they have done no good? Won't the people work at them, or haven't they time, or what is it?" Pressed in this way, the good man was a little vague and indefinite. I think his notions were rather mixed, and that when he repudiated allotments so vigorously he really had in mind small holdings for peasant farming—quite another matter. But he certainly led me to believe that the allotment-holders wouldn't work at them with sufficient interest and vigour to make them good for anything. However, he proposed to look round the neighbourhood, and we were soon straddling over gates and stumping across fields telling of poverty and neglect, and crops hardly worth gathering in. A delightful old soul my friend the rector. How heartily he abused the Government that did nothing but the dirty work of the Liberals! Just wouldn't he like to scarify the "demoniac miscreants" who had framed that new Tithes Act, that would so cruelly rob the poor clergymen, himself among the number! What a hearty dislike he had for "Joe Chamberlain!" And we wrangled and laughed, and discussed the universe at large and Essex in particular. Now he would clap me on the shoulder in hearty assent, and the next moment we tumbled apart to the political antipodes. But there were the allotments. I was fairly taken aback. I had expected to see them as barren and miserable-looking as the rest of the cultivation in that part of the world, and lo! they stood there like an oasis in the desert. I think the good rector could hardly have been round that way lately. He made the most he could of a few weeds, and declared the potato crop was all diseased. I flatly disputed it, and would have it they were not diseased, but ripe and fit for digging. We pulled up a root, and the rector tried to find some specks of disease about the handsome little tubers, but couldn't find me one.   With the doggedness inborn in the out-and-out Tory, he wouldn't admit that he was wrong, but the potatoes were certainly good, and every allotment was as full as it could hold of cabbages and beans, potatoes and carrots, onions and parsnips—all good valuable food produce —while all around were thousands of acres producing nothing but docks and thistles.   It was the most luxuriant and thriving object I had seen in a morning's travel, except the cottage-gardens and the fruit-trees, which everywhere down here look as though they *will* grow plums and pears and apples, whether the Postmaster-General will give us a parcel post that will bring them to our homes or not.   The allotments certainly looked thoroughly thriving, and paid well even at the stiff rent of £2 an acre.   And yet that good man still, I have no doubt, believes that by no possibility of social readjustment can those broad acres be made to maintain more than the dozen or so of struggling and despondent peasants still left in his parish.   I ought to have stated that the rector told me some of this land had just been taken by a Scotchman ; and, since writing the above, I have heard that large lettings have been effected in the neighbourhood I have been describing.   There seems to be quite an invasion of some parts of Essex by Scotchmen, who are coming down, I am told, in considerable numbers.   I was informed at one point that for sixteen miles the road ran along land that had been taken by Scotchmen who were going in for dairy farming, somewhat after the fashion of the good old times.   They will give no employment for Essex hands, for they are bringing their families with them to help in the work ; and I hear of bonnie lasses with short petticoats and bare feet, and a general muscular development worth a couple of the labourers left on the soil.   I don't know whether they have brought the pianos.   The only house I have seen occupied by a North Briton was a nice, stylish little new brick farmhouse, which I was told was not furnished much better than the labourers' cottages around.

LETTER V.

A MODEL VILLAGE.

August 22.

IN my last letter I described a part of Essex in which the land was poor, a vast proportion of it altogether out of cultivation, where crops were of the scantiest, where the cottages were bad, and almost everything wore a general aspect of poverty and depression. To-day I have walked for some hours through a locality in all respects different. Many of the crops I saw were first-rate. There had been room for more labour, but everything looked prosperous; and as to the cottages in the village of Stisted, which I found at the end of my walk, between three and four miles out from Braintree, they must be among the best labourers' cottages in all England. They were put up by the late squire, Mr. Onley Savill-Onley, to whose memory a handsome stained-glass window for the parish church is being subscribed for, and who seems to have endeared himself to everybody. The squire, I am told, was a man of cultivation, a clever landscape artist, and took great pride in designing cottages, not only healthy and commodious, but pretty and artistic. He was, by the account of the Rev. Canon Cromwell, Rector of Stisted, in all respects a model landowner—lived among his people, spent his money among them, won their esteem and confidence, and generally acted the part of an earthly Providence to them all to an extent that one cannot but fear must have tended seriously to sap independence of character in the village. Pensions have been so freely granted to widows that they have accumulated in Stisted in numbers sufficient to have deterred Mr. Weller, senior, from even venturing to drive his coach through the spick-and-span little place. To add to the prosperity of the village, allotment land has been let at twopence a rod, and the farmers in the neighbourhood are men of capital, and have habitually kept on their hands all the year round. If the labourers under such circumstances are not to be kept on the land it is difficult to see what is likely to keep them, apart from some totally different economic system. They have good and cheap cottages—£4 a year is about the rent —permanent work, cheap allotments without stint, while in Canon Cromwell they have a large-hearted, liberal-minded friend, earnest in every effort to provide education, rational entertainment, and everything else that may be practicable for them.

Such a combination of advantages must be very rare, and yet from this model little village the young men are streaming away into the towns or the colonies, just as they appear to be in almost every other part I have visited, and nobody seems to be able even to suggest a possible remedy. The truth I am reluctantly driven to by my visit to Stisted, more than by anything I have seen yet, is that this question is one of wages, and wages alone, and that unless means can be found of bringing up the standard of wages to a point which every farmer in the kingdom would scout as utterly preposterous, this shifting of the population cannot be decidedly stopped, and can be retarded only in proportion as that standard is approached. I was attracted in this direction by a report in a local paper that the labourers at Stisted and Pattiswick had refused to set about harvesting till the farmers would come to their terms, and that virtually an agricultural strike was on foot. The men in this neighbourhood get ten shillings a week during the winter and during summer eleven. When harvest comes round this arrangement is suspended, for it is the custom here for them to form companies and to make bargains with their

masters to cut, bind, cart, and stack the crop at so much an
acre. Fifteen shillings an acre is an ordinary figure, when
the men find their own beer. Some masters prefer to pay
the whole in money, but the common arrangement is for the
farmer to pay twelve or twelve and sixpence an acre with a
certain allowance—not of beer, for the Truck Act forbids
that—but of malt and hops, which the men brew into beer
for themselves. There is a small brewhouse in Stisted,
where the men, for a payment of eighteenpence or so, may
brew their beer, which they generally do in the night. It
is an obvious infringement of the Truck Act in spirit, if not
in letter. It ought to be stopped, and if need be the
amended Truck Act should be amended again. I am told
that some of the masters manage in this way to get rid of
the bad barley they cannot otherwise find a market for, and
those who are trying to promote temperance among
harvesters find it a difficulty and a discouragement. This
beer-making material is worth about thirty shillings, and
the men, one of them told me to-day, reckon to cut ten
or twelve acres of wheat per man, the whole earnings being
divided among the company. Suppose each man harvests
eleven acres, at twelve and sixpence, his share will be
between six and seven pounds for the harvest, to which must
be added the thirty shillings' worth of malt and hops. Of
course, if the crop is heavy, there is more work to the acre
than when it is light, and the men and masters have to
haggle until they can come to terms about it. This year
there was a difference of a shilling or eighteenpence they
couldn't get over, and the men refused to go to work. Two
or three days appeared to have been wasted in this way, while
one after another the masters gave in, the largest and
probably the wealthiest holding out the longest. However,
terms were eventually agreed on, and when I reached the
locality nothing but the drenching showers prevented the
cutting of some very fine crops.

c

I jumped over a bank into a field, where a party of them were waiting, and had a long talk with the men, as well as with several others I met in the course of my walk, and their testimony was practically identical. It was with them all a question of wages.. It is the big shilling, they told me. "But are there no other reasons why men are leaving the country?" I asked. "Do you dislike the work, or don't you like living in a village?" No; it wasn't that. They would stay in a village if the pay was right, and they didn't mind the work, but there was too much of it for the money. The masters had had them under their heels far too long, and unless things were changed there would be "ructions." If things weren't altered they would all go. "When you go back to Lon'on," said one brawny fellow, ensconced deep in a shock of wheat, "tell them iron-mongers up there they needn't make no more o' them things"—indicating the sickles—"we ain't a-goin' to use 'em." "But don't you think men are better off down here at the pay you are getting than they would be in London at a higher rate? You know a man's expenses down here are very much lighter than they are in London." "There ain't much difference for single men," was the reply, "and there's a lot o' difference in the pay." In the course of the morning I talked with a respectable-looking working woman, who afforded rather a telling illustration of this. "Well," I began, "and are the people leaving Stisted and going into the towns, as they are doing in other parts?" "No," said the woman; "I don't know as they are—except the young 'uns; they keep going!" "Except the young ones! But they are just the ones who ought to be staying to do the work." "Yes," laughed the woman, "that's true enough; but you see they likes to better themselves if they can. I got a boy as has jest gone from here." "Ah, and why did he leave?" "Well, sir, he couldn't save nothing out of his pay. All through the winter he got ten shillings a week,

and when he'd paid me for his board and lodging and had
dressed himself—he is a young fellow of two-and-twenty,
and dresses pretty well—there was nothing left. ' Mother,'
he says, ' I shall never be better off at this game. I'm
a-goin' to try my luck in London.' " "And did he find
work when he went to London?" "Yes, he went over
somewhere down Penge way and got on at once with a
contractor or some't to drive a cart at a pound a week, but
he soon giv that up and got on to the railway. I ain't quite
sure what he gets there, but I know it's over a guinea." We
talked of working hours, and I asked the woman what the
people did with themselves in the winter evenings. " Some
on 'em goes to the reading-room up in the village. That
was where my boy used to go when he had had his tea and
washed. He'd go up there and read the paper." " Ah,
and I suppose it was there he picked up his idea of going
to London?" " Oh, yes, sir. He see the advertisement
about the place he got in the paper." "And does he like
it? Wouldn't he like to come back again?" " No, sir ; it
suits him very well indeed. He's been down once or twice,
and he looks hearty and well, and says he's very glad he
went."

"Yes," said Mr. Cromwell afterwards, "I know the lad
you are referring to. He and two friends of his used to
come up to the rectory to educational classes. Those two
friends made up their minds to go out to Canada, where
they got employment immediately. I forget exactly what
pay they got, but something like five times what they were
getting here. And these young fellows have friends in the
village, and these things are known by everybody." Can
there be anything more natural than this exodus from the
villages? Can there be anything more inevitable than the
virtual depopulation of our agricultural districts unless some
radical change can be effected? Some of the farmers will
tell you that ten or eleven shillings a week is but the

nominal wage, and that at times they earn considerably
more. There is some truth in it. A labourer's wife and
children will sometimes earn a little by picking stones off
the land. For a month or six weeks a woman may earn as
much as eighteenpence or two shillings a day by pea-
picking; so that the Tory rector may have been right when
he told me that a cottager and wife and children sometimes
had as much as a pound a week coming in. It is possible
they may have, just while the pea-picking lasts. But if you
tell this to the men they are instantly down on you with a
contra account. "They calls it eleven shillings a week,"
said the men in the harvest field to-day, "but what about
the days o' pourin' rain when you can't get into the fields ?
Don't they stop yer pay for them ?" "I should think they
do !" cried the fellow buried deep down in the corn shock.
"They'll say, 'hullo, here's a shower of rain. Go and send
them fellows home. Darn 'em ! They'll all be under the
hedge.'" "Ah," said another, "many's the time as I've
been home with five or six shillin's for my week's pay." Of
course there is a great difference in masters, and things vary
somewhat according to local circumstances, but in Essex, so
far as I have seen it, I don't think it would be far wrong to
put down the income of an able-bodied labourer at from
five to ten pounds at harvest, and for the rest of the year
ten or eleven shillings a week when in work. The best of
the young men among agricultural labourers find no difficulty
at all in getting employment in the towns. It is not they
who drift to the dock gates and the casual wards, but they
oust others who have to do so. Why should a young man
stay down in his village when he is practically certain of
finding employment at double wages, with all sorts of
indefinite possibilities in the towns? As things are, he will
not stay. The whole conditions of his life will have to be
changed. The farmers down here can tell you why. As a
rule, with very few exceptions, they have always been against

education. With very few exceptions, they are dead against it now. If they speak candidly—as they will sometimes—they tell you that this restlessness and shifting are simply the results of education. And they are undoubtedly right. Schools and newspapers and ballot boxes, and trade unions, and penny postage, and cheap travelling are all educating our peasantry. It is of no use to rely upon old remedies now that you have got new men with new cravings, new ideals, new sense of power and importance, and new resolution to live a life a little more worth living. There is no going back. "The proper remedy for the evils of liberty," said Fox, "is more liberty." The proper remedy for the evils of education is more education. Every agency by which men can be made out of drudges and dolts and mere beasts of burden must be kept in operation with redoubled energy, and they must be got back to the land which so sorely needs them under conditions affording some of the stimulus of hope, some little scope for enterprise and ambition.

LETTER VI.

A WAYSIDE PARLIAMENT.

August 27.

IN my last letter I gave, I think, good reasons for believing that the one great cause of the flocking of the agricultural labourers into the towns is the poorness of their pay, and the further I inquire the more certain it appears to me that nothing will stop this disastrous influx but a very material advance in wages, or something equivalent to it. I have just been out eight or ten miles from Thurston Station on the Great Eastern line, in Suffolk, where I was met on all hands with pretty much the same story as in Essex—land labour-starved, wages about eleven shillings a week, young men going into the towns. At one point in the road I found a large gang of men who had just done dinner and were snoozing or smoking their pipes, and I got into conversation with them. They talked quite freely to me, and several of the men very sensibly and intelligently. The impression they gave me was pretty much the same as that I had received from the other party of reapers I mentioned in a previous letter, the impression of deep dissatisfaction with existing conditions of life and a strong disposition to revolt against them. Men had been going off the land, and they would continue to do so, as fast as they could. Was it likely, they wanted to know, that they were going to stay there at ten or eleven shillings a week while they could get thirty in town? "Where do they get thirty shillings a week?" I inquired. "At the breweries," said the man. "Do you know anybody who did it?" "Yes, a chap in our village went to a brewery and got thirty shillings straight off." Apparently they all knew of somebody who had left the land and "bettered themselves."

"Now, tell me," I said to them—I suppose there were about twenty men there, a fairly representative gathering of Suffolk labourers in the heart of the county—"now, tell me what you think would be likely to keep the labourers on the land? What do you think would be satisfactory?" One man thought "twelve bob" would do, but his moderation was scouted. Others candidly voted for all they could get. After a wrangle which, to an ear not accustomed to Suffolk vernacular, was a little confusing, one solid-looking man said he thought fifteen shillings a week would be fair wages. "Give me fifteen shillings a week and a bit o' ground," he said, "and I'll be content. You wouldn't ketch me a-going into a town." Content, alas! is but a Will-o'-the-wisp, and it would be rash to predict that a general rise in wages, even to that extent, would finally settle the difficulty. But the suggestion of fifteen shillings a week and a bit of ground seemed to be generally approved. "What do you mean by a bit of ground ?" I asked. " Well, say a quarter of a acre." " But some of the men tell me that a day's work on the land is quite enough, and that they don't care for more of it when they have done that." " Well, I got a quarter of a acre myself, and I finds I can do it very well." " And what is it worth to you now, all the year round ?" " Well, I reckons it's as good as two shillings a week on to my wages." "Then fifteen shillings a week and a quarter of an acre of ground would keep the men in the villages, you think ?" Yes, that might do it, and nothing much short of it would. What is the probability of any such remedy being arrived at is a point upon which the readers of the *Daily News* may be left to form their own opinions. Some of the horse-keepers I have found getting fourteen or fifteen shillings a week, and able to rent a bit of ground. But the nearest approach to it by ordinary labourers in this locality that I have heard of is in a village eight or nine miles out of Bury St. Edmunds, where a short time before harvest began the men struck for twelve shillings, and got it. How long they will keep it is a matter that may perhaps be positively decided shortly after the completion of harvest. These men had been getting ten shillings a week.

My charioteer was an intelligent man who knew the country all round, and his conversation was instructive. He had no idea of my purpose beyond the intimation that I was interested in the condition of the land and the labourers, and he talked very freely. Yonder was a village where lots of people went away last summer. Over there was another where the farmers last week wanted thirty men to begin harvest, and couldn't get them anywhere. Yes, there was no doubt things were in a bad way. There was land at Stanton that hadn't had a plough over it for five years, and Mr. So-and-so somewhere else had got so many acres of turnips you couldn't see for weeds. " I tell 'e what it is," said a man who had come up driving a van while our discussion was

going on on the roadside, and pulled up to take his part in
it, "the farmers ain't half doing the land." "No, that they
hain't," broke in another. "Why, there's five crops in that there
field. There's thistles and docks, and poppies and curloch
and squitch, besides the barley." "They don't do nothin'
to the land," resumed the man up in the van. "What they
mean to do is to get all they can out of it, and then when
it's got down till it's good for nothin', they'll chuck it up,
and then where are you?" This man had a good deal to
say. He spoke like a capable, intelligent sort of person,
but with a certain rancour I couldn't help noticing. When
we moved on, my driver explained to me that that man had
been in the employ of one of the farmers in the neighbourhood, but had left on some ground or other, intending to get
employment with some other farmer. But he found it impossible. "If a man don't put up with whatever a master
likes to do, and leaves him, there's no chance of his getting
another job with any o' the others. They hang together,"
he said. I don't, of course, know the details of the case of
this particular man, but I noticed that he was not driving a
farmer's vehicle, and the remarks of my driver entirely tallied
with what I had heard in other quarters. In many localities
there seems to be a sort of league among the masters against
the men, always ready to repress and punish any display of
independence. "The masters," said a picturesque yokel a
day or two ago, "ha' had we like that," striking a particularly
ludicrous attitude, and bringing down a ponderous hob-
nailed hoof on a clod of mould, supposed to represent the
neck of the labourer. "The masters ha' had we like that;
and now we mean to ha' they." One mustn't, I suppose,
take too literally poor Hodge's rebellious expressions. My
driver, as we jogged along, gave me very droll accounts of
some of their attempts to get up strikes over the harvest
work. As I have previously explained, the gang of labourers
work together in getting in the crops, and before beginning

they have to arrange terms. For this purpose one of their number is selected as "lord," and he has to conduct nego-tiations, trusting, of course, to the moral support of the rest. " Maybe there's ten of 'em, and they'll all on 'em swear like fury as they won't do't under so much, and you'd think as they'd rather die fust. They be all agoin' to have it and no mistake. Well, they go to the master, and then p'r'aps there's two on 'em 'll hold together and all the others 'll give in without sayin' a word." The unlucky " lord " in such a case comes in for the brunt of the bullying —or "mobbing," as they call it here—which it seems to be generally al-lowed many farmers and bailiffs indulge in very freely on the smallest provocation.

" Yes," said a Nonconformist minister who had been working among the Suffolk labourers for seven or eight years—" low wages is the first thing that makes these people so anxious to get off the land." " They are going then from here also ? " " Oh, yes, continually going. Only a week or two ago I lost two of my young men." " Low wages the first point. And what is the second ? " " The second— indeed, I am not quite sure whether it ought not to be put first —is independence." By this the speaker proceeds to explain that he means that these young men, who are continually leav-ing the villages, are largely actuated by the desire to get out of that serf-like condition in which they find themselves, and the abject subjection they are under to the farmer. " Unless you have lived among them," said this minister, " you can have no idea of the gulf that separates the two classes." The tyrannical, domineering, nigger-driving sort of treatment the men have to submit to I have heard about in many quarters. " And there's another thing," said the man up in the waggon, who, as I have explained, probably had specially good reasons for knowing what he was talking about, " 'ere's many o' the men got to live in the farmer's cottages ; they be on his land. If you offend him it ain't on'y yer work as you

loses. It's a clear kick out—work and house and neighbourhood too. Very like there ain't another house to be
had for miles, but out you must go. Is that right? Ought
a man to be dependent on a master like that?" "No; he
didn't oughter," was the clamorous response all round.
" O'course he didn't." It was this question of cottage
accommodation that I had mainly come out here to inquire
a little into. I have loitered so long on the way, however,
that I must leave the subject for another letter. It might
be supposed that as so many are continually evacuating the
villages that deficiencies in cottage accommodation must be
a difficulty rapidly solving itself. It does not appear to be so,
however. There are many of these villages in which there
can have been no cottage building for years. Some of the
houses become totally uninhabitable, and large numbers of
them are far too closely packed, and if by chance a house is
vacated there is a rush for it, while many of the people, as I
have shown to some extent in a previous letter, are compelled
to live in cottages that are a scandal and a disgrace to all
who are responsible for them.

LETTER VII.

HOW THE GUARDIANS DIDN'T PROVIDE THE COTTAGES.

August 29.

AGITATORS are of course very dreadful people, but in
moving about among the rural population of Essex and
Suffolk one cannot help fervently wishing that he could let
a few agitators loose among them. There is a stir among
these dry bones, but oh! for a few prophets to breathe
upon them and set them shaking mightily! All sorts of
things are wrong. To a large extent the land is not half
cultivated. The people are not half paid, and consequently
many of them are badly fed and abominably housed and ill

supplied with water. Existence with them is a dull, dead-alive, hopeless sort of drudgery, without interest, without enjoyment, without any practical result except the mere keeping of body and soul together, and the end of it all is the workhouse, while the community at large is of course the loser of all the added wealth the land might have been made to yield. And yet you cannot talk with these people for a quarter of an hour without being impressed with a perception of the truth that all these evils might so easily be remedied if you could but kindle and sustain the energy and aspiration you clearly perceive within them. Put into these men just that same mainspring of legitimate and healthy self-interest which keeps going so many busy wheels all the world over, and at once you will fetch out of the soil the wealth to give them plenty of food and good water and comfortable houses and everything else they want to keep them on the land in contentment and prosperity. Why don't we turn our attention to the problem of fetching out of the men and the land what is really in them instead of vainly endeavouring to put things right on a wretched basis of ten shillings a week, supplemented by poor-law doles and rate-aided cottage building? In the mass of agricultural labourers we have got a great wealth-producing steam-engine. Set that steam-engine going, and all that is requisite will be produced. But instead of getting up steam we are shoving behind—painfully labouring to push round the wheels. Of course, if you are bent on getting your engine along, and can't raise the steam, you must push behind ; but it is really weary and disheartening business. My meaning will become apparent, I think, to anyone who will listen to a simple narrative of the attempt to get cottages for the poor people of Ixworth.

Ixworth is a considerable village about four miles from Bury St. Edmunds. Mr. W. F. H. Millington, whose extremely able essay on the " Housing of the Poor " won

the Warburton Prize at Owens College, Manchester, last
year, and who is resident here near the borders of Suffolk,
tells me that it is not conspicuously worse in its sanitary
condition than many other villages in this part of England ;
but it is fairly representative. I went over there a day or
two ago, meeting by the way market-day carriers' carts one
after the other laden with young country-women with their
boxes and bundles on their way to service in the towns.
Ixworth strikes the stranger as a pleasant and prosperous
village, and anyone driving through it would certainly have
no idea of overcrowding or ruinous homes or pestilential
fever dens suggested by the appearance of the place. Tory
guardians and Tory parsons, being of a caste altogether
separate from the cottagers, would never have found out
that anything was wrong in it. The Church living is a very
poor one, I am told, and in the past, right poorly it seems
to have been filled—if one may judge by results. About
two years ago, however, the Rev. F. D. Perrott, a liberal-
minded man of private means, took over the charge of the
parish, and set about trying to get in touch with the
cottagers. He found, I am told in other quarters—for Mr.
Perrott has left home in ill-health—that the Church had
scarcely anything to do with the people, and the people
scarcely anything to do with the Church. He soon got
things on a better footing, however, and succeeded in
forming the Ixworth Agricultural Labourers' Association.
The labourers were brought together for the discussion of
subjects bearing on their social welfare, and then, of course,
came out the facts of their home life. Up till then the
people had been hopeless and helpless, but now they began
to make their troubles known, and in the depth of last
winter men came in from villages miles away to meetings in
Ixworth. I have before me particulars of some of the
Ixworth cottages, got together by a house-to-house visitation
of a resident in the place, and they are shocking enough.

Numbers of houses have not so much as a back door, to say nothing of garden plots. Numbers of them are reported "not wind- and water-tight." "There is a row of houses in this lane, the total number of inhabitants is forty-four, and there are three closets for their use. In one house, consisting of two rooms, there are ten in family. In this row there are no back places at all." "Water comes into both bedrooms," in the report on another house, "and walls and roof are very bad." In another house "the wind and rain come in, and the rats. The woman showed me a bed-quilt covered with holes made by the rats." In another case "Doors are very bad, and the walls tumbling down. When it rains much, the water runs from the back kitchen into the sitting-room, and forms a pool in the centre." "I have asked several tenants to come forward and give evidence, but they are afraid to do so. They have told me they feared being turned out." Can anything be more abject and pitiable than the condition of people condemned to exist in such places, and afraid even to indulge in the satisfaction of a grumble about them? Dr. Thresh, whom I have mentioned before as the medical officer for the joint unions of Chelmsford and Maldon, was called in as a specialist to report on the state of things. After giving similar details, Dr. Thresh says : " These wretchedly small, overcrowded houses not only affect the morals but the health of the inhabitants. Rheumatism and chest affections are caused by sleeping and living in such damp, draughty dwellings. Infectious disease cannot be isolated, nor can any case of illness be properly treated in them. Apart from serious illness they are the cause of depression of vitality, generally affecting the bodily vigour as well as the spirits, and rendering the system unable to withstand the actual onslaught of disease."

I myself visited several of the cottages, and some of the people seemed quite scared by the few simple inquiries put

to them, evidently regarding them as the preliminary to
their being cleared out. One woman told me she had been
on the look-out for months for another cottage, but the only
one she could find was four miles off. What was the good
of a cottage four miles off your work? she wanted to know.
" If they turn me out I'll die on the roadside," she said.
" I wunt go into the work'us, I wunt, I wunt," she exclaimed,
fiercely striking a stick she held in her hand on the seat of
a chair beside her. While she spoke she stood beneath a
beam in her low ceiling that looked as though it only wanted
somebody to stumble in the room above to give way and
bury her and her children. In one room, not so bad but
that it probably could be repaired, I found, by the way, a
very interesting old man, whose reminiscences quite belied
the belief that the agricultural labourer is so much better off
now than he was a generation or two ago. He sat by his
broken fireplace shaking as if with the palsy. He had had
a sunstroke, he said. He was incapacitated for work, and
was dependent on the parish for his maintenance, after
seventy-two years' work upon the land. " I be seventy-six,"
said the old man, " and I was set to work 'most as soon as I
could walk. There warn't no schoolin' much in them days."
" It is a pity that there wasn't," I put in. " Ah! 'tis a pity.
If I'd on'y learned to read and write I could ha' done a
good deal better nor I ha' done. Why, even now," continued the old fellow, bristling up with an energy that his
seventy-two years of toil had not quite exhausted, " if I
could on'y write I could do some't or other." " Nonsense,"
grunted the old dame on the other side of the fireplace,
" what could you do, I should like to know?" " Do!"
retorted the shaky old fellow, resenting this disparagement
of his capabilities. " Why, if I could write down names and
figures couldn't I go round wi' coal or some't?" and he
looked as though, even now, it wouldn't take much to
persuade him to try for as much scholarship as would suffice

for the coal business. "They talk about labourers bein' so much better off nor they used to be," he said, in response to a remark of mine. "Why, when I was a boy we used to do t' thrashing wi' the flail, and we'd be at it in the barns all the winter through. There was one-pun' notes in them days, and many's the time when I was a boy o' fourteen and worked wi' the flail wi' my feyther we'd taake home a one-pun' note for our week's work. Why, if they were to pay 'e a one-pun' note now they'd think as they were goin' to be bust up." Perhaps the old man's memory was at fault, but on another point he was confirmed by his wife, and I think he spoke the truth. "So you've really been at work seventy-two years?" I said. "Aye, that I hev, and for years I used to walk eleven miles a day in goin' to and from my work. The walkin' takes it out of e' wus nor the work." Nothing is commoner than to find cases in which men walk two and three miles to their work.

One of the cleanest and most beautifully kept little homes ever seen in a village was one in which a delicate-looking elderly woman said she was never well. She showed me the brick floor and walls all reeking with moisture, and she took me out at the back to see the source of a terrible smell, which, when the wind was in a certain quarter, rendered her cottage almost unbearable, and made her feel sick and ill. It was the cesspool of an old closet, slightly boarded over, and within ten or twelve feet of her back door. She would give the world to get out of the house if she could only find another. Like scores of others in the village, however, she was condemned to live in this pestilential place, where any day fever or cholera might quite naturally break out.

All this clearly tends to hasten the influx into the towns. The proper and radical remedy would of course be to improve the earning power of the people. If by any modification of our agricultural system we could bring

science and capital to bear on these labour-starved fields of
Suffolk, and give the people such an interest in their
occupation as would really make them work, all the evils
would remedy themselves.   No doubt we should require an
Act of Parliament for obtaining plots of ground by some
simple and inexpensive procedure.   That is an urgent
necessity in any case.   But we should want no Act of Parliament for putting up houses if the people could pay for them,
and if they can't pay for them there must be something
radically wrong.   Why do not we fearlessly face this radical
wrong?   Why doesn't that land support these people?
That is the question, but we do not squarely face it.   We
shirk the question, and we pass Acts of Parliament for
shoving the engine along without getting up the steam.
Last year Parliament passed the Housing of the Working
Classes Act, on the whole an admirable measure, and under
our existing social circumstances very necessary.   In the
towns it was especially desirable.   But in these rural
districts the problem of housing the people is quite a
different one, and the provisions it contains for the providing
of agricultural labourers' cottages have at Ixworth so far
broken down, and will, I fear, prove a dismal failure.

First the "Rural Sanitary Authority" had to be prodded
on to action, that is to say, the Thingoe Board of Guardians
—every man of whom I am told, by the way, is a Tory—
had to be induced to do something for the poor at the
expense of the rates.   Mainly, as it would seem, by the
alarming result of the Stowmarket election, they were got to
move in the matter.   They applied to the County Council
for leave to put the Act in force.   In accordance with the
provisions of the Act, the County Council appointed one of
their number, Lord Francis Hervey, M.P., to go to Ixworth
and hold a formal inquiry whether new cottages were
necessary, whether there was no probability of their being
provided without the operation of the Act, and whether, all

things considered, it would be financially prudent to undertake the business. Well, this was all done. Mr. Theodore Dodd represented the labourers, Mr. J. J. Spark was for the Guardians, Mr. R. H. Wilson for the lord of the manor, and Lord Francis Hervey made, by universal admission, an excellent president of the court. Overwhelming evidence was adduced; the case was abundantly made out, and the Council were ready to issue their certificate, and then—the whole thing collapsed. It had been proposed to build, I believe, a dozen poor cottages for people exposed to wind and rain and foul stenches. Probably two-thirds of the cost would have been represented by the rents the people would pay. The other third would have had to come out of the rates. At the last moment the Guardians were horrified to find that this frightful expense, owing to their having omitted to make an application to the Council to the contrary, would have to be spread over the whole of their district instead of being limited to the place immediately benefited. They therefore begged that the Council would not grant their certificate, and that they might not be permitted to put up the cottages. They still pretend they want to do it, and they are going to begin the business all over again, and I hear that over this question of the incidence of the rate there will be a dogged and determined fight. When they have held their inquiry and settled about the rate, and the Council have authorised them to proceed, then it will become a question whether they had better proceed. If they decide that they will, the landowners may refuse to let them have the land at a reasonable rate, and they may have to put in force compulsory powers, ruinously expensive and provokingly dilatory. And all this because the people working on the land for nine or ten hours a day can't fetch out of it enough to pay for a decent roof over their heads, and enough food to keep body and soul together. It is quite time that the day of the democracy had begun to dawn upon us.

D

LETTER VIII.

COAL AND BLANKETS.

September 1.

I HAVE to-day travelled for some hours through the by-ways and villages of that part of Suffolk that borders on Norfolk. The country is much of it very pretty. It is beautifully wooded, here and there traversed by small streams, dotted about by the most charming little cottage homes, with now and then a pleasant rectory, a picturesque old church, a lordly-looking mansion, an undulating park, or a richly-laden orchard. From such a round as I have taken to-day, one brings home with him a mental panorama made up of almost everything that is peaceful and pleasant in rural life. Here is a vicarage garden with a party at lawn tennis ; yonder through that woody vista is a little company of harvesters ; now you have a rosy-looking woman shaking down the plums for a fair-haired child, and further on you see a venerable-looking dame sitting by the open door amid flowers and beehives. Peace and quiet, beauty and fruit-fulness, prevail everywhere. The village shoemaker is deliberately stitching away in a breezy little workshop, with the scarlet blossoms of kidney beans glowing in at the open door, and hollyhocks and rosy apples peering in at the window, out of which the good man now and again gazes as though in heart he is out with the reapers yonder in the waving cornfield. We push our way through the stalwart, standing corn down towards a cottage clad in grapevine and half-buried in the brown rustling wheat, where stands the village blacksmith, not under a spreading chestnut-tree, but, better still, within the shadow of a well-laden pear-tree, planted knee-deep in the corn on the margin of his own cornfield. Sickle in hand, and with two or three young men about him, the burly smith, with his cornsheaves and his pear-tree and the cosy cottage just over the hedge there all combine to make a picture such as, one cannot but think, must often haunt the memory of the emigrants from rural England into the docks and railway depôts and warehouses of London. "A good deal more fresh air 'ere than in Lon'on," says the blacksmith, as he mops round his brow, wet with honest sweat, and looking with pride on the splendid sheaves of corn he and his assistants have just bound up. "Aye, aye ; they keeps on going off," and then like everybody else the village blacksmith proceeds to explain the depletion of the villages by s'posing they want to better themselves, and suggesting as the only possible means of preventing it the payment of better wages. There's no doubt he thinks the farmers are very short-handed. He laughingly mentions one man who has four hundred acres of corn and has got four men to cut it—a hundred acres apiece before them.

In this village of Barnham wages for a considerable proportion of the men are slightly better than in any other neighbourhood I have gone through. They are getting twelve shillings a week—a fraction over twopence farthing an hour it comes to—and seven pounds ten for the harvest. One cannot but suspect, in moving about these rural districts, that the wages received by the people really have little or no relation either to what they earn or to what the master can afford to pay. As Mr. H. L. Smith says, in his paper on the "Migration of Labour," read at the National Liberal Club last year, the rates of wage in rural districts are largely customary, and every here and there it strikes one very forcibly that if the people were strong enough to form a good strong union among themselves the whole situation would undergo a total change. In this village of Barnham the monarch of pretty nearly all he surveys is the Duke of Grafton. He pays, as I have said, seven pounds ten for the harvest. Why does he pay that? Is it a sum based on any calculation of the quantity of corn to be cut, the number of hands to be employed, the chances of weather, and so on? I suppose there must have been some sort of calculation some time or other, but, so far as I am informed, such considerations enter very little into the matter. It seems to be assumed that at harvest time an agricultural labourer ought to earn from five to ten pounds during the time within which the corn is fit for cutting and carrying, and the Duke of Grafton chooses to pay seven pounds ten for some weeks of incessant toil from sunrise till sunset, and very often a spell of work by the light of the harvest moon. The Duke sits up at Euston Hall and offers seven pounds ten, the men down in the fields want eight pounds, and the agent runs backwards and forwards between the negotiators. The harvest certainly is great, and the labourers few, and if they only had the pluck to hold out they would probably get ten pounds, but not one of them dares to take the lead in insistance on a material advance upon what is customary—though, by the way, I think I was told that in previous years the payment had been seven pounds—and they meekly give in and go to work. "If you offend the Duke and his agent in these parts," said one, "you may as well go to the devil at once." Not that, so far as I can learn, the Duke of Grafton is open to much criticism. His labourers are better off than those of most landowners in the neighbourhood His cottages are good and cheap, and the general conditions of life among his people are unquestionably good. As John Bright would have said, he is a very respectable Duke.

By the way, there is a very interesting little relic of the *régime* of the last Duke of Grafton standing by the roadside in Barnham. It is a little wooden Primitive Methodist chapel on wheels; at least, that is what it has been, though it appears now to have been turned to some industrial purpose, having been purchased, I am told, for the sum of five pounds. I talked yesterday with a shrewd-eyed, ruddy-

faced, stubbly-chinned old villager, whose share in putting
up the little conventicle had cost him some years of exile
from the place. They wanted the Duke to let them have
a bit of land to put up a Primitive Methodist chapel, but he
refused them. So they built this wooden shanty, and put
it on wheels in one of their gardens. The agent remon-
strated, and tried to persuade my old friend here to take his
conventicle to one of the "free villages." But no, said the
sturdy peasant, all villages were free to worship God as they
thought proper, and he wouldn't budge. He found, alas!
that the freedom was only theoretical, and in the end he lost
his employment, and had to clear out, leaving the little
schism shop behind him. Eventually, however, after some
years, he found his way back, and now looks a hale and
hearty old man, about whose brow one fancies there are
the marks of troublous times, softened, however, by an even-
tide of comfort and prosperity. I am told that the obduracy
of the Duke was ultimately overcome by the prayers of the
Primitives, who couldn't and wouldn't pray for the death of
the man who thwarted their evangelising efforts in the
villages, but were very earnest in their supplications to
Heaven that "every obstacle might be removed." The
Duke seems to have got an intimation of what was going on,
and thought it prudent to answer the prayer himself.

In this village of Barnham the cottagers seem to be as
comfortable and prosperous as good management of the
property and considerate treatment can make them. They
have good cottages, gardens, allotments, good water, and, as
things go, good wages. Yet the population of the place has
slightly gone down since the last census, and the universal
testimony is that "the young 'uns all go." An intelligent
villager—not a labourer, but a man of the working class—
gave very emphatic evidence to that effect. He was a
member of some Nonconformist Church — now freely
tolerated—in the village, and he said they found invariably

that as soon as they got hold of a young man and set him thinking a bit, he began to think of going. They lost all their young men that way he said. No sooner does a young man begin to think at all than he begins to think of getting on, but as a Dissenter he instinctively feels that on a great ducal estate all the powers that be will most certainly be against him, and that all chance of any sort of advancement will be prejudiced by his religion. It strikes one as curious that all the farmers—even those who may reasonably be presumed to have plenty of capital—seem inclined to pinch and save in the matter of labour. I had mentioned to me 2,000 acres of land on which, upon the highest reckoning, not more than seven men were regularly employed, and as one spins along through miles of cornfields you see every here and there unmistakable evidence of the labour-starving of the land, and men will tell you of the reductions that have been made within their recollection. When I drove from Thetford through Barnham, Livermere, Troston, Honington, and Euston into Thetford again, the day was breezy and dry, and thousands of acres of corn stood ready for cutting. With the men actually at work it looked as though the harvest wouldn't be got in till Christmas. Here and there reaping machines were going, and I hear that the American reaping and binding machines are gaining extended use in some parts of the Eastern Counties. Every innovation of this kind, of course, tends to the immediate displacement of hands.

Some of the little glimpses one gets into life in the remoter villages are really very curious. In one place a woman incidentally alluded to the blankets that were lent to the people. I was surprised that she should have the loan of a blanket, for she seemed a respectable and spirited little body, who might have been supposed above it. But it appeared that everybody in the village had the loan of a blanket. " But," I said, " are there no people in

the place who are unwilling to borrow bed-clothing?"
"No, sir; everybody has 'em—unless it is the estate brick-
layer. I dunno' whether he has one. They seal 'em up
in the spring, and they unseal 'em in the autumn." "Seal
them up?" I said, in perplexity. "Yes, sir; I'll show you
mine," and the vivacious little woman whisked upstairs and
brought down a calico bag, the mouth of which was sewn
up with string, the ends being sealed with black wax. She
proceeded to explain that in the spring they all had to
trudge up to the rector's wife with their charity blanket
folded up in its bag to have it tied up and sealed. They
took their bags back home till October, when they again
went to the good lady to have their seals broken and the
blankets released for winter use. Every cottager in the
village had the loan of a blanket and seven hundredweight
of coal. There was a clothing club too, to which they all
contributed, but everybody who went to town to buy clothing
had to take the parcel from the shop straight away to the
parson's wife, who would minutely inspect them to see if
they were suitable for persons in their state of life. Here is
the clerical beneficent domination on the one hand, and on
the other there is the squire who owns all the cottages, and
whose agent requires them to mind their P's and Q's if they
want to remain. They pay their rent yearly, but they all
sign an agreement that an eight days' notice to quit shall be
sufficient. They have to be very careful. Their children
mustn't wander from the pathway in the park, and dreadful
things would happen if they were known to bring home
a few dry sticks.

Now, I know nothing of the clergyman or his wife, or
of Lord De Saumarez, the owner of the property, and I have
not the least desire to represent them as oppressors or
tyrants. They may be the most amiable of their race. I
can quite conceive that the vicar's wife may be actuated by
the kindest and best of motives in going to the trouble of

minutely inspecting their purchases and sealing up their blankets. It keeps them clean and ensures fair usage and proper storage when they are not wanted. The woman certainly had one point on which, evidently, her mind was a good deal exercised. They used to have nine hundred-weight of coal when the population was larger. But latterly it had been only seven, and although the population of the village had gone down recently and there were several houses empty the coal still kept at seven hundredweight. If there were fewer to have it, surely there ought to be more to have. How it was she couldn't make out. Apparently these things are all managed over their heads. But I dare say it is all right. Nobody, of course, ever heard of charity funds going to pay the organ-blower at church, or to wash the choir surplices. The thing is inconceivable, and no doubt some satisfactory explanation would have been forthcoming if I had had the enterprise and the time to look into the matter. But suppose that all these things are just as they should be, can one conceive anything more pauperis-ing and degrading than the kind of tutelage under which these villagers live? Can you wonder that young men of spirit are eager to clear out of such an atmosphere of serf-dom? As to such "charity," a clean sweep ought to be made of it. It is a mere relief to the wages list of the employers. I am not quite sure, but I think I was told that ten shillings a week was the rate of pay prevailing here, and I was certainly informed that young men—"quite grown chaps"—had been working for five and six shillings a week, and eight shillings had been paid to a young man of twenty. Only last week two of them left the place. In the next village all the houses and all the land, except one small plot on which a chapel had just been built, belonged to one man who has consolidated several farms, putting his labourers into the farm houses and pulling down the cottages. He and his labourers had entered into a compact

for ten shillings a week from Michaelmas to Michaelmas. The men had tried to get a revision of the bargain
recently, but without avail. "When a says a thing,"
observed a buxom dame, "you can't move'n, and," she
added emphatically, "I like'n all the better for't."

LETTER IX.

LARGE AND SMALL FARMS.

September 3.

DURING my rambles in the Eastern Counties I have found
the general state of things—the condition of land and crops,
labourers' wages, hours of work, cottage accommodation,
facilities for getting allotments, and so on—all varying from
place to place. But two things I have found almost invariable. Wherever I have been, I have found, as I have
repeatedly said, that as a rule almost without exception
population has been dwindling, and small farms have been
consolidating into large ones. This increase in the scale of
farming operations I find to be quite as striking a feature
of the agricultural situation wherever I have been as the
decrease in the population, and, as I have shown, it is
indeed to a great extent the cause of that decrease. The
consolidation of farms is not, of course, always a voluntary
proceeding. In some instances I find it attributed to the
folly and infatuation of landowners. Only yesterday a
gentleman told me of a case within his own knowledge in
which a farmer was giving thirty shillings an acre for land.
At that rate it was impossible to get on. He went to his
landlord, told him that his difficulties were such that it was
impossible he should continue to pay that rent. He offered
eighteen shillings as the utmost he could afford. The offer
was refused, the tenant left his farm, or at all events took
steps for securing another, and then apparently the landlord

discovered his mistake, and sent to say that he would accept
the eighteen shillings.   But it was too late, and eventually
the land was let at twelve and sixpence.   Several persons
have said to me that if landlords would be content to take
from small farmers rents as low as they are continually
having to take from large ones, the small man would not
have to give up.   No doubt that is often the case; but it is
safe to assume that, in a general way, landowners know their
own business best.   Here and there the short-sighted folly
of an individual may drive out a small farmer, and hand over
his land to a large one; but we may rest assured that
wide-spread movements—general changes such as this from
small farms to large ones—are not brought about by individual folly, but by the operation of great economic forces.
To a very large extent at least it is the landowners who are
assuming occupation of land for their own farming.   With
the price of wheat low, and seasons unfavourable, many
small farmers will tell you that during the past few seasons
they could do no good for themselves, even though they
were rent free.   Small farms have been given up because
they could not be made to pay.   Fresh tenants could not be
found for them, and landlords, rather than let them go to
ruin, have taken them into their own hands.   In Essex and
Suffolk I have again and again shown that the migration of
labour into the towns has been very largely due to the
reduction of the staff of men consequent on such changes.
In a short incursion I have made into Southern and Central
Norfolk I have found just the same thing going on.   " This
joining of one farm to another has been the curse of
Norfolk," said Mr. George Rix, a rather remarkable leader
of the agricultural labourers in the Eastern Counties.   " It
has been the curse of Norfolk," he repeated.   " It has made
a difference of a man to every hundred acres of land."   It
has done here, in fact, pretty much what it has done everywhere else.   It has reduced the number of hands employed,

it has in some localities overstocked the labour market, and, of course, has tended to keep down wages. From the agricultural labourer's point of view, it has been an unmitigated curse. The shopkeepers in the small towns have complained bitterly of it too. They say that instead of four or five households coming into a little town with their orders for farm implements, and household necessaries, and groceries and clothing, there is but one family, and that one as often as not gets supplied from the big co-operative stores in town. I have heard this again and again from shopkeepers. At the same time there is, of course, general complaint that instead of the rural population increasing and growing more profitable, it is continually dribbling away.

At present, then—observe that I am only quoting current opinions on the present phase of things—this consolidation of farming is extinction for the yeoman class, it is bad for the agricultural labourer, it is bad for the provincial shopkeeper, and it is bad for the community at large, not only because it is, as things stand, against the interests of entire classes of great importance, but because very commonly this large scale farming fails to produce as much as the land is capable of producing. A large farm wants an immense amount of oversight. The farmer cannot see to it himself. He has to trust to others, and he does not get good work out of his men, and his land is not well tilled. Another argument I have heard against extensive farming is that stock is not bred upon such farms to anything like the extent it should be. Animals at certain times require special attention, which they do not get because they are not under the master's eye. Losses are very frequent, and those who farm on a large scale prefer the branches of the business which are attended with fewer risks. I have already quoted the opinions of those who speak favourably of extensive operations. They say that as a man of capital—and in many cases with private resources quite apart from his land—

the big farmer can buy largely; he can get the best machinery; he can fully employ his horses and his men all the year round, and if the market for his produce is bad, he can wait till it improves. All this is universally admitted. But even with all his advantages, it is contended that for the large farmer himself the system is not entirely satisfactory, while for everybody else concerned it is absolutely bad.

All this is seen more or less clearly, and there is an intense and widespread feeling that something ought to be done by way of remedy. All sorts of speculations and suggestions are rife. Let us have technical education, say some who appear to think that if Hodge could only be persuaded to do his turnip-hoeing on scientific principles, his enjoyment of the work might make all the difference between ten shillings in the country and five-and-twenty in town. Certainly let us have technical education. Educate, educate, educate, by all means in your power. It will all help on towards the final solution of the question. But do not let us be simple enough to suppose that that alone will do it. By general consent it is the many-sided education of the rural districts that is emptying our fields and swelling the huge population of our towns. The agricultural labourers must have better cottages, say others. Of course they must. For us, as a community, to rest content that either in town or country people shall be penned up in such pig-sties as many of them are forced to put up with, would be a foul disgrace to us. We democrats must keep hammering away at this question of the housing of the working classes without pause or intermission, until every working-man's family has a house that is fit to live in. But, as I have already shown, young men are streaming away from villages in which the cottages are beautiful, absolutely all that could be desired for them, and allotments to boot. Cottage building will not do it alone. Others say, let the law be altered that compels the hapless fathers of families struggling to exist on eleven

shillings a week to contribute a shilling or eighteenpence of
their week's earnings for the maintenance of their old fathers
and mothers. Aye—something is wrong here, too. It is
right and proper that a man should help his old parents
when they can no longer help themselves ; but it is pushing
a right principle to a brutal application when half-starved
peasants have 10 or 15 per cent. of their scanty earnings
wrung out of them every week of their lives, to save the
pockets of ratepayers. Nor is the cash payment the whole
of the matter. Pitiful tales could be told of days of lost
labour and weary tramps over long miles, and of fruitless
appeals to Boards of Guardians to relieve poor wretches of
burdens they are not able to bear. Everywhere the labouring poor speak bitterly of this demand upon them. " I
stuck to th' old man as long as I could," said a labourer,
"and I 'ould do it. Th' old 'un 'ad a seat by my fireside
and a bit o' some't to eat while I could gi't to'n. But when
he went into the 'ouse 'cause I couldn't afford to keep'n at
'ome and feed the young'ns, they didn't aughter a come
down on me for a shil'n a week, and I told 'em so." " You
went before the guardians ? " " Yes, and I 'ad to walk five
mile through a drenching rain and five mile back over it,
and then they wouldn't let me off. They said as I must
pay, and I wa'n't workin' above half time, and they know'd
it." In the abstract principle the law is right ; the practical application of it by rural Boards of Guardians—largely,
of course, composed of rate-paying farmers—is often a cruel
wrong. There is urgent need for alteration here. But here
again I fear amendments are not likely to have any material
effect on the solution of the agricultural question.

Yet another suggestion is made in a letter which has
reached me from a gentleman who is strongly of opinion
that, "whatever the Liberal party may do in the future,
unless the curse of drink is stayed in some manner, you can
never do any permanent good for the people of the villages."

I sincerely hope that the Liberal party will do whatever may be thought wise and practicable to " stay the curse of drink " in the villages, and the towns too. I cannot say that in the course of these rambles I have come across much evidence of it. In some of the villages there have been no public-houses. I went through three in one afternoon, in which my attention was called to the fact that there was no public-house. I must not pretend to say that I take this to be evidence that all the people were teetotallers. In many parts they are given to brewing their own beer, and, for cheapness at all events, they quite cut out the brewer and the publican. They give, I am told, four and six or five shillings for a bushel of malt, and a shilling a pound for hops, and out of this they brew eighteen gallons of beer, for which at the public-house they would have to pay two-pence-ha'penny a pint. But, apart from this, some of the big landowners won't have a public-house on their estates, and I was told more than once in answer to inquiries that drunkenness was not very rife among the villages. How could it be, I was asked, on village incomes? Now let me entreat the teetotal readers of the *Daily News*, whom I already see in imagination sitting down as one man to pen an indignant protest against my gross misrepresentation of village life in this respect—let me entreat them to observe that I am not speaking of village life in general, but only of so much of it as has come under my own observation. I know that in other localities it may be different, and even here there may be more of the evil of it than meets the casual eye or the chance inquiry. I am fully alive to the grave difficulty that is presented in the drinking habits of the labouring class to every advance of social progress. We must battle with this difficulty by every means in our power, especially by means of intelligent recreation and opportunities of social intercourse apart from the public-house. We have got to battle with drink and all its evils, but do not let

us delude ourselves with any idea that the putting down of
drink and making the people sober is a solution of the
agricultural problem by which we are now confronted. All
these points I have alluded to are worthy of the most
earnest consideration ; but something more will have to be
done, or the agricultural problem must remain unsolved.

LETTER X.

ALLOTMENTS ONLY AN ALLEVIATION.

September 8.

THE Allotments Act, I suppose we are all pretty well agreed,
has proved a wretched failure so far as any direct action
has gone ; but the attempts that have been made to put it
into force, and the discussion it has called forth, and the
attention it has been the means of directing to the subject
of allotments have not been without their effect, and if small
holdings could solve the agricultural problem it would, I
think, be in a fair way of solution. Public opinion has
done much, and in moving about the country I am struck
by the extent to which allotments are being provided. Dr.
Wallace suggested in a letter to the *Daily News* the other
day that I should make a point of inquiry of every labourer
I talked with whether, if he could get land of a good quality,
at a fair rent and on a practically permanent tenure, he could
not make a good living out of it. I have not acted on Dr.
Wallace's suggestion, for it has seemed to me unnecessary to
do so. Without any exception, so far as I can call to mind,
allotments not of the best quality let at anything but a fair
rent, and on a tenure terminable at the caprice of the landowner or his agent, have been taken with an avidity which
renders it quite needless to inquire whether labourers would
be glad to have land on the terms suggested.

I have seen a great many allotment grounds, but I do

not remember coming across any instance of a plot unable
to find a tenant.   I have seen some to-day on the Duke of
Marlborough's estate near Woodstock, not by any means
the best of land, let in plots up to two acres at a rental of
thirty-five shillings an acre.   As allotment rents go that is
moderate ; yet an overseer informed me that the farm out
of which the plots had been taken was let at either thirteen
and six or fourteen and six, he was not quite sure which—
certainly not more than fourteen and six.   They were all
readily taken at this, and the general opinion was that they
would pay very well, though none of the men I talked with
seemed very enthusiastic over them.   "It's better nor nothin'," said one man.   "It'll put a few taters in yer pot."
Very grim and sarcastic was the smile that puckered the old
fellow's face as he told me the rents the poor labourers had
to pay for their bits of plots as compared with the farm rents
around.   He didn't know exactly what the farmers paid,
but he knew the allotment rent was some't over twice as much.
" They does a little charity and they doubles their income,"
said he, with a sardonic grin.   I talked with many persons
in this village on the subject of allotments, and I found
pretty much the same feeling everywhere.   These bits of
ground were a very good thing, some assistance, but nothing
at all calculated to keep young men in the village.   " They
ha' been goin'," said an intelligent thatcher, "and they 'ool
go."   The state of things in that village he thought was
scandalous.   There wa'n't nigh cottages enough.   People
were bound to stay where they were.   There was nowhere
for 'em to move to, and they had to " pig in " just as they
could.   " There's quite big families in the village," said one
woman, "and they on'y got one sleepin' room.   It's no
business to be."

" It's pretty nigh time somebody came round and spoke
a bit for poor people," said one young married woman as
she stitched away with unflagging energy at a white glove

she was making.   She was in one of a row of cottages with their backs towards the public highway and their fronts looking out over long strips of garden, beyond which were the new allotments that had been taken possession of last September, and were now full of a good crop of potatoes and beans and wheat and barley.   The little places looked extremely pretty and pleasant with their vine-clad fronts and clean-looking rough-stone paving, and picturesque old well and smother of flowers, and chubby, rosy-cheeked children playing about, the pictures of health and bucolic content. " He don't look bad on bread and lard and fat bacon, do 'e ? " said a proud mother of a two-year-old cherub, who had come up towards us gnawing a green kidney bean by way of varying his somewhat monotonous diet.   " No, he really doesn't.   Is that all he gets ? "   " Yes, sir ; that's about all."   " Well, he won't starve while he can get plenty of bread and lard and fat bacon."   " No, sir, that's true enough, if us could on'y be sure o' getting enough on't."   The little places looked the very picture of peace, cleanliness, and comfort, and yet the impression one brought away after ten minutes' chat with the people was that they were constantly engaged in a hard struggle for existence, and were worried by a sense of the precariousness of their living.   Just now there was work for all, but it was the winter that was the great dread, when the women very often had to keep the men.   Yes, there was a bit o' glovin' round about there, and that helped 'em wonderful, and it was work as they could do at home and look after the children.   But that ain't so good as it was.   Prices had gone down a penny and twopence a pair, and the Duchess of Marlborough had set up a factory in Woodstock for makin' gloves by machinery.   No doubt she meant it kind, but it had done 'em a lot o' harm.   They found a'ready as there ain't so much work to be got, and prices was lower.   They didn't know what'd come of it.   The summer wages were twelve

E

shillings, and some o' the men were very often out for three months and goodness knows 'ow they lived. Twelve shillings a week wasn't none too much.

I tried to get these women to give me some statement of the way in which they spent their twelve shillings. "Now just tell me," I said, "how people manage to live on twelve shillings a week." "Oh, Lord ha' mussy! I can't tell 'ow they does it," said one of them. "I dunno myself 'ow the money goes. There's seven of us—me and my husband and five children, all too young to do anything but eat 'earty and kick out shoe leather." "Well, now, what do you manage to do with twelve shillings?" "Well, there's two goes for rent to begin with, and five and threepence a quarter for club money." "That is in case of sickness?" "Yes, sir; if my 'usband was sick he'd get ten shilling a week and the doctor." "Well, that 'is about fivepence a week, so that you have nine and sevenpence for feeding and clothing the seven of you?" "Yes, I s'pose that's it." "And how does that go?" "Blessed if I knows, sir. You goes to shop with five shillins, and it don't seem to go nowhere." "No, that it don't," chimes in another. "I often says to myself 'I dunno 'ow the money goes.'" "Oh, drat the money!" exclaims another in the innermost corner of the room. "I wish there wa'n't none." It is a pleasant little scene of rural life this. There is no pressing anxiety as to the immediate future. The women now and then sigh, it is true, but they jest and laugh at their troubles, as we are all apt to do when our troubles are at a distance. It is the high tide of the year's prosperity, or it would be if the skies would only clear. And these villagers are among the most fortunate of their class. Some of them have a little supplementary industry to rely upon, and the summer pay of the men is twelve shillings. I have just left an Oxfordshire village where the normal summer pay till two or three weeks ago was ten shillings, and I have had indicated to me villages in this part of the country where wretched families have to subsist as best they can on nine shillings a week all through the winter. What wonder if now and again people die outright of cold and starvation.

Since beginning to write this, my attention has been directed to a case that came before an Essex Coroner just after the last bitter winter. A woman died, and her husband was charged with "culpable neglect." Oh, the ghastliness of some of our judicial jokes! The poor fellow had struggled and striven through the cruel winter, he and his wife and family, on nine shillings a week with stoppages for wet days and snowy days, and days when the ground was frozen hard as the heart of the world around. It was proved that when in full work he had but nine shillings, and sometimes he had but two or three days' work a week. A short time before the inquest he had been out of work for a month at a stretch. The coroner said the man couldn't be charged with culpable neglect. No ; clearly not. Poor fellow ! he had battled with hunger and despair and misery, and had come bravely through till towards the spring, when times would be better. But the wife had grown thin and feeble. She had pined and starved, and presently came what the doctor called "accidental hæmorrhage," syncope, and the children were motherless. There must be an appalling amount of this kind of thing coming within only a very short step of the final catastrophe in some of these remote villages especially, even where, in harvest time, all looks so peaceful and pleasant and prosperous. As I have said, I have just left a village where till recently ten shillings was the weekly wage. The agricultural unionists have been round there, however, and two or three weeks before the ordinary time of harvest the masters consented to give twelve. "Do you think that will stand good after harvest?" I asked a man likely to know a good deal of the masters as well as the men. "No," he said, "I reckon it won't. As soon as harvest is over the

farmers will get rid of all they can anyhow do without."
" Are all the men kept on here during the winter?" I asked
a labourer in one of the villages. "No; not all on 'em in
the winter," he replied. "How many should you think are
out in the winter?" The fellow took a puff or two at his
pipe and looked out across the garden. "I should say
there was a dozen or fifteen." "Married men?" "Most on
'em." "And what do they do?" "God knows. Starves,
I s'pose."

When a man has got a piece of ground it seems pretty
clear he need not starve, even when he gets out of work in
the winter. "Thank God I be independent o' the farmer
this winter," said a labourer to an intelligent artisan with
whom I was talking yesterday; "I get half an acre o' wheat,
half an acre o' barley, and a quarter of an acre of potatoes."
There was wheat for his bread and barley meal for his pig.
"With bread and bacon and potatoes I shan't starve, and
it'll go 'ard wi' me if I can't find a job or two as'll pay the
rent and a bit o' firin'." That looks like a solid, unquestion-
able advance in comfort and independence; but it is the
special perplexity of a task such as mine—the task of moving
about the country and talking with everybody—that one
no sooner gets hold of a bit of firm and solid footing
than he is sure to meet somebody who pushes him off of
it. "My dear sir," exclaims a leading Liberal of lifelong
standing in this constituency of Mid-Oxford, repeating almost
word for word the opinion of the Essex Tory parson, "this
talk about affairs in the villages being put right by allotments
is the sheerest humbug." His contention is that the advantage derived from the allotment, though real and substantial
enough, will prove only temporary, and that the man who
can make a little in this way will be able to work for rather
lower wages, and that sooner or later he will be bound to do
so. John Stuart Mill argued in the same way, as one of
the correspondents of the *Daily News* pointed out the other

day. The force of this argument may, however, be somewhat modified by the fact that the population of the villages
is going down and labour becoming scarcer. On the other
hand, the demand for labour is growing less. Machinery is
still displacing men, and grass lands are extending. There
is a balance of arguments for and against, and I must leave
the readers of the *Daily News* to say which side has the
preponderance.

I may have further opinions to quote on the subject of
allotments in another article. Meanwhile I may say that I
was very much struck by what I found in an Oxfordshire
village to which I had been directed as one of the poorest
and most ramshackle in the county. I strolled through
the place, and felt at first that I had been misdirected. I
leaned over a garden wall, and talked with an old man who
had just been digging up half a barrow-load of splendid
potatoes. They were " magnum boneys," said the old fellow,
and very nice taters, and he proudly held up one or two for
my inspection. I suppose the fine turn-out of potatoes put
the old man for the moment in an optimistic frame of mind,
for everything about that place seemed highly satisfactory.
The cottages weren't so bad and rents were very reasonable,
and they all had gardens and there were plenty of allotments
and work for those who could do it, and hardly anybody on
the rates and nobody had left the place so far as he knew.
Sons ? Yes, he had sons, but no, they weren't in the village.
One was in " Birnigham " and one was gone to Ameriky
and another to Australia, and I rather think he said another
had gone to Yorkshire. Why hadn't they settled in the
village ? Why, 'cause they could do better. The old man's
wife now came out to call him to dinner, and they both agreed
that it was a poor, beggarly place, and no good for nobody.
They didn't want their boys to settle there. " I don't want
my children to settle too close round me," said the little old
woman, whom I put down to be over seventy years of age,

with a healthĭly bronzed face, wrinkled all over, but full of
vivacity. "I don't want 'em too close round me. I'd like
'em to be in Banbury or Oxford, where I could go and see
'em sometimes ; but drat 'em if they be close round 'e, they
al'ays runs to the granny, whatever's the matter. I like 'em
best a little way off, and it is a poor, beggarly place this.
But there, the Lord al'ays makes a way for them as wants to
do," and the dame chattered on, all the time seeming to
hurry her spouse away to his dinner. She had been up that
morning at six o'clock, had had a turn in the garden, and
swept round her house and run round the village with her
papers. Yes, she sold papers. She had got fourteen customers, and she got a halfpenny a piece out of 'em, only she
had to pay two-pence for carriage. Bless the Lord, very
few people could do as she could at her age. I don't know
how many yards o' lace she hadn't made since the New
Year, and there were "arrands" to run, and one thing and
another. I was told afterwards that she was considerably
over seventy, and if anybody would offer her sixpence she
would think nothing of trudging away to Bicester, four miles
off and four miles back again, to execute any little commission ; and it is, I am told, no unusual thing to see her
come in with a basket on each arm and another tied round
her waist.

Now these were the first people I spoke to in the village,
and I found that when the old folks united in pronouncing
it a beggarly place they were quite correct in some respects
at least. This was the village I have already alluded to as
the place in which ten shillings a week had been the rate of
wages up till just before harvest—a shilling a week lower
than in any village I had found in Essex or Suffolk as the
summer pay. Yet in this village allotments are to be had
in abundance, and I am assured that the number of people
who are doing well with them and who have pigs in their
sties is quite exceptional. I ought to add, however, that the

cottages, bright and pretty as they looked outside, were, some of them, of the most beggarly description, and are actually letting at threepence a week, or, with a bit of garden and a chain-and-a-half of allotment ground, at fourpence-ha'penny. These, it must be understood, are not the rents to the labourers alone—the old man with the "magnum boneys" had not worked for a farmer for five years, and paid fourpence-ha'penny—so that low rents are not to be regarded as equivalent to pay for labour. This village struck me as affording a remarkable illustration of the tendency referred to by the leading Liberal whom I have quoted—the tendency for wages to keep down to bare subsistence. Here are the cheapest cottages, and the most thriving allotments, and the lowest wages I have found anywhere yet. In 1881 the population of this village was about 360 souls; now it is 325, and still dwindling. These are facts, whatever may be the inferences from them.

LETTER XI.

PUBLICANS AND PARSONS.

September 11.

It has been difficult to move through our English villages during the past two or three weeks, and then to sit down and write about them without gushing a little. Even the stormy weather of this memorable summer, trying as it has been for all who are concerned in harvesting, has in many respects enhanced the loveliness of the village and its surroundings. The drenching rains have kept the grass in the fields, and the mosses and lichens on the cottage roofs exceptionally brilliant, the roadways white and clean, the orchards and woodlands fresh and verdant. Never can rosy apples have looked rosier, or apricots sunnier, or plums jucier, or flowers gayer than they do this year in their

setting of lustrous foliage, quite free from dust, and as yet
scarcely touched by any indication that

> " Winter comes to rule the varied year
> Sullen and sad."

Even the lowering rain-clouds, that to the farmer have kept
rolling up behind the hills like demons of destruction, do
but add sublimity to the peaceful and pastoral scene,
and, combined with sudden bursts of sunshine, often lend
a breadth of effect and vividness of colour surpassingly
beautiful. Step for a moment into this little ancient church,
with its ivy-mantled tower and hoarse-ticking clock, its open
doorways overspread with nets to keep out the birds, its
massive stone walls with their queer little nooks and niches
telling of holy water and images of saints, its venerable font
and antiquated wrought-iron work, and worm-eaten old
seats. An appropriate place to wait out of a thunder shower
for a few minutes—to wait and muse how

> " Out of the old fieldes, as men saithe,
> Cometh al this new corne fro yere to yere."

And now, while the last big drops of the storm are streaming
down slantwise through a dazzling flood of sunshine, step
out again under the roof of the liche gate, with the rain-
bespangled grass and the mossy gravestones at your back,
and before you on the other side of the way an orchard with
its ten thousand ruddy apples blazing like gems under the
pattering rain-drops. Over the top of the broken wall you
can see through beneath the tangled boughs of the shady
orchard into the sun-flooded meadow, where brown and
white cattle are grazing in groups of indescribable charm.
Away to the left the pretty cottages with their thatched roofs,
their steps of unhewn rock, their windows full of geraniums
and fuchsias, and their porches overgrown with autumn
roses and canariensis, are hobbling down the broken pathway in a picturesque, irregular line, their red chimney-stacks

gently streaming out into the trees above the soft, blue smoke of the wood fires, on which busy matrons are beginning to prepare the evening meal for father, whose work has been stopped by the drenching downpour, and who will presently be home. The rain is over now; stroll down the village and gossip with the people. There is nothing very startling or sensational to be gleaned, but you get some valuable side-lights on village life, and most of the folks have something worth listening to. Here is a venerable patriarch with a marvellous memory for what "I says to he" and "he says to me says he" fifty years ago. His father met with an accident when he was a young man, and died in a day or two, leaving his wife to the care of the parish. And the grey-headed old man tells you—as no doubt he has been telling for many a year—how that the next day was relieving day, and the guardians made an order that he was to keep his mother as well as his own family on his eight shillings a week. Indignation still sparkles in the old man's eyes as he tells how he met Muster Sumkins, and Muster Sumkins said as he was to keep his mother. "I says to'n, I says I oon't keep my mother. He says, 'You oon't?' and I says, 'No, I oon't, for any on 'em,' I says, and I oon't neither. I'd ha' sell'd my sticks, and gone to Ameriky." Here is another villager who has withstood the powers that be, and, as he says, was "bunked out o' the place" neck and crop, with seven young children at his heels. Physically, the man is a splendid specimen of the agricultural labourer, and tells his story with evident satisfaction, though it doesn't seem to be entirely to his credit. He had just lost his wife, and the lady of the village wanted him to send some of his children to school, but he wouldn't. "Why wouldn't you send your children to school?" I inquired. "Cause I oodn't," said the man, with a smile of dogged obstinacy. "I'd a mind to do as I liked." Seemingly the lady was right in her wish, and the man was wrong in his refusal. But to evict him from home and work and village in this fashion was just one of those high-handed exercises of absolute power that do so much to widen and deepen the chasm between the two classes of the village.

At another place in the same neighbourhood I hear a droll story, and yet another display of insubordination on the part of a labourer. A fine stalwart fellow, with a shrewd, intelligent face, stands at his cottage door in his shirt sleeves, with his hands tucked down deep into the pockets of his fustian trousers, and tells me of somebody or other who'll have to go up to the hall to-morrow over some charity bread. In a certain parish bread is given away to the cottagers every Sunday after church. So many residents in the parish take it in turns, and, till recently, the wife or children of the men entitled to it could receive it. The churchwardens, however, lately resolved that this should no longer be permitted, and that the man who didn't personally come and take his sermon should have no bread. The truant villagers resented this, and one of them, who had lost his turn at the loaves, went the following Sunday and helped himself, at the same time dealing out to the good people at the church some of his private opinions about them. My informant, a Radical politician, was evidently in sympathy with the insurrectionary villager, but he shrewdly suspected that he would have to pay for his audacity. He'd just like to see one o' the newspapers get hold o' that story. They'd make sommit on't, he'd bet. The man would certainly have to pay, for they would make it out that he had been brawling in church, and he would have nobody to defend him. "What 'e wants," said the man, "is a good sharp lawyer to tackle 'em for 'im. If 'e could only get Sir Charles Russell to tak't up for'n he'd let 'em know. They'd soon put their tails atween their legs when they sin 'e." I am afraid the occasion is gone now, and that Sir Charles has lost a fine

opportunity of acquiring undying fame. Before the day
was out I was destined to hear a little more of this case. I
stopped at a village inn and called for a cup of tea. The
landlord refused it point blank, and I was immediately
invited by the company in the tap-room to "have a pull"
at their quart pots. As graciously as I could I declined the
beer, and insisted on the tea, and after some little wrangling
I got my way. While the tea was brewing I studied village
life in the tap-room, and out of curiosity I brought forward
the charity bread. Oh for a phonograph that would reproduce for me just now the little tit-bits of dialogue that
ensued! as the wizened little old man in the smock frock
and the wideawake told how as they did say as Joe
Stuggins, or whatever his name was, had in the height of
argument bobbed his nose again' the churchwarden's. It
was inexpressibly droll. In the course of the discussion it
was asserted and evidently believed by the men that in the
village in which they sat a hundred pounds had been left
for charity and had entirely vanished, and there were dark
allusions to money that had been paid to hush up somebody's theft of brasses from the church.

The scene was amusing enough while one could shut
one's eyes to all but the humour of it ; but it had its painful
and unpleasant aspect from another point of view. It is of no
use crying down public-houses. We must have houses of
entertainment, and before I close this series of articles I
hope to be able to say something on the subject of what
they ought to be in the villages. This place I chanced to
go into affords a fair illustration of what they ought not
to be. I got my cup of tea ; but suppose one of those
labouring men had preferred a cup of tea to a pot of beer,
what would have been his chance of getting it ? One of the
party when I went in was quite evidently drunk, but he
called for another quart, and the landlord brought it to him
without the least hesitation. What hope is there of

rendering our peasantry sober, and thrifty, and self-respecting, with dens of this sort in their midst? Where is the parson of that old ivy-mantled church? Why doesn't he put his foot down and say this shall not be, and that a landlord who turns a drunken man out into the village shall have the rector of the parish to deal with before the magistrates next licensing day? What is the good of having a " Christian gentleman " in every village if that gentleman can't tackle a flagrant iniquity of this kind and by hook or crook put an end to it? I don't like to attack the clergy indiscriminately. I can see, and I am sure that many of the country clergy are men entitled to every respect, and are doing an invaluable work in the dark corners of the land. But as I move about and talk with the people I cannot shut my eyes to the fact that half the evils of village life could be remedied if the parsons were worth their salt. Half of them seem to me to be mere nonentities, with no understanding of the people, no sympathy with them in their hopes and fears, their struggles and sufferings, no sort of fellow-feeling with them whatever. " Haven't you got a clergyman here? " I inquired of one woman in reply to her plaintive and spiritless wish that somebody could look after the poor a bit. " Yes, sir," was the reply, " we got one, but we don't see much on 'im. I been here ten years and I don't know as he ever been near my house." " He ain't much good to us," said a bystander. " Oh, I dunno," said another, anxious apparently to say what she could; " I never 'eard as he done nobody no harm." Damning with faint praise, this, with a vengeance. Few of the villages I have been through have any place where men may go and talk over the news together, and smoke their pipes and sing a song without the necessity for beer drinking. I passed through one village and talked with a Nonconformist local preacher, who told me that an effort had been made to set up something of the kind in that place, by the joint action

of three or four of the Dissenting bodies.   They had built a
hall, and it was to have been a place for healthy recreation
and entertainment.   But none of the good people seemed to
understand the necessity for anything but religious service,
and as it was not specially identified with the "cause" of
either sect, the scheme fell through.   One of them has now
monopolised the use of the place, in which services are
occasionally held, but ordinarily it is shut up, while five or
six public-houses are in full blast—two of them I noticed
actually standing back to back.

LETTER XII.

DUCAL LAND-GRABBERS.

September 14.

I AM afraid the people of Woodstock have imbibed something of the discontented spirit that appears so very generally
to be animating the agricultural world around them, and
that they are not sufficiently thankful for the blessings they
are privileged to enjoy.   Not unto every small town is it
given to have a great ducal landowner overshadowing it as
the Duke of Marlborough overshadows Woodstock, and one
would think that the inhabitants of this interesting old town
could not be too grateful for the happy fortune which has
given them one Providence above and another at Blenheim
Palace.   Possibly there may be some of them who have a
due sense of their happy lot, but if there are I have not yet
met with them.   I have been moving, I fear, in rather a bad
set, and they have been doing their best to prejudice me
against great landowners and the sort of influence they
exercise.   Clearly there is a democratic ferment at work in
this part of the world, as in so many others, and after what
I have seen to-day I cannot help feeling that it is quite
time there was.   Starting from Woodstock, I have had

to-day a most interesting and instructive drive through
Bladon, Handborough, Combe, Kiddington, Glympton,
and Wootton. One or two of these villages are beautiful
little places—in some respects all one could reasonably
desire. Bladon, for one, just outside the wall of Blenheim
Park, is quite a little show place. It is nearly all owned by
the Duke of Marlborough, and though he and the vicar of
Woodstock are at loggerheads over a matter which I am not
concerned here to discuss, they have between them given
the people good cottages and gardens, a fine church, and
free schools, and many other things that must contribute
largely to their comfort and welfare. Kiddington and
Glympton—owned by different wealthy landlords—are also
quite model villages. But the democrats of Woodstock
seem even fiercer in their condemnation of these pet villages
than of such places as Handborough, where the conditions
of life are in many respects the very reverse of all that is to
be found in the others. Both Kiddington and Glympton
have within living memory been largely reduced by the
ruthless pulling down of cottages. At one time this was
done for the simple purpose of clearing out poor people,
who were not wanted for the profit and convenience of the
landowner, and who were likely to be a burden on the
rates. "Here are we, the great landowners, the only
people on earth of the slightest importance. We don't
want these cottagers; turn them out and pull down their
houses, and let them drag their wretched carcases to the
workhouse in the next parish, where we shall not be
responsible for their maintenance. What have we to do
with them?" I don't know whether the present owners
have done this; possibly not, for it is many years now since,
by the union of parishes, this sort of thing was checked.
But other motives have led to the demolition of cottages,
and a resident in the district told me of many small houses
he could remember to have been swept away. These

places now apparently contain just about the number of dwellings required for the estates—not the least reference to the number of people the land could and would maintain, but just what the squires choose to have there. I am assured that it is literally true that if in one of these places a young man wants to get married and settle down, it is of no use merely to woo and to win the young woman. He must induce the squire to consent also. "Where's So-and-So?" "Oh, he's gone out of the neighbourhood. He wanted to get married, and the squire wouldn't put up a cottage and wouldn't hear of anybody taking in a lodger, so he had to go."

In these villages attempts to introduce Nonconformist ideas have been found to be quite hopeless. "In that cottage yonder," said my guide, "a man became a Nonconformist and had the audacity to hold a prayer meeting in his own room. He got notice to quit, and was turned out of house and home and employment—not of course for the prayer meeting; oh dear no." A Liberal politician here told me that in some election recently—County Council, I think he said—there were eighty voters in one such proprietary village, and he could only get one solitary individual so much as to speak to him. "No, sir, excuse me, I really can't. I don't want to lose my coals at Christmas." That is the sort of thing with which the forces of progress have to contend, and it is not surprising that there are many about here who regard "good landlords" with utter abhorrence. They are beneficent, but their beneficence implies the forfeiture of every particle of freedom, and the submission of the people to whatever may be imposed upon them. I heard to-day of a poor widow who shortly after her husband's death had a call by the estate agent. He came on Sunday evening, and told her she must get out of her cottage and shift into another. Certain changes had been decided on, and she must make

room for somebody else. The poor woman didn't want to
leave her home, and protested against it. Even if she went,
surely she was entitled to some notice. Yes, no doubt—
legally. For all that she must go, and at once ; if not she
must expect no more benefits. And, poor soul, she meekly
submitted and went—swept out like so much dirt before a
besom. "You have no idea what a condition of serfdom
the people are reduced to on some of these big estates,"
said a resident here to me to-day. The squire owns the
cottage, he can give or withhold allotments, he is practically
the sole employer; his wife and daughters give coal and
lend blankets, and look after the people when they are sick,
and the parson finds schooling and religion, and there is
no resisting any of them in anything. There is literally
nothing for the people to do but plod quietly on as they
are told, take what is given them, and be thankful. It is
all well intended, all beneficent and beautiful, but it is the
abnegation of all manhood, of everything like citizenship.
The power of the clergy, when they happen to be men
of independent means, is often a deadly blight upon
the freedom of the poor. Just combine this power
with that of the squire to turn out a man, with wife
and children, from his house and his village and his
employment, and add to this combined power the blandish-
ments of the Primrose dames, and you have a phalanx
which—though thank God it is even now being broken,
and shall one day utterly be put to rout—will yet give us
many a long day's hard tussle.

Deeply conscious as one cannot but be of the tremendous
weight under which the liberty and independence of spirit
of the agricultural poor are being crushed, it is with grim
and hearty satisfaction that one comes across here and there
manifestations of a little good English pugnacity—aye, even
though the pugnacity may be not altogether in the right. I
could not help feeling this in the little village of Combe.

Combe is on the far side of Blenheim Park from Woodstock, a benighted little place if its reputation counts for anything. In driving into it from Woodstock you pass a ruinous old structure, which I had pointed out as a stable put up by a former Duke of Marlborough for the shelter of his horse while he was paying his respects to Miss Glover in the village. His workpeople were always long in arrear with their wages, and they used to waylay his Grace near this stable and dun him for money. "Oh, you shall be paid; you shall all be paid," he would say. "Ah, but when and wheer, yer Grace?" demanded the men. "I remembers 'em doing it many a time," said a countryman to me yesterday. I suppose his Grace—let us be careful to give the most noble duke his proper title—I suppose his Grace found this unreasonable dunning of his starving labourers troublesome and inconvenient. They were thorns and brambles in his primrose path, and the lady was soon transferred to Blenheim, and the villagers will tell you now how Duchess Glover used to come dashing about Combe in her carriage. A little further on in the village you have another interesting little object in the shape of a Liliputian Wesleyan chapel. I don't know how the bit of land upon which it stands came to be available for the purpose, but I was informed that it was the only bit in the place that could be got, and, in order to make it do, one side of the building had to be planted in a pond, and the consequence is that it has always been damp and uncomfortable. A little higher up is the church, and an intelligent native with whom I strolled round pointed to one of the porches as having been at one time the Sunday-school room. There was no Dissent in the village at that time, and the parson's deputy in the school was one of the gardeners at Blenheim. The parson would look in and have a bit of chat about the gardens and flowers up at the palace, and as soon as he was gone old Jemmy Whatever-his-name-was would send one of

F

the children over to " The Cock " for a pot of beer. " Many's
a time I've sin children goin' into Sunday school with a pot
of fourpenny," said my informant.   Under this spiritually
minded and enlightened *régime* of the Church on the
one hand and the great landed proprietor on the other,
Combe seems to have been in the past a bye-word and a
scoffing to all the villagers around.   Anything specially
simple-minded and stupid it has been the habit to put
down to "Silly Combe," and in the country around you
may hear how that one native of the place sat on the branch
of a tree while he sawed it off, forgetting that he would let
himself down ; how that another turned a horse out to graze
with the nose-bag on, and so forth.   Practically, all the land
and all the houses belong to the Duke ; but it is far from
Blenheim Palace, and the management of it seems to be
left to agents, and they do or they don't do just as it seems
good to them.

As I moved up the village past the old stable and the
Wesleyan Chapel and the parish church, I noticed the wall
of a cottage bulging outwards to a degree which I thought
looked quite dangerous.   I examined the house further, and
it struck me that a good strong wind would be sufficient to
bring the whole place down in a mass of crumbled ruin.   I
was told that an old couple lived there, and I stepped into
the garden and spoke to the woman.   The poor, miserable-
looking, old creature—I should say between seventy and
eighty years of age—was full of complaints that they would do
nothing to the place.   She couldn't remember that they had
ever done anything.   " Come and look round 'ere, sir," she
said ; and I made my way through what had been once a
thriving garden, full of raspberry-canes and standard fruit-
trees and strawberry-beds.   The rafters were all broken
away, and were projecting over the eaves ; the thatched roof
had sunk in in the middle, and there was a hole through
which you might have dropped a wheelbarrow stopped up by

nothing but a few old rusty tea-trays, or something of the kind, loosely thrown into it. The walls were cracked and broken, and the window of the bedroom was lacking half its glass. " How do you manage with that bedroom window ? " I asked. " Oh, I got a bit o' board as I stop that up wi'," said the woman. " I never remember as they put a bit o' glass in the window, and I never lived nowhere else," she added. There were two bedrooms ; the one with the hole in the roof was totally uninhabitable. The water during all this wet, squally season had literally poured in there, flooding the place from top to bottom. The thatch over the smaller bedroom was not so bad as in the other room, but it let the rain in freely, and, as I have said, the window had only about half its glass in, and the wind must have blustered freely about every corner of that wretched hovel. Yet, up there, under the driest corner of that ruinous roof, lay all last winter a poor, bed-ridden old man said to be eighty-six or eighty-seven years of age. If anybody wants to verify this, he is there still, and the neighbours say that in the night-time they sometimes hear him crying and moaning piteously. The condition I have described must have been pretty much the state of the place for years past, yet the Duke of Marlborough's agent has, I am assured, been taking three pounds a year rent for it, and, if he cannot be said to have turned a deaf ear to all appeals to him, has again and again met them with promises that have never been fulfilled. As I have said, these people do or they leave undone just as they think proper, and there is no public opinion which dares express itself. But where's the parson ? Where's the one Christian gentleman in the village who goes to the agent or, if need be, to the duke, and says, " I am the friend of these poor people. This is wrong, and it must be put right " ; and when it isn't put right goes again and says, " This is wrong, and if it isn't put right I'll raise the devil about your ears ! " Where's the parson? Why, not a hundred yards off. "What sort of a fellow is he?" I asked an intelligent old man in the village. "Oh," he said, with a smile, "he never interferes wi' nobody, 'e don't."

Nor is atrocious neglect of this kind the only thing of which this village has to complain. One would like, if one could, to discuss these rural matters in cold blood and with level judgment. But I confess that it has made my blood boil to drive round about Blenheim Park, and see how the labouring poor have been and are being defrauded of what belongs to them. There has been common land enough about some of these villages to make every family in them comfortable and prosperous. It would have given them room for cottages and gardens and allotments, or when, by-and-by, we get local councils, it would have afforded the means of some form of public co-operative husbandry which would have made agricultural labourers only too eager to get into the district instead of scuttling away from it as they are doing. Every man will tell you of somebody who has gone off to the railways or to the mines in Yorkshire, or to try his luck in London. Here, as elsewhere, farms have been con- solidated into large holdings, expenses have been cut down, and machinery has supplanted labourers. "The corn at one time," said a man, "used to give the labourer about here nine and ten shillings an acre at harvest time; but machinery does the work now, and all the labourer has to do is to pick up the sheaves that the machine has cut and bound, and stand them up in shocks." He gets now about ninepence or tenpence an acre. The winter wages for many of the people, I hear, are nine shillings, with stoppages for wet days. But still, if the common land could have been well tilled for the common benefit, it would have made all the difference between starvation and comfort in the winter- time. But what has become of the common land? Nearly all of it belongs to the Duke of Marlborough. Here are these men, whose park wall I have had variously estimated at from nine to fourteen miles in length, and with unnumbered thousands of acres, and whole villages of property outside, have been generation after generation gobbling up piece after piece of the common lands of the poor, and they are doing it still. " Look there," said an influential Liberal of Woodstock, " the Duke of Marlborough has no business whatever with that land, but as Lord of the Manor he just simply takes it, and nobody dares oppose him." The thing looked plain as a pikestaff. There was the park wall bounding the duke's private property. Between that wall and the road was a space of waste land, common property. The transfer from public to private ownership is begun by sticking up a notice, " All persons depositing rubbish on this land will be prosecuted.—Marlborough." A little further on comes the next stage, and a low stone wall skirts the road and shuts in the open land. It is now the duke's, and if the people want it for allotments he has no objection to let it them at five-and-twenty shillings an acre. Again and again men said to me, " we are paying for our own land." For a mile or so before you get into Combe the road runs through some pasture land. There is not a doubt, I think, that that was all common land. Some of it is still unenclosed, but on both sides the road throughout the greater part of it a double railing and a quick-set hedge have been planted within the past year or two. All the people in Combe believe it belongs to them, and a pleasant walk that men have trodden from time out of mind has been taken away.

One old man told me he remembered his grandfather having a flock of sheep on that land, and it was all open and common property. Another said he couldn't recollect it being open, but the first he knew of it was that a farmer, whose tomb he pointed out in the graveyard, had rented it of the Duke at ten shillings an acre. One Sunday he remembers the agent getting the people together down in a field yonder and telling them he was going to drain it and otherwise improve it, and they could have it in plots at two pounds an acre. "It was their own land," said the man; "however, they took it at two pounds, and had it for years, and got it into good condition. Well, th' old dook died, and the next dook took it away from 'em. I remember it well." Up in the little old church there is a painted board stuck up in front of the gallery, registering a solemn compact that for one piece of this "common or waste land" the Duke of Marlborough is to pay six guineas a year. Whether that six guineas is still paid to the overseers for the benefit of the parish I cannot say; but it is unanswerable evidence as to the original common rights in the land, and everybody in Combe will tell you that in exchange for their rights of cutting furze and turf on another piece of the same common the Duke of the day solemnly pledged himself to send into the village loads of faggots on certain days. The Duke of Marlborough still, of course, holds that piece of land, but never a stick of their firing do the poor people get. How long will the common-sense and right feeling of the people of England endure this sort of thing? Not very long, I think, unless all the signs of the times are utterly misleading. In just the same way the Duke of Marlborough has acquired that piece of land at Combe by engaging to perform public services that are no longer rendered—to say nothing of a good deal more that they appear to have taken merely by cool impudence—so were their manorial rights acquired in exchange for duties that are no longer required of them. These matters must be thoroughly overhauled, and the great reforming party of this country must administer to these great, lawless landowners of insatiable maw emetics powerful enough to make them disgorge. On some system or other the people must get back to the land, and there could hardly be a better beginning than to begin with the lands that are justly their own. Even here in this little obscure corner of the rural world the people are beginning to put down the foot, and when a little time ago another piece of their common land was going to be appropriated to a purpose to which they had given no consent, they doggedly refused to permit it. " We ha' had enough of our land filched away from we," they said, "and we'll ha' no more on't." In this case, to which I had intended to refer at length, but which I must leave for another letter, they were, I think, unfortunate and wrong ; but, notwithstanding that, the mere fact of their resistance is a healthy sign of the times, and such signs are multiplying on all hands.

LETTER XIII.

A MODEL VILLAGE CLUB.

September 17.

I CLOSED my last letter by alluding to a point on which the inhabitants of Combe had taken a firm stand against an attempt to appropriate a piece of common ground to a purpose to which they had not given consent—a gratifying manifestation of spirit in one respect, though in another unfortunate and mistaken. It will be well worth while to give some account of this affair, because in one or two respects it is interesting and instructive. The village in summer is a pleasant little place, with a triangular expanse of greensward in the heart of it. It was a very small slice from the edge of this village green that it was proposed to take for the purpose of enlarging a little the plot of ground required for a sort of village club. Few places could require it more. Across Blenheim Park, Combe is, I suppose, between two and three miles from Woodstock, but it is a long drive round by road. It seems far out of the world, and in the winter-time must be a depressingly dull, sequestered little nook. It has an old church, a couple of chapels, and several public-houses ; apart from these, any facilities for social intercourse were not only entirely lacking, but, as the people were nearly all of them extremely poor, and there were no leaders to set anything afoot, any such facilities seemed quite hopeless. Some few years back, however, a couple of ladies, mother and daughter, settled here, and the younger, Miss Adela Brooke, planned the institution I have referred to. I am giving now an account of the matter in general terms. In some points of detail I may be subject to correction, but substantially the affair may be taken as I give it. This institution was to be wholly for the public good. The scheme, I understand, was entirely Miss Brooke's; it was to be for the recreation and enjoyment of the villagers—a public-house without the drink, one reading-room for men and another for boys, a room for games, to be used occasionally for a little music, or a lecture, or such entertainment as might be found practicable; there would be a skittle-alley, a quoit-ground, and so forth. The village could not possibly afford either to put it up or to maintain it when it was up. The money would have to come from Miss Brooke or her friends. Nothing could have been more reasonable than for this lady to expect that the people would have been delighted to give up a piece of their common land to such a purpose; "and," said one of them to me yesterday, "if her had a gone the right way to work her 'd ha' had it sure enough." It might, I am afraid, have been by no means easy for this lady to have hit exactly on the right way. Miss Brooke is a High Churchwoman and a Conservative, and many of the villagers are Dissenters and Radicals. For her to win their confidence in an enterprise of this sort would, no doubt, have been difficult, and, so far as I can learn, she made no attempt to do so. She adopted the good old Tory plan of setting about to do the thing for the people over their heads, and without consulting them, instead of proceeding on the democratic principle of taking the people into her confidence and working with them. The land, however, she could not get without the consent of the copyholders—the villagers themselves. The Duke of Marlborough, the Lord of the Manor, of course gave his consent to this appropriation of the land, but the proposal was brought before the court-leet, and a plain question was put to the lawyer present. " Muster lawyer, if us gives this land for the café, whos'n 'll it be ? " " It will be Miss Brooke's." " And her can do as 'er likes wi' it ? " " Yes, it will be hers to do as she likes with it, but ——" " And her could sell it if 'er'd a mind ? " " Yes, no doubt she could if ——" " Then us won't gi' it. We ha' had enough o' our land filched away from we, and we'll ha' no more on't." It was in vain that it was urged that the new institute was to be devoted to the popular good, and that, as other people would have to find the money, the people themselves might reasonably be expected to give what was in their power. Insuperable and unreasonable distrust took possession of the villagers, or some of them at any rate, and on the other side, I fear, there was engendered a supreme contempt for " ignorant Dissenters " and Radicals. The work, however, went on ; appeals for funds were made, and many of Miss Brooke's personal friends responded liberally. Land was bought at a cost of a hundred pounds just on the borders of the green, and right in the centre of the village the new institute was put up, at a cost, I am told, of six or seven hundred pounds. The breach, however, widened, and before I had seen the new building I had heard a good deal about it. Miles away from Combe I heard of a lady who was begging in all directions for money to put up " a kaffy or some't, and they do say as when the lease is out er'll go and live there, and ha' it for 'er own house." Another opinion was that the place would prove the ruin of the village by encouraging gambling, and a Nonconformist villager was strongly of opinion that young lads would be drawn in there, and become so hopelessly abandoned to

bagatelle and draughts and that sort of thing that they never
would be got to chapel any more. So strongly had one
good man felt the impending doom of all that was good and
respectable in the place that when, in the early stages of the
business, Miss Brooke had put some posts tentatively on the
coveted bit of ground, he had gone by night and sawn them
down, and later on, I understand, other saviours of society
had gone during the hours of darkness and smashed in the
patent ventilators, thus spiting the unfortunate contractor
for the building, who, of course, had to renew them.

Well, I subsequently learned that the lease of the land
will run on for a good six hundred years or so, and when I
came to look at the place it was obvious at a glance that at
the end of that time it would not be easy to effect its conversion to a convenient dwelling-house. It was I found, in
fact, a handsome and quite unique little village club—quite
an ideal little place—in red brick and red tiles and white
timber, all designed with a practical sagacity and forethought
and wise adaptation of means to ends altogether remarkable.
The room to be devoted to games had in it a nice bagatelle-
table, the gift of a gentleman in London, and on a small
platform at one end of the room was a brilliant-toned little
piano. On entertainment evenings the women of the
village will come here, if they choose, and get a little music,
or a little recitation, or a reading. There is a hatchway
opening into a well-appointed little kitchen, where tea and
coffee and other refreshments will be provided ; and there is
a reading-room and library, to be provided with papers and
periodicals and books, also communicating with the kitchen ;
while upstairs there is another room for the boys, who are
apt to interfere with the comfort of the men. There is a
covered skittle-alley for the younger men, and for the older
men "four points" will be provided, while out on the lawn,
where members may sit, and smoke their pipes, and watch the
play, arrangements have been made for quoits. Everything

is built in excellent style, solid and substantial and durable. " It is quite an ideal little village club," I couldn't help remarking when I had been all over it, "a delightful little place. There is only one possible point of criticism in con- nection with it." "And what is that?" inquired Miss Brooke, " I shall be glad to have any suggestions." " It wants absolutely nothing but a democratic—a popular com- mittee of management." "There will be a committee of management." " I am glad to hear that." " But why, now, do you wish to bring in politics into a matter of this sort?" " I am not using the word democratic in any political sense. You have set up a beautiful little place for the people; let it be managed by the people, and it will do incalculable good." Miss Brooke took my suggestion with the utmost amiability, but I fear she will hardly act upon it. There will be a committee, but, as I gathered, not a popular committee in the sense of being a committee of the people who are themselves to use the club. She herself not unnaturally expresses her determination to be a " sleeping partner," and seeing that, with some of the people on full wages in the winter—when, of course, the place will be most in request— making only nine or ten shillings a week, it will be impossible for the club to be self-supporting, it is clearly desirable that she should maintain her interest in the institution. But even as a mere matter of education it would be wise to give the villagers considerable latitude in the management of the club set up for them. Miss Brooke fears that management by a committee of labourers would result in all sorts of things she does not approve of.

Miss Brooke, of course, not unnaturally feels that as she has created the place for a definite purpose it cannot be expected of her that she shall hand it over to those who may possibly set about thwarting that purpose. At any rate, she declares she will not do so, and I fear that she may meet with a good deal of opposition and prejudice. I am dwelling on this because the difficulties besetting this invaluable enterprise at Combe are likely to be found in the way of similar efforts in hundreds of other similar places. It is really rather depressing and discouraging to find that in the villages we have not yet managed to lay down first principles, and that many of the battles that have been fought and won and almost forgotten in the towns seem to be only just beginning in many of our rural districts. In the great towns of the kingdom this question of recreation has been threshed out, and all the most intelligent and influential of our social reformers and leaders are absolutely unanimous in their opinion that recreation is good for body and mind. Clubs and institutes and polytechnics and schools and colleges all over the land are acting on the assumption that amusement is as desirable as work. In the villages almost everywhere I have been I have found that this belief in recreation has yet to be established. Miss Brooke proposes to issue a financial statement, and to appoint a committee of management. She has raised the whole money except £85 still required to meet the expense of building and equipment, and, if any word of mine shall have tended to bring her assistance to this extent, it will be a source of great satisfaction. To brighten the lives and relieve the tedium, and to wage war upon the public-house in the most effective of all ways, is work in which Liberals and Conservatives, Churchmen and Nonconformists, may cordially unite.

LETTER XIV.

NO "HARVEST HOME."

September 21.

It is pleasant to wake up in the morning and find yourself able to peep out upon the broad, white roadway of a small country town, with its fringes of trees and turf, and its quiet, old-fashioned houses, and its beautiful, ancient church, and to remember that you have planned a long day's ramble amid cornfields and cottage-gardens, hamlets and villages, and little country towns. Down in the hotel coffee-room are three or four gentlemen who are discussing over their eggs and coffee the thrilling tragedy they have attended the night before at the travelling theatre, the proscenium of which is blazing in gold and crimson out on the green yonder—not of course that they could possibly be interested in the thing as a histrionic performance, but, as they seem anxious to assure each other, merely as a study of life. They have patronised the side-door, and have figured among the aristocrats in the orchestra stalls at the modest outlay of fourpence apiece, and they all agree that they have had excellent entertainment for their money. It is not only bacon and cottages that are cheap in the country.

Talking of bacon, by the way, it is one of the signs of the times that the village shopkeepers all with one accord declare that they have hardly any sale for it, and that fat bacon nowadays won't go at any price. In one village I had the falling off in the sale accounted for by the fact that most of the people had allotments and kept pigs, and so fed their own bacon. In another place it seemed to be agreed that, upon the whole, the labourers were rather better off of late. There had been a slight improvement in wages, and the people had been enabled to get enough fresh meat to put them out of conceit with bacon. Even those who still ate it had grown fastidious in their choice of it, and would have none but the best. It must be nice and "streaky." In Smithfield the meat salesmen will all tell you that a similar change in the taste of townsfolk set in years ago, and has for a long time constituted one of the difficulties of the meat trade. People will not eat fat meat as they used to do. It is curious to see the rural districts following in the wake of the towns in a matter of this kind. I was told that in one country town a provision dealer who had not been sufficiently alive to this change found himself with four hundred sides of bacon for which he could get no sale at any price, and my informant believed that most of it had to be buried. On the other hand, the proprietor of a country inn who drove me for some miles through mid-Oxford told me that most of the cottagers' pigs about his part had, he believed, been eating their heads off lately. Feed had been so dear that most of the pigs would have to go to the miller.

How quiet and clean and pretty the little country station looks, with its gravel platform and white palings, banked up with asters and petunias, phloxes and dahlias, and its single line of rail meandering away yonder into the grey morning mist. Rosy-faced lasses in their best clothes, and with the most brilliant of nosegays for their friends in the big town they are off to, are standing in little groups, furtively eyeing the two stalwart young sportsmen with their dogs and guns, or watching the curling white steam from the approaching train as, like the giant released from his bottle, it stretches upwards and spreads out over the stubble-lands. And then the engine comes flashing and snorting in, and all is bustle and confusion. I seat myself in the train, and the cheery and obliging guard hands me in a financial paper that he has found in a neighbouring compartment. With one eye out of window and the other on the paper, I sit for a while ensconced in a corner of the carriage, ruminating on the perplexing fact that for Eiffel Towers, for gold-mining, for cattle-ranches in South America, for railways in mid-Africa, for cork-forests in the middle of Spain, for waterworks in Bessarabia—for any and every purpose under the sun, only let it be far enough off—in Santa Fé, or Topeka, or Riobamba—abundance of capital appears to be always ready for the smallest opportunity, while half the land one is rattling over is manifestly starved for want of a little. " Farming over

.much of the land round about here," said a gentleman of
long residence in mid-Oxon, " is very poor. No capital, no
capital." " In such-and-such a locality," said another
similarly well-informed witness, " there are so many acres of
land and hardly a sheep upon it. In another direction "—
giving names and places—" there are so many acres and no
sheep—four hundred acres here, five hundred acres yonder,
and very few sheep, if any." Said my driver yesterday, as
we rattled along towards Wychwood Forest, through a
purely agricultural district, " They are most of 'em hard up.
Bless your soul ! they sell everything—straw and hay and
stock—and I've known some of 'em run things so close for
ready money that they had to buy back a bit o' straw and
hay just to get along with. They can't make nothing out of
farming that way." " Why haven't they made more progress
with the harvest here ? " I asked of a woman who had kindly
invited me into her cottage to rest while waiting for a
conveyance. " I don't exactly know, sir," she replied.
" Not hands enough ? " " Yes, they have been pretty
middlin' off for hands. I wonders they ain't got more in.
But they stopped seven of the men as was a getting it in to
go and thrash some on't." One cannot be surprised that in
these days when, as a " Middlesex Farmer " recently said in
the *Daily News,* our agriculturists are practically in competition with all the world, their business carried on in this
hand-to-mouth fashion should be a failure. I had a long
conversation with a gentleman who apparently had a great
deal of knowledge of agricultural affairs in his own locality—
or at all events of the affairs of those engaged in agriculture,
and I was fairly amazed at his statements. One after
another he named men who had at one time been reputed
to be worth three, five, ten, or fifteen thousand pounds, but
who had now given up altogether, or were struggling with
all sorts of disadvantages for want of money. The statements were certainly startling, but I am bound to say that

the appearance of the country he referred to, and through which I have driven to-day, fully bears them out. The land in many parts bears unmistakable evidence of neglect and half-culture. The last farm I had my attention directed to this evening was one to which a man had brought five thousand pounds a few years ago, but from which he was retiring a broken man. His land, I understood, had been taken by another tenant, but at a much lower rental.

In thus bringing together a number of instances of failure I am conscious that there is some danger of giving an erroneous impression. Nobody contends, and I do not wish for a moment to suggest, that farming generally is going to the bad. No doubt, it is often far less of a failure than it is made to appear. The much-respected Vicar of Bampton made a remark which I thought both humorous and suggestive. By the way, there is but one Vicar of Bampton now. There used to be three, who took it in turns to perform certain duties and to pocket certain emoluments. This man would this year take the tithes and the duties of the church at Bampton; next year he would have the rent of the glebe-land, and would do duty at a village a little way out; the third year he would minister at a third church, and pick up such crumbs in the way of fees and other odds and ends as fell in his way, coming back in the fourth year to his starting-point again. "To quarrel like the Vicars of Bampton" was at one time a proverbial expression in this part of the world. This arrangement has long been altered, and there seems little quarrelling now, for the vicar and his Nonconformist neighbours seem to be on the nicest terms with each other, and there is apparently little to fall out about, unless it may be over the public-houses. Bampton has about 1,350 people and fourteen public-houses—rather more than one public-house for every hundred people, men, women, and children. But, to get back to the land, the vicar threw a humorous light on the

subject when he said, I thought with just a touch of the
subacid in his humour—that in. estimating the season he
found that there was a marked difference between those
who were farming his glebe land and other farmers around.
" Pretty fair," is the estimate of the farmers round Bampton,
or of many of them. " No doubt things might have been
worse." But the incumbent has 400 acres of glebe land,
and when he talks matters over with his tenants, with
especial reference of course to their bearing on rent, there
are dolefully long faces. Things never were worse, and
there seems not the slightest prospect of their ever being
better. We must not take literally the pessimism of the
farmers. But, by universal consent, times have been hard
and have severely tried the weaker of them. And now, by
consent equally general, a still further strain is to be put
upon them. " I can see," said a gentleman of great experience as a farmer on a considerable scale between
Bampton and Burford, "that there are going to be changes."
" The farmers will have to pay higher wages, you think ?"
" Yes, I think so." He had himself lost none of his men,
and was on the best of terms with them. I had heard of
this gentleman before I reached his village, and understood
that he had been one of the kindest and most considerate
of masters. I was quite prepared to believe him therefore
when he said that he had done his best to promote the welfare
of his men. He paid them wages that have involved him
in some blame, and had provided them with allotments,
had carted their manure for them and their crops of potatoes,
and in many other ways had. striven to maintain a good
feeling between himself and his men. But notwithstanding
it all, and though personally he was on the best terms with
his labourers, he appeared to be quite conscious that none
of them would be able to go on as they had been going, and
that great changes were impending. " There have been
great alterations of late years," I remarked ; " for instance, it

G

strikes me as significant that I have nowhere found any survival of the old-fashioned 'harvest home.'" "No; it is quite gone. The Union killed that. There used to be the sheep-shearing supper and the hay-harvest supper, as well as the harvest home in the autumn, but nobody thinks of such a thing now. It is quite gone out."

I had been reminded of this by finding myself that morning confronted by a picture in my hotel bedroom of the bringing home of the last load. A sunburnt rustic with a fiddle, and a boy by his side with a flageolet, led the way ; then came the team, with a child striding the fore horse, and other children with flags on the top of the load ; swains with their pitchforks, and damsels with bundles of corn on their heads and aprons full of flowers, came capering alongside ; and in the rear of all was the farmer, on his stout nag, looking jolly and prosperous, and contented. Through the three or four weeks of harvest, big, flat hampers would have been sent down to those harvesters in the field from the farmer's kitchen, and fine steaming joints and abundance of vegetables, and substantial plum-puddings would have put heart into the men and the women and children helping to tie and carry the sheaves, and the whole business would have wound up with a jovial supper in some big barn, swept and garnished for the occasion. All pretty and pleasant, but all gone. I was, indeed, told of one farmer who still kept up the old custom, and whose men are now being regaled with good dinners, and who are to have a feast when it is all over. He farms three hundred acres, and last year made five hundred pounds net profit. But this is the only instance I have met with. "The Union killed that"—upset the old dependent, subservient, "patriarchal" sort of relationship, which I suppose we are all of us given occasionally to deplore as though it had been something purely beneficent and good, but which was often enough quite consistent with seven shillings a week for a man and his family, half of it paid in the patriarch's unsaleable corn, dealt out at a good stiff profit on Protectionist prices. It was the old National Labourers' Union that broke in upon that relationship, and set up in its place something like two hostile camps. That Union to a greater extent broke down, but you will find that all the more intelligent of the men who are not thinking of leaving the land still have ideas of it, and would be only too glad to act upon the idea if their fellows, as one of them expressed it to me yesterday, "was only men." The thing has by no means died out. In the stony, picturesque little town of Burford I found an intelligent young fellow—one of those dreadful agitators—representing the Dockers' Union, down there for the purpose of seeing what could be done to enrol the labourers in an organisation that would prevent the great capitalists in towns from sweeping the agricultural districts whenever they may be confronted by demands they are not disposed to concede. As the labourers on the land diminish in numbers they increase in individual strength for a tussle with their masters, and strong and determined trade unionism in the fields will certainly be a factor in the near future. Every here and there one meets with trivial little facts that are striking in their significance. In Burford I talked with a very shrewd and experienced road-surveyor, who every year requires large quantities of stone for the roads under his charge. The depletion of the country of its labour—though I think scarcely so great about here as in some localities I have visited—has been such as to tell very perceptibly on his business. Even in the winter-time he does not find it anything like so easy as he used to do to get men to break stones, and in the summer he very often cannot get them at all. He has to get his road-making material from a distance ready broken. This is done by machinery, the use of which for stone-breaking must thus be largely developed by the very same influences that are depopulating our fields and filling our casual wards. Round about there farmers have been at their

wits' end for men, and have whipped in all they could get from
any quarter.   The surveyor had sent in an order to a local
stonemason, but could not get his order executed because
the stonemason's men had gone harvesting.   These men and
slaters and carpenters had been turning to with the sickle
and pitchfork around Burford.   They would not of course
be the most efficient of harvesters, and they have to be well
paid.   The consequence is that the farmers are turning their
thoughts more and more to machinery, and the advantages
and disadvantages of the American inventions for reaping
and binding are just now everywhere being anxiously discussed, and at many points they are being adopted.

Thus on all hands one perceives indications that town
and country are finding common interests, and that social
equality and the brotherhood of labour are asserting themselves, while art and science, and invention and education,
and the rise and fall of markets, and the vicissitudes of the
seasons, and the very failures and calamities of our farmers,
are all combining to produce changes, the ultimate issue of
which few among us appear able to conceive, but which we
may rest assured will go on whether we understand their
drift or not.

LETTER XV.

MOVING FORWARDS OR BACKWARDS?

September 23

I HAVE received several letters urging upon me the desirability
of giving details of the results of the allotments and small
holdings that have come under my observation.   To tell the
truth, I have kept no very precise account of them.   I set out
with the intention of doing so, but I soon found it impracticable—impracticable at any rate so far as any really useful
purpose could be served.   It is of no use to record the fact
that a man gets out of a quarter of an acre of ground so

many bushels of potatoes, so much wheat, so much barley, and so forth, unless you can give a great many other facts also—the cost of the seed and manure, the time the man may have lost from his regular employment, the value of the help he has had, and several other items, none of which a farm labourer will ever be able to give you. One might of course easily pile up facts and figures showing that a labourer of merely average intelligence and industry can make out of a plot of ground far more than the average farmer gets out of his land, and if one were to take some of these figures, he would be driven inevitably to the conclusion that that way lies the solution of our agricultural problem.

Such figures are often, I fear, entirely fallacious. Yet I have talked with many a man who, on the strength of such calculations, seems to be consumed with a feverish hankering after such access to the land as will enable him to realise some such result. In a remote Oxfordshire village I talked with an intelligent, hard-working man, who seemed to be one of these. Poor fellow! I couldn't help feeling the greatest sympathy with him. He was a strong, squarely built man in the prime of life, but looked fagged and jaded. He had three-quarters of an acre of land. " Three-quarters of an acre," I said ; " there must be a deal of spade-work in that." " Yes," he said, with something of a sigh, " it robs a man of a good deal of his rest." " Yes, it do," chimed in his wife, who stood by. " It's a shame that a man should have to work so 'ard for a living." " You think that a man who does a good day's work for his master ought to be able to live upon his earnings ? " " Yes, sir, I do Why shouldn't he ? If he's a mind to do more, let 'im do it ; but 'e didn't ought to be obliged to do it." It was impossible to dispute the reasonableness of this. A man who works from seven in the morning till five in the evening, and pretty nearly all the hours on the clock during harvest, ought to live in decency and comfort on his wages, and if he chooses to work on his own ground after hours it should be as a provision for rainy days or old age, or for little indulgences and luxuries. "I'm sure 'e works harder nor 'e ought to work," continued the woman, "and yet us can't seem to get on. It's everlastin' slave and worry. Us never gets no peace o' mind." Every line about the woman's thin, pale face, and every tone of her voice, testified to the genuineness of her complaining, and the force of her eloquence was strongly enhanced by the grim visage of the husband, who stood by with hands thrust deep down into his pockets, and a hard, dogged sort of hopelessness about his whole appearance.

I strolled with the man down the beautiful little village, with its old church, and its rugged elms and broken stone cross, its cottages capped with vivid sheets of moss, and clad in ivy and clematis, and the gorgeous crimson of Virginia creeper, or fragrant with ripe fruit—apricots, and pears, and plums. What a little Arcadia it might be, and how beautifully suggestive of peace and plenty came the huge waggon-load of corn, tottering slowly along under the russeting boughs of the trees skirting the little broken lane winding round the churchyard wall. I drew the man out and encouraged his confidence, feeling that the practical experience of one labourer with three-quarters of an acre of land must be in many ways representative of that of labourers generally. He had had his little dream of the prosperity and progress that were to be ensured if he could only get a bit of land. Well, that bit of land had been obtained, and undoubtedly some good had resulted. Both man and wife had agreed that it had helped them wonderfully through the winter. "I dunno what us'd ha' done without it," said the woman. But much of his dream hadn't been realised, and he seemed to be in despondency and doubt whether it ever would. The work was exhausting and hard—this cultivation of three-quarters of an acre in

addition to his day's employment. But he didn't mind
that. He was used to hard work, and was willing to do it.
A few years ago he found himself giving way to drink, but
he cut it short off and had been eight years a teetotaller.
He thought he could do if anybody could, but his three
years had shown him the difficulties of allotment cultivation.
"You see," he said, "you can't be in two places at once,
and jest when the master wants 'e is jest the time when you
wants to be on your own ground." I noticed this morning
some rather dismal illustrations of this very fact while jogging
along a country road on a carrier's cart. There were long
stretches of allotments, with crops all choked up with weeds,
and tons of potatoes, that ought to have been up long ago,
still lying in the ground. The owners, of course, were all
harvesting. Last year this man was just getting up his
potatoes between the showers, when his master sent for him.
His crop was spoiling, and he thought he would finish his
job. For that very excusable act of insubordination he
found himself discharged, and for weeks last winter the poor
fellow was out of employment. "The farmers hates us to
have allotments," he said, "and that's 'ow they pays us out.
Let 'em go and get fat on their allotments, they says."
Once again I say, Where was the parson? Did he learn
what had happened, and did he befriend these poor,
struggling people in their distress? Did he go to the
farmer and rebuke him for his unreasonableness and his
cruelty, and point out his folly in thus embittering and exas-
perating the people by whose sweat and sinews he had to
live? Did he urge that the man had a fair excuse for not
coming the moment he was sent for, and that, since the man
was only a day-labourer, he had a perfect right to decline an
engagement for that day, if he thought proper? Did he
endeavour to make the farmer understand what it must be
for a man who has been struggling to make headway against
poverty and anxiety to be thus flung back and compelled to

stand idle and wretched, while all the ground he had gained
slipped from under his feet, and debt and difficulty accumu
lated upon him ?   If in a case of that kind he couldn't show
these poor cottagers a little sympathy, if he couldn't go and
preach that farmer a straight and pointed little sermon about
justice and mercy and common-sense, what is he good for?
What does he do in that picturesque old church and pleasant
parsonage?   I made some inquiries about the reverend
gentleman, but could find no trace of his influence with the
people outside his church, while within it his teaching
seemed to be largely calculated to set churchmen and
dissenters by the ears.

"What I should like," said the labourer, " 'ud be to 'ave
as much land as I could do.   I could get twice as much out
of the land as the farmers do ; they don't 'alf do it.   Give
me plenty o' land and I could do well."   " Just as you are
now, without any capital ? " I queried ; and the man's face
dropped.   " No," he said, looking thoughtfully down the
road.   " I s'pose I should want a bit o' money to go on wi'."
Now I have given this man's experience because, roughly
speaking, it exactly coincides with the experience of all others
with whom I have talked on the subject.   They are all
seemingly eager for a bit of land, all believe they could do
well if they could get it.   All who try it under fairly good
conditions—tolerably good land, near their house, at a
reasonable rent—find an indisputable benefit in it.   But
they soon find that the advantage has its drawbacks and
limitations.   Said a man to me the other day—" I sometimes
think I likes the winter better nor summer.   In winter, when
you done your work, you can go 'ome and rest and ha'
a bit o' comfort.   But in the summer you has to do yer day's
work and then go out on the allotment."   The young men
of course do not feel this ; but after a certain time of life
they do.   " They talks a good deal about short hours and
Saturday half-holidays in the towns," said a shrewd old

villager; "I don't see why people in the country shouldn't
have 'em as well. When a man's done his day's work, why
ain't he to go 'ome and rest and do a bit as he likes, same as
people in towns?" That is a feeling which we may depend
upon it will grow stronger as time goes on, but farm labourers
do not generally overwork themselves in the field, and the cultivation of as much land as will supply them abundantly with
food for their own consumption is easy and pleasant. I find it
generally agreed that they can add about two shillings a week
to their income, and it is better than an addition of two
shillings in cash, because much of it comes in the form of food
for winter consumption. Practically, I may say there is no
difference of opinion about this. Of course, in some cases,
this two shillings a week will enable a man to save. He will
accumulate a little capital, and then he may very advantageously, perhaps, take a little more ground, and in course
of time, by a compound accumulation of success, a sort of
geometric progression, he may develop into a small farmer.
I have met with many men who have done something of
this kind, and whatever there is in our land laws and land
tenures obstructing and hindering this should certainly be
swept away. Such men are invaluable. But, speaking
generally, the agricultural labourer cannot advantageously
do more than raise produce for his own consumption. This
is well within his own strength, and he is quite sure of his
market. The moment he steps out beyond this—has to
employ another man to help him, to interfere with his own
wage-earning, and to find a market for his produce—I am
speaking only of land tillage—he is out in the great commercial world, subject to its vicissitudes and fluctuations,
needing capital and experience and business knowledge.
"Two acres of land!" I said to a man early in these inquiries; "how does he do it? He can't dig this?" "No;
he gets it ploughed." "Whom does he get to do it?" "Oh,
there's a man over there brings his plough round, and ploughs

up allotments at so much a pole." "But I thought the special advantage of this small husbandry was the thorough work the man could put into it himself. I thought it was his own spade that was to do so much." "Well, that's how they does it." "And what do they grow?" "Potatoes and wheat and barley, and so on." "And what do they do with the wheat?" "Grinds it, some of it, and what they don't grind they sells." "How do they thresh it?" "Oh, the best way they can. Some on 'em pays a trifle to have it threshed aud winnowed." "And how do they grind it?" "They sends it to the mill. The miller comes round once or twice a week and takes a bag o' wheat away, and brings back a bag o' meal, and charges so much a peck for grinding." "And each family make their own bread?" "Yes, and do their own baking, or some of 'em take it to the bakehouse." One listens to all this, and looks round upon the country and sees tiny corn-fields no bigger than a London back-garden multiplying by the thousand, and he begins to rub his eyes, and to ask himself, Can this possibly be the way forward, or are we slipping back into the thirteenth century?

LETTER XVI.

ARCADIA REALISED.

September 25.

ONE of the most interesting and instructive scenes of rural life in England may be found in the villages of Lockinge and Ardington, on the estate of Lord Wantage, in Berkshire. Lord Wantage owns somewhere about 22,000 acres of land in this part of the country, comprising these two villages, with their 800 inhabitants. He farms eight or ten thousand acres himself, the consolidation of farms having gone on, and still going on, here as in so many other parts of the country. I went over yesterday, because two or three years

back I understood that the owner of this vast estate was
going to crown and complete the remarkable little social
system he has created here by admitting his people to a
share in the profits of his farming, and I wished to learn a
little about the result of it.   In previous articles I have
already dwelt upon the undisputed advantages of farming
on a large scale with sufficient capital.   Some at least of
these advantages were obvious enough before I had gone
far on to the estate.   On scores of other farms I had seen
thousands of acres of over-ripe corn still exposed to the
caprices of this cold and rainy autumn.   At Lockinge all
was gathered in and stacked safe and sound in splendid-
looking ricks ; much of the land was already under a heavy
manuring, and not a little of it was ploughed up.   Abundant
capital, the finest appliances, and a full staff of men had
enabled Lord Wantage to take advantage of every hour of
fine weather.   I understood that magnificent crops had been
gathered in in fine condition, and the owner of the estate
and his agent, Major Carter, both military men, were able
to betake themselves to the German manœuvres, while small
farmers all around were still struggling with their corn and
growling at the weather.   The one disadvantage of such
extensive farming is the great difficulty and expense of
supervision.   A large body of labouring men, spread over a
great area of land, cannot be kept going as they can be on
a small farm with the master himself working among them.
Many recorded co-operative experiments show, however,
that if you can manage to give the labourer a real interest in
the success of the farm this difficulty disappears.   A little
book I have been reading while moving about the country,
written by the Rev. C. W. Stubbs, and entitled " The Land
and the Labourers," gives particulars of several interesting
experiments in co-operative farming.   From one cause or
another they all of them failed.   One of the most remarkable of them collapsed solely in consequence of the bank-

ruptcy of the person who financed it, and who, " though a high-minded and benevolent man, was disastrously given to gambling." Nothing in these narratives is more striking than the heartiness and vigour with which the most stolid of farm labourers will work the moment they fairly realise that they have a real personal interest in the enterprise. It is no longer necessary to look after them ; they look after each other, and the man who skulks and shirks will immediately have his fellows down upon him. It struck me when I first heard of Lord Wantage's profit-sharing scheme, a couple of years back, that it would be a most notable experiment, since it promised to combine all the advantages of the large farm with the thoroughness and vigour of the small.

In many other ways these villages of Ardington and Lockinge are well worthy of a visit. Seen in the early summer especially, as I saw them on a former occasion, they strike one as quite a little rural paradise. The estate is beautifully timbered ; the cottages, with their ornamental eaves and pointed gables, their fanciful chimney-stacks and pretty porches overgrown with ivy and roses, their grassy slopes and lawns and shrubs and flower-beds, all present innumerable points of view with which the artist would be enraptured. Every villager has, or may have, his allotment. There is an admirable reading-room and a public-house in charge of a salaried manager who has no interest whatever in pushing the sale of drink, but who is especially required to provide good soup in winter, and tea and coffee and other non-intoxicants at all times. There is a first-rate co-operative store, with commodious premises, at which the people can get all the necessaries of life—clothes, grocery, bread, meat, and provisions, on profit-sharing terms. The bakery is a beautiful little place, with patent ovens and the newest machinery. In addition to all this, over a hundred of the villagers are employed in municipal workshops, so to speak—shops fitted up with all kinds of the latest machinery and the best appliances—saw-mills, carpenters' shops, blacksmiths' shops, painters' shops, wheelwright's shops—all for the building and repairing and general maintenance of the property on the estate. There are two churches and an excellent school. In short, it is a little self-contained world in which nobody is idle, nobody is in absolute want, in which there is no squalor or hunger, while in the midst of it all is the great house of Lockinge, the beautiful home of Lord and Lady Wantage, always ready to play the part of benevolent friends to all who need their help, and who, indeed, by all accounts, seem sincerely desirous of promoting the happiness and well-being of their people. The regular pay of the labourers on the estate is not higher than elsewhere. I understood that it was a shilling or so higher at one time, and that in consequence Lord Wantage has the very cream of the labourers in that part of the country, but that it was reduced to ten shillings a week when the profit-sharing scheme was promulgated, the expectation being that this reduction would be more than counterbalanced by the dividend that would be distributed when the farm accounts were made up.

Having said so much in favour of this delightful little Berkshire colony, it seems ungracious to turn round and declare that the whole thing is radically rotten and bad, and that the whole system of things here is another illustration of that "model" village life which is merely another name for social and political death. Lord Wantage is not to be attacked. He stands high in the esteem of all his neighbours and friends—unless it may be some of the tradesmen in the little town of Wantage, who are naturally angry with his co-operative supply stores—and he has most laudably and consistently carried his Conservative principles into action. Materially, the result on the face of it is delightful, and as a means of keeping the control and management of the people by the aristocracy nothing could possibly be better. But for all the purposes of political life and social progress and human development it is utterly bad. Lord Wantage has done for the people, in the true spirit of benevolent Toryism, what the people ought to be able to do for themselves—not individually, of course, but collectively and unitedly, and by their own sturdy, independent, and manly effort. I don't know what Lord Wantage's personal wish may be with regard to the voting power of his people, but I am sure that those people themselves have no idea whatever that they are free electors. "Any politicians here?" I asked an old man as I walked up the road with him through Lockinge. "What's them?" said the man, with a puzzled air. "Politicians," I bawled, thinking the old man was a little deaf or very stupid—" Politicians—you know what politicians are." " Be 'em animals they goes out to shoot?" said the old fellow, and then I saw the waggish twinkle of his eyes that told me plainly enough he was only making a fool of me. He knew very well what politicians were, but he wasn't going to talk about such matters at Lockinge, and I couldn't induce him to. All around I heard Ardington and this village spoken of as a little political Dead Sea, in which no public opinion ever was known to manifest itself. Nobody would say that Lord Wantage was a man to exercise any improper influence on his people; but he is a strong Tory, has been a member of a Tory Government, his agents are Tories, and he owns all the land and all the houses, and can give or take away employment. I could not find anybody who knew of a political meeting having been held in these places. I heard it rumoured that there was one man who dared to avow himself a Liberal, but I couldn't find him. "Oh, yes, sir," said a woman in the place, "they all votes Lord Wantage's way, of course. It wouldn't do for 'em to go again 'im." I am assured that the admirable little public-house in Ardington is to a great extent a failure, because the men find that they are not free to talk there, and that whatever they say is liable to be carried by the birds to the agent's or bailiff's ears. The people are managed and governed and controlled without the least voice in their public and collective affairs, and, though they undoubtedly have strong opinions on certain matters, they dare not give expression to them. For instance, the people have allotments for growing their own vegetables, but they must not keep a pig. They have flower-gardens in front of their cottages ; if they don't keep them in order the bailiff will be down upon them. A labourer doesn't quite like his cottage; there is no possibility of shifting without the bailiff's consent and arrangement. " They daren't blow their noses over at Ard'n'ton without the bailiff's leave," said a labourer in the neighbourhood. The people control nothing, have no part whatever in anything like public life, nor any voice in matters directly affecting their own welfare.

In the management of the stores certain changes have been made. At first, I believe, the customers had a five per cent. dividend on their purchases—that is to say, a person laying out ten pounds in the course of the year had ten shillings as his share of profit on the trading. Then they had a dividend of seven-and-a-half, and one year they divided ten per cent. Lord Wantage makes certain alterations involving greater cost of working, and the dividend goes back to five per cent. Of course, he has a perfect right to do so. He finds the capital, taking, I think, only a very moderate interest as his share, and letting the profit, whatever it may be, go to the people. They have no right to complain, but they do complain in private ; and since it is a matter affecting their own pockets, they have, however unreasonably, a vague, grumbling sort of sense that things are not managed quite as they should be. This little central depôt for the economical buying and distribution of all the necessaries of life on real co-operative lines is admirable so far as the mass of the people are concerned, whatever individuals may think about it. It is based on the sound economic principle of producing and distributing at the lowest possible cost. But, to be completely satisfactory, the people in these villages ought to subscribe their own capital, as they would soon be able to do, if, as I thought Lord Wantage was going to arrange for them, they could only be got to work upon the land with a real, solid, stimulating interest in the result of their work, just as they have on their own allotment. Let a man feel confidence in the management, and be assured that if all goes fairly well he will have a good substantial share of all the land can be made to yield, and he will put his back into the business. But I hear that the profit-sharing has resolved itself into a mere bonus of two pounds at Michaelmas, and, indirectly, I am given to understand that the people grumble that they have got this bonus of two pounds a year instead of the shilling a week in wages, and that Lord Wantage really pockets twelve shillings a year. I ought in fairness to add, however, that when this reduction of wages took place it was general with the farmers all round, and that the concession of the bonus, therefore, was a real one, since in any case the reduction would have been made. You cannot imagine a labourer working on a farm of eight or ten thousand acres being in any degree influenced in his work by such a profit-sharing scheme as this. For their village stores the men ought to subscribe their own capital, pay interest, if at all, into their own coffers, and pocket the profit of the whole business. The management would, of course, be in the hands of the people themselves, who would elect their own officers and control their own affairs. Whatever advantage there might be would be public advantage, and it would all be consistent with everybody's perfect freedom and independence. There need be no fear of anybody, no cringing to agents, no concealment of opinions—absolutely nothing inconsistent with free, individual, manly life and sturdy citizenship. There is nothing Utopian, nothing impracticable in this—everybody knows it is being done on all hands. In the little town of Thetford the other day they invited me to go and see their co-operative stores, and they told me they had been so successful that they had a surplus of capital they positively didn't know what to do with. Where the limit of this sort of collective action is to be drawn I don't know anybody who has told us or who can tell us, and why the whole social and industrial life at Lockinge and Ardington should not go on upon the same system I can see no reason but the difficulty of effecting the change and of fitting the people for the fuller, freer, happier life it would open up to them.

As this article is of the nature of an attack on Lord Wantage, I think it only right to append his reply to it, addressed to the Editor of the *Daily News :*—

TO THE EDITOR OF THE " DAILY NEWS."

SIR,—I fully believe that by your courtesy I shall find a place in your columns for a few remarks on subjects connected with the letters of your Commissioner concerning village homes. The object he has in view is, as I understand it, to gather together information with reference to the management of landed properties, showing in what instances certain practices have been found beneficial and worthy of being more generally adopted, and where the reverse is the case. Such a scheme impartially and intelligently carried out cannot fail to be interesting and instructive, and deserving of support. It is not my desire or intention to enter into any controversy ; but I feel it would be unfortunate if some of the systems in operation on my estates, which your Commissioner describes, were to be discredited by erroneous statements which would have the effect of discouraging their adoption elsewhere.

H

A correspondent of yours who signs himself "Lockinge," makes many and varied complaints on behalf of the labourers of this district. Among these the allegation that the "bonus" system has caused universal dissatisfaction among the labourers on this estate can only have a misleading and mischievous effect. In spite of what this correspondent says, I strongly (after an experience of some years) recommend the system as an incentive to industry, and as conducive to a widening of interest on the part of the labourers in the prosperity of the farm on which they work. The bonus is, as your Commissioner points out, given over and above the regular wages paid to farm labourers on this estate, which are in no way affected by it, and which rise and fall according to the fluctuation of supply and demand. It is not intended that the bonus system should be worked on strictly profit-sharing principles, which at present involve considerable practical working difficulties, but which further experience may possibly overcome. But the amount of bonus given is dependent on the profit realised. Certain farms of mine, which till recently made no profit, and consequently gave no bonus, have since last year paid their way, and have yielded a bonus, which I hope may be gradually increased in amount as the farm profits improve. The enforcement of sanitary regulations naturally falls upon the landlord, whether he happens to hold town or country property, and the insurance of healthy conditions by means of estate rules must in some cases override other considerations. The convenience of a pig-sty close to the cottage backdoor is more than counterbalanced by the contamination of the neighbouring well. But it by no means follows that, because a pig-sty is not allowed close to a cottage, the cottager is forbidden to have one elsewhere. The allotment is the most suitable place for a pig-sty, and on this estate every man can, if he wishes, have one put up at cost price, and removed at his convenience. Allotments should, where possible, be in near proximity to the village. Such is the case on this estate, and the proof that they are not "failures" is that the demand for them is such that none are ever vacant. The management of the public-house is so well and fully described by your Commissioner that I need say no more about it, except to observe that the sole restrictions enforced are such as the law of the land imposes, namely, those restricting the supply of liquor when men are in a state of drunkenness. The co-operative stores established in these villages distribute the whole of the profits among their customers, being worked on what is known as the Rochdale co-operative system. This mode of distribution was adopted, after full consideration, in preference to another plan, also on the Rochdale principle, which disposes of the profits in the shape of dividends among the shareholders. But when there are shareholders who take these dividends, the money returned to the customers on their purchases is to that extent diminished, and this consideration has guided the managers of these stores in their adoption of a system which is working very satisfactorily.

It has been said in your columns that it is easy to draw pleasant pictures of the condition of the agricultural labourer under the care of a beneficent landlord. But why assume that such a condition can only be purchased at the expense of freedom to think and act for himself? The fact that we live in democratic days is no reason for disparaging and discouraging the legitimate influence landlords may exercise over their neighbours and tenants by helpful supervision and by friendly interest in their affairs which ought not, and which do not, interfere with the freedom of speech and liberty of action which are the right of all alike, of labourers as well as landlords.—I am, Sir, your obedient servant,

WANTAGE.

Lockinge House, Wantage, Berks, October 3.

LETTER XVII.

THE PEOPLE AND THE PARSONS.

September 29.

I HAVE again been making a circuit through a number of villages under the guidance of another Radical Dissenter. Some of the correspondents of the *Daily News* seem to have been very angry with me because, as they suppose, I have made Radical Dissenters my chief source of information, and they are inclined to believe apparently that some of my comments upon the clergy are to be accounted for by the prompting and instigation of the guides I have chosen. As a matter of fact, I can scarcely be said to have chosen my guides at all. They have been chosen for me in most cases by circumstances over which, as the phrase goes, I had no control. I have gone down into a district with the simple purpose of inquiring into the condition of our agricultural population, and my first step has generally been, when I have wanted guidance, to inquire right and left for those who know most about the people. In one district I had a consensus of opinion pointing to a chimney-sweep as the man who had the most intimate knowledge of the village labourers, and to the chimney-sweep I went—only to find, by-the-way, that the good man had no opinion ot " them newspaper chaps," and would have nothing to do with me. Alas, for the dignity of the fourth estate! If I had been assured that a village rector or a zealous young curate had been manifesting a special interest in the homes and lives and wages of the poor, I should certainly have compassed sea and land to get at him. I know one village where, I am informed, a young curate of this character really created a stir among the labourers around. The farmers immediately raised such a disturbance about the rector's ears that the young curate had to clear out bag and baggage.

"Now let me understand," said a vicar to me last night, "before I say anything, is my name to appear?" "Certainly not if you object to it." "Well, I do object. You see," continued the vicar, settling himself back in his chair more at his ease, "I am dependent on the rent of my glebe for my living. It has already been reduced by two-thirds of what it used to be, and if I offend the farmers the other third will go. I have a wife and family to think about." It was right candidly put, and if I further add that in one parliamentary division I was in, in which there were a hundred and twenty-seven parishes—all of them with one clergyman and some of them with two or three—there were only eight parsons to be reckoned on the popular side of politics, it will, I trust, enable some of my angry critics to understand why it has been that when I have wanted to get at an actual knowledge of the people, I have had, as a rule, to go, not to the parson of the parish, but to "rabid Dissenters."

I started from Steventon, a large and pleasant old village a little way down beyond Didcot, on the Great Western main line, in company with a Radical shoemaker, who I had previously heard had been making himself such an unmitigated nuisance in his own locality that I felt sure there must be grit in the fellow. He was, I found, a Wesleyan "local preacher," a Sunday-school superintendent, a fighting politician, a regular "firebrand" among the labouring people about there. This turbulent and irrepressible shoemaker had had the audacity to poke his nose into matters pertaining to village charities and the management of common land let out in allotments, and had been stirring up the people to the assertion of their rights. For this outrageous conduct he had actually incurred that enmity of the surrounding farmers which the candid vicar dreaded, and his cobbling business went. He had had two customers left till lately, but they were labouring people, and they knew their master, a farmer, objected to their dealing with him, and they supposed they must give him up. He is now trying to make a living out of a bit of land, but fears they will get him out of the place yet. And yet that man is an upright, conscientious, philanthropic, and eminently useful labourer among the villagers for miles round. Himself a poor man struggling with difficulty, he had nothing to give them; but he had been fighting the poor men's battle, had walked miles every Sunday to preach to them without fee or reward; he thoroughly understands the people, and is in entire sympathy with them, and the consequence is that they trust him and talk over their troubles with him. I found that everybody knew him, and he knew everybody and all their circumstances. Himself a totally uneducated man, he has for years been travelling the country all round as the advocate of the free education which the Tory parsons were opposing with all their powers. I am dwelling a little on these points because this man is typical, and because these matters of the established and the unestablished teachers and preachers are vitally bound up with the life of the village. I am told that I have been hard on the parsons, and that I seem to have a prejudice against them. I have no such prejudice. I declare emphatically that I would ten times rather have it in my power to speak in respectful and appreciative terms of a village clergyman than be compelled to make him an object of ridicule and disparagement. I do not forget that he may have his own burden to bear, his own personal griefs and anxieties; and I am not altogether incapable of realising the state of intellectual and moral isolation in which some of them are placed, and which in some of these outposts of our civilisation must put all that is best and strongest in a man to the severest strain. Here and there I have had glimpses into clerical life in our villages suggestive of much that should entitle those concerned to sympathy and forbearance. I don't wish to attack men whose circumstances I do not know and whose characters I may misjudge. But though as men I would rather let them alone, as State functionaries and office bearers they must be judged by their public utility; and I cannot be wrong in pointing out the mischiefs of a system which puts into the position of teachers and guides and guardians of our rural population men who may be very excellent, but many of whom are utterly unfit for their duties.

Let me illustrate what I mean. I went last evening into a certain little village which I had passed through the day before. It was charmingly situated, and looked delightfully pleasant and pretty ; but if you came to look a little narrowly into its condition you could see poverty and decay written in every feature of it. In point of wages, it was the poorest place I have been into all along—all through the year, except just at harvest time, nine shillings a week. I strolled about among the cottagers and talked with them at their doors, and later on in the evening I had quite a little gathering around me under a tree spreading over the roadway, discussing their troubles. There was nothing essentially different from what I had met with in scores of other places, only there seemed here rather more general depression. How did they live on nine shillings? They didn't live. It was a lingering death, the people said. Bread and potatoes had been their food all through the winter, and they hadn't had enough of that. At least a dozen men in that place had been out of work altogether in the winter-time. As to the cottages, I was assured there were not three good ones in the place, and I heard of the utmost wretchedness last winter. The wind had blown them pretty nearly out of their beds, and the snow had come in upon them. One poor woman, shortly after her confinement, had had the stairs break under her, and had badly injured her breast, and was ill for a long time. And now winter was coming round again, and they seemed to have had hardly any harvest. What with machines and the wet weather and the stinting of labour, their earnings had been less this harvest than they had ever known before, and how they were to pay their rent and clear off their accounts with the shopkeeper, heaven only knew. It was a dismal little conference altogether, but it was not quite all in one tone either. From out of the darkness under that spreading tree came one or two stern and resentful voices. How was it all? There was plenty of land, and it used to maintain a good many more people. Why shouldn't it again? Were people to starve and rot in dog-kennels because the farmers couldn't or wouldn't employ them on the land? Something would have to be done or there'd be a row.

Well, there were the people full of grievances, embittered by suffering and anxiety, chafing under a sense of injustice and unmerited hardship. There were the people; yonder were their ramshackle houses that they couldn't pay for; and all around, spread out beneath the solemn stars, were the broad acres that would keep them in comfort and competency, ay, and if well tilled would keep the squire, the parson, and the lord of the manor too. But now everything was all wrong; the village was dwindling away and rotting; the charities had gone astray; wages had gone down; the people were in misery and anxiety and degradation. I noticed that the women were given to swearing—a sure sign of a wretched and demoralised village. There was no reading-room, no sort of amusement, no meeting-place at all but the church and the public-house. And what had the parson to say about it all? Even in such a wretched place surely an earnest and well-qualified man might have made himself heard and felt a little. Of course he knew all about them? Of course he was indignant that these unfortunate people were so vilely housed and cruelly underpaid? He was full of sympathy with them, no doubt, and if he couldn't say all he would like, of course he could say enough at least to let them all feel that he sided with them and suffered with them ? Well, I called upon him, and he was good enough to give me a little instruction in these things. It was all, he explained, a matter of supply and demand. These people were really making more than nine shillings a week, and if they weren't there was nothing to compel them to stay in that village. There was nothing to prevent their going elsewhere And this was the good man whom the Church of England had planted in the midst of a population such as I found here, with the strict injunction to address them twice a day on Sundays as " Dearly beloved brethren," and to be

> "In his duty prompt at every call,
>   To watch and weep and pray and feel for all."

I hope I was civil to the reverend gentleman, but I didn't stay long.

I was the next day in a neighbouring village, where wages were a shilling higher, and here, again, I had heard the most distressing stories of the difficulty of living and the discomforts of home life. Here, again, times were harder than they used to be. Here was the same dreary old story of land badly cultivated, of labourers thrown out of employment, of cottages that had been pulled down, and young men who had gone away. I was taken into the houses and shown where the wind, whistling through the crevices, had actually blown the paper off the walls, and one woman told me how last winter she had had to knock her neighbour up in the middle of the night to borrow some sacks to cover up her children with because the rain had saturated everything about them as they lay in their beds. She pointed to a delicate-looking daughter who had been brought to death's door, as the doctor said, from want of the common necessaries of life, and she had the most piteous tale to tell of illness and privation and suffering. Another woman, less vehement, but hardly less full of grievances, told how she had had a daughter lying at the point of death, and of her anguish when the doctor ordered beef-tea and brandy, and she couldn't get it, and there was not a friend in the village to whom she could run in her extremity. This woman explained in the most intelligent and circumstantial way how it was that they were earning less this autumn than they have ever done before, and I found that every indication I met with and all sorts of testimony pointed to this as ˙the general condition of the labouring poor of the village.

Well, and what had the parson here to say about it all? I called upon him, too. A large and beautiful house, a most courteous and polished gentleman; everything suggested that he would be eminently fitted to take spiritual and educational charge of this village. I had heard of his refusal to make the rectory a relieving-office, and I knew of one child at least running about the village unbaptised in consequence of his refusing to respond to an appeal from a sick-bed. But I did not feel altogether willing to endorse some of the opinions I had heard expressed about matters of this kind. It is shocking to see the extent to which the people in many of our villages are degraded by weak and injudicious alms-giving, and a firm stand of this sort is by no means inconsistent with sympathy and earnest effort. But I had seen a good many cottages, and I had listened to a good many tales—discounting some of them, of course —and I was convinced that in this village also earnings were dreadfully low, cottages in a shocking condition, population going down ; surely something must need putting right, and the rector would have a decided opinion about it all. Well, he had. He was decidedly of opinion that a man with seven or eight children couldn't be said to have to live on ten shillings a week, because two or three of them would be sure to be earning something.   He thought it would be much nearer the mark to put down the wages at fifteen shillings, and referred to the report of a Royal Commission in years gone by which made out the income of labouring men to be seventy pounds a year. I was assured that, though poor, the people have a surplus for amusements. They could go up to the Exhibition, and occasionally had a day at the sea-side, and a cigar on Sundays. And a great deal more to the same effect. In short, the rector, I found, looked at the whole subject from the squire's and the farmer's point of view, and I understood quite well how it was that " somehow the parson and the people didn't seem to hit it." I left that gentleman and made my way out of the village, musing much on that room full of poor, rough, ignorant fellows amidst whom I had stood last night. It was the taproom of the public-house. One little paraffin-lamp shed out a feeble light over the uncouth company, all enveloped in a dense cloud of rank tobacco smoke. Old men were there and boys, and one or two girls and a woman or two. They were drinking, of course, but they were all sober enough, and presently came a thumping of the grimy wooden tables with the bottoms of the empty quart pots, and somebody was going to oblige with a song. A square-built, sturdy man stepped into the middle of the room, took a draught of his beer, and broke forth in a husky, rugged voice with " The Labouring Man."

" You Englishmen of each degree, one moment listen unto me,
   To please you all I do intend, so listen to these lines I penned.
   From day to day, you all may see, the poor are frowned on by degree,
   But then you know they never can do without the labouring man."
      Chorus—
            " Old England ofttimes leads the van,
               But not without the labouring man.

" The labouring man will plough the deep, till the ground and sow the
         wheat.
   He'll fight their battles when afar ; fear no danger nor a snare.
   But they are looked upon like thieves by those who are kept at home
         at ease ;
   And every day throughout the land they try to starve the labouring
         man."

" Have you any sort of reading-room or any kind of evening entertainment for the men in the village?" I asked the rector, as I parted with him. " No," he replied; "we used. to have, but we have given it up." But the publican keeps on. What a pity it is the publican won't do the giving up, and the parson the keeping on!

LETTER XVIII.

THE VILLAGE PUBLIC-HOUSE.

October 3.

THE village public-house is an institution which will have before long to receive a good deal more attention than it has hitherto done. It is a subject upon which—if one may judge by some of the letters that have reached me—it seems to be extremely easy to lose one's head and to pour out any amount of intemperate nonsense. There is, I suppose, no question with any of us as to the evils of drink, and there have been times in the course of my village exploration when I have been sadly impressed with a sense of the formidable obstacle the wretched habit of beer-drinking—as a mere habit and not from any necessity—must present in the way of all efforts at social amelioration in rural districts. Again and again, with wearying monotony, I have been assured that it is of little use to give the labourer better wages, for it will only mean that there will be more money for the public-house; and again and again I have met with facts that seem to give support to this doleful foreboding. " Do you get a company such as this every night?" I inquired of an intelligent young village publican. " No," he replied, " it's mostly Fridays and Saturdays this year." "Not much money about, I suppose?" " No. You see it's a bad harvest for them. With a good harvest there would be pretty good trade all the week." Said a village blacksmith, " They don't very often get drunk ; but they would if they could. How be they to get drunk out of ten shillings a week, and a family to keep ? " I am very much afraid it is deplorably true that if by any dead lift you could add half-a-crown a week to the wages of every labourer in the kingdom, one at least of the immediate effects would be to pour in a stimulating shower of gold to every brewery in the kingdom, and to afford the means for a good deal of drunkenness. Only old fogies of a specially stupid type, however, would think of arguing that therefore it is of no use to endeavour to improve the position of the labourer. He will certainly have to be better paid, and, like the rest of us, he must be free to get drunk if he will. He will have to find out for himself the mischief and the misery of it, and it will be for moralists and philanthropists to help him to acquire habits of sobriety and self-restraint.

How this can best be done is a problem which should engage the serious attention of every Liberal in the kingdom and every religious teacher in the villages. I have been through some places, as I have before stated, in which landowners have in their own high-handed fashion sought to make their tenants and labourers sober by refusing to have a public-house on their estates. Whether they have accomplished this object or not I have no means of judging. But even if they have, it is not a method that will be likely to commend itself to Liberals. It savours a good deal too much of the autocratic and despotic. Whatever objection there may be to making men sober by Act of Parliament, there is certainly a far more valid objection to making them sober by the act of a domineering squire. Whether the majority of any community ought to be invested with the power of putting down public-houses in their midst may be a question fairly debatable ; whether such a power ought to be in the

hands of any one man in a village, be he who he may, seems
to me to be a question which no Liberal should hesitate for a
moment to answer by an emphatic negative ; and where, as
in many cases, the village inn is forbidden, and no meeting-
place of any kind is provided, it is an exercise of the
grossest tyranny.   If public-houses of the present type are
to be shut up, most certainly something better should be
substituted; and if the conversion of the people to
temperance and sobriety could be effected without any sort
of coercion, and simply by gaining them over to higher
interests and better associations, I think we must all feel
that the social advance made would in every way be more
real and substantial.   I am bound to say that the little
institution set up by Lord Wantage, to which I have already
referred, struck me with especial admiration.   It was neither
more nor less than a comfortable little public-house, managed, I take it, virtually on the Gothenburg system ; that is
to say, it was established merely for the public convenience,
and without any object of making money out of it.   As I
explained, the manager of it has a fixed salary, and has no
inducement to push his business, and will be just as ready
to serve a customer with a plate of soup as a glass of beer.
The villagers may go there and smoke their pipes and chat,
and, if they please, may take nothing at all, and anything
approaching drunkenness would be discouraged.   Of course,
this will not by any means satisfy all our more zealous
teetotal friends, but even they must admit that if all our
village publics could be advanced thus far in the pathway of
improvement, it would be a great thing.

Earnest teetotal advocates will naturally regard with
more approval the other village institution described in a
previous article, the pretty and attractive little place set up
by Miss Brooke in Coombe.   This, it may be remembered,
is to be a sort of literary institute and lecture-room and
concert-hall and place of entertainment for the people of the

village, who may get here anything they want except intoxicating drinks of any kind. Of course, it would be a great
thing for this village and the neighbourhood if all the people
would take kindly to this beautiful little social home thus
liberally provided for them ; and if by-and-by the managing
committee should be able to report that the attractions of
their new public-house have succeeded in entirely emptying
the old ones, and compelled them all to shut up, it would
be a matter of great encouragement to social reformers ˙
throughout the land. I do. not care to predict failure, but I
could not help noticing, as a significant fact, that Miss
Brooke had among her cordial well-wishers and supporters
one of the four or five publicans of the place. The worthy
man, no doubt, wished to please the lady, and knew his
customers too well to be seriously alarmed at anything she
could do on tea and coffee and ginger-beer. The place is
admirably designed for the improvement of the people, and
ought to succeed, and, no doubt, will effect much good in
course of time ; but the people will require educating up to
it before many of them can be brought within the sphere of
its influence.

Another beautiful example of a village public-house, or
club, I visited a day or two ago at Gaydon, in Warwickshire.
This a gentleman resident there, an ardent philanthropist
and Radical reformer, has had the public spirit to put up at
a cost of about a thousand pounds. It is altogether a
beautiful little place, comprising a large and pleasant hall, a
pretty little octagonal committee-room, a refreshment-bar,
and a residence for the caretaker. The hall is of wood.
Externally it is of split larch, employed in rustic fashion ;
within this is a layer of felt and an inner boarding of stained
pine or something of the kind. The interior decoration is
simple and effective. There are maroon curtains at the
windows, artistic photographs on the walls, and a dado of
matting all round gives an appearance of comfort and finish.

On the floor are tables and chairs in polished black wood; there are two handsome sideboards, and the ornamental mantelpiece is of solid oak. At one end of the room is a platform with a piano upon it, and over this platform is the only inscription about the place; it is in gold letters on a red ground—"God and the People." Ordinarily this hall serves as a reading-room, and is supplied with a library of books and with magazines and papers. In the winter-time it is too large to be quite cosy and comfortable, and arrangements are made for screening in a large floor-space round the fire with thick curtains, the lighting being effected by bright-looking little metal lamps with white opal shades. Now and again concerts are given, by the aid of such talent as may be available in the neighbourhood, and twice or three times in the course of the winter evenings a village ball is held. It is a village club to which members have to pay an entrance fee of sixpence and a penny weekly subscription, the management being vested in a committee of the members themselves, with the donor of the building as chairman. Under this committee the refreshment-bar is, of course, managed, and they have found it, upon the whole, expedient to sell both beer and tobacco. Mineral waters, too, are supplied, but nothing else. I understand that tea and coffee were tried, but there was little or no demand for them   The place, of course, is not used during the day-time, the people being out at work, and it has been found that after their work they go home to tea, and if they turn in here for an hour or two in the evening they don't want more tea, but prefer a glass of beer. The supply of it, however, is strictly limited to three glasses. It is contended, and I am bound to say I think with great force, that by having no intoxicating drinks a large number of those whom it is most desirable to get to a place of this kind will be repelled. If they are inclined for a glass of beer they will certainly have it, and if they cannot get it at their reading-room they will simply go to the village public. I think I understood that at first the limit for beer was placed at two glasses, but subsequently was altered to three; but, notwithstanding this, it is a most instructive and significant fact that the consumption of beer per head of the members of the club has steadily declined since the opening of the place. This is a very interesting fact, but not, I think, at all a surprising one. It is indeed exactly what might be expected. Men who would fuddle indefinitely or as long as money held out in the public-house, where everybody was drinking and where there was no diversion but drink, would find themselves in a place of this kind in a different moral atmosphere. There would be other interests, there would be no idea of having to drink "for the good of the house," there would be sure to be some who would drink little or nothing, and gradually and insensibly they would then be brought to think less of the drink as essential to an evening's pastime. This system certainly commends itself as a compromise between the unlimited sale of drink on the one hand, and the entire prohibition of it on the other, and if in every village such a place of public resort could be established and maintained for a few years, the effect would be incalculably good. Alas! how is it to be done, or anything approaching it? Where is the philanthropist in every village who will give £1,000—as has been done in Gaydon; or collect six or seven hundred, as has been done in Coombe? And if they are put up, who will maintain them? The Gaydon institution, I am told, costs about £20 a year to maintain. There are many to whom it is thought that the entrance fee and weekly subscription are a bar; and even with them the expenses cannot be raised without the aid of the liberal benefactor who has created the place, and who has to contribute a yearly subscription of eight or ten pounds. Yet some such social centre as this will have to

I

be provided in every village if civilisation is to make much headway among the people ; and the means of providing it, and maintaining it, and managing it, will have to be regarded as one of the problems for our local government councils before the world is much older.

———

LETTER XIX.

THE VILLAGE SUNDAY.

October 6.

How does the village spend its Sunday? I yesterday devoted one of the most delightful of autumn days to a quiet stroll from place to place in order to see. I had got into Buckinghamshire by the south, and on Saturday evening found myself in the pleasant little town of High Wycombe. The good people of Wycombe are very proud of their place and its busy factories, and of its development of late years. I was told, I think, that they make a chair every four minutes, that fifty thousand pounds a year is taken by the Great Western at the little station here, and I had hints at a quarter of a million of money's worth of business being done every year in its staple industry. But yesterday all was as peaceful as the morning sunshine. Its factories were at rest ; its shops, of course, were closed ; no vehicle disturbed the slumberous stillness of its streets, and as I passed out in the direction of West Wycombe, quiet folk in their best clothes, and with something of the Sunday rest in their faces, seemed to be streaming towards its churches and chapels. Soon I leave Wycombe and its sunny streets and tinkling church bells behind, and I am out in the open countr .

> " Mute is the voice of rural labour, hushed
> The ploughboy's whistle and the milkmaid's song."

I, too, catch something of the restfulness of the day, and I would fain for a few peaceful hours drop the troubles of labour, and the price of allotments, and the shifting of the people, and see a little of Hodge in his Sunday clothes, and quietly observe the way in which he spends his one day of rest. It is not, however, an easy matter to do this. I make a casual inquiry of a woman—the first person I speak to— as to an old church, and in two minutes I am once more under the doleful douche of a sad story of trouble and anxiety. They are going to have a sale in that neighbour- hood next week. A big landowner is giving up farming, and everything is to be sold off. She is very sorry for her neighbours. The man has worked on that farm most of his days, and now he is getting on in years he has got to turn out with his wife and family and find a new home and new work. He has been to one or two hiring fairs ; but what 's the good ? Nobody will take on an old man like him, especially now that the harvest is mostly over. What a pathetic figure—a man who has laboured all his life and lived honestly and respectably, now that his grey hairs and bent form begin to tell of the coming on of age, standing there in the market-place waiting for somebody to come and save him from the dreaded workhouse ! All he wants is a mere hovel and the privilege of working hard for ten or eleven shillings a week, and these he can't get. He has to stand mutely by while younger and stronger men are en- gaged, and then go sorrowfully to the home from which he must soon turn out into the bleak world. The woman I am talking to has her own trouble also. Her husband is engaged in the chair-making, like so many more in this part ; but that has been poor of late. It isn't like what it used to be. Machinery, she thinks, accounts for this. Anyhow, her husband in years gone by spent sixty pounds in tools for doing work all of which machines now do, and there are the tools indoors all rusty and useless, and it is of no use trying

to sell them, for it is the same with other people as it is with
them. She has written to a sister in Australia asking her to
help them out to that part of the world. Things are getting
worse here.

I see only two other people in the course of a couple of
miles' walk, and they are labourers on the land. A cheery
greeting and an inevitable allusion to the weather and the
remainder of the harvest, and once more I am in for a
story of discontent and change. The farmers treat their
men like dogs, but, says one, he'd put up with that if they'd
pay them fairly ; but they won't, and he for one is going the
first chance he can get. Five times as much could be
fetched out of the land if it were only well done. But he's
had enough of farming and is for the town. It is rather a
relief to shake off the two rustics and their grievances, and
turn up a green lane between hedges all alive with birds,
and bedizened with hips and haws and the scarlet berries of
" lords and ladies," and honeysuckle still flaunting its blossoms out in the sunshine. The birds, at all events, are
prosperous and happy, the long-drawn-out harvest having
enabled them to take their tithes at leisure, and they are
now busy gleaning along all the hedgerows where the laden
waggons have trailed their burdens, and left a part behind
them. The larks are carolling this morning as though it
were May instead of October, and the rooks here and there
are as blythe and as noisy as though they were busy nest-
building.

And now my path winds away into the beech woods for
which the neighbourhood of Wycombe is famous, and which
have given facilities for the special industry of the place.
What a glorious scene of peace and beauty ! A dazzling
flood of sunshine steeps the tree-tops that rustle against the
deep blue, lights them into amber and gold, smites their grey
trunks into columns of silver, and dapples the russet carpet
of leaves with flecks of quivering light. On my left the

wooded hillside stretches upwards against the sun, and down an opening avenue comes a broad torrent of sunshine sweeping along a pathway all vivid moss and dainty hare-bells, and yellowing ferns, with here and there a belated foxglove, and myriads of tiny cobwebs still wet with dew, and shining like frosted silver. My footfall is in the softest of moss, and only the dreamy hum of insects and the gentlest rustle in the tree-tops break the Sabbath stillness of those pompous and majestic aisles. But listen ! I am nearing the verge of the wood. Yonder is a soft curl of smoke, and through the trees the village green gleams out under the blue, and from the further side comes a droning of some musical instrument under the hand of an inexpert player. It is the Sunday-school harmonium doing its best to give out a tune, and presently a company of sweet young voices come swelling across the greensward in a bright and spirited hymn. How entirely right and natural and fitting comes the sound of praise and adoration in those solemn avenues. Standing there under the quivering canopy of autumn foliage one cannot but feel that life is beautiful if it is only simple and healthy and free from pressing care ; and when the little ones come trooping out in their Sunday finery and bright little faces, and hand in hand quietly disperse over the green, or stroll into the shadow of the beech woods, or away down the village, one feels that it is a thousand pities that children should ever be brought up in the stony streets of towns. What matters that some of their bits of finery are threadbare, and that some of their shoes turn up at the toe because they are two inches too long, and may probably belong to their mothers? Who cares about their boots when their faces look so pleasant and happy as they jog off with the turf beneath and the sun above, home to the dinners, which at this time of year are sure to be plentiful, though frugal enough? Outside the chapel railing are two or three of the men of the village smoking meditative pipes

and watching the pretty groups of children. I and they
are soon chatting things over, and how can we help coming
again on to the old ground? It is wages and work and
homes and life in the winter, and the farmers and their
doings. Quite unasked for by me, and altogether incidentally, I am told how all the land about there is in the
hands of four or five farmers; and an intelligent operative
who works in Wycombe but lives out there tells me how
within his recollection one after another five farms have
been taken into one, and so it has been all the way round.
He ridicules the idea of farming not paying. The fact is,
lots of people are farming who never ought to have had
anything to do with it. If it doesn't pay, why are all these
farms snapped up by big men as soon as they are given up
by incompetent little ones? I make some inquiries about
the habits of the people, and am assured that if there is any
drunkenness in the village it is on the part of those who
come out there from other places—people who come out
pleasure-taking in the summer time. The villagers themselves don't get drunk. Service there in the morning?
No, there is now only Sunday-school for the children.
There's service afternoon and evening. The greater part of
the people go; but there is no church within two miles, and
some of them don't go anywhere. Yes, that man's off to
preach at the next village, and there are friendly greetings
as the preacher in black clothes and a clerical wideawake
and the beaming face of one who has had a good dinner
bustles across the green and disappears down the slope like
a ship going out to sea. We discuss a little the sweet-
smelling stocks and the great clumps of scarlet dahlias and
the luxuriant verbenas, and then I move on, but am soon
again in conversation with four men, seated like so many
crows on the top of a fence, each burly fellow with a short
clay pipe in his mouth. They have had dinner, and now
they are doing a siesta on the top rail, while the children

play about them in and out of the cottage-doors close at hand. Yes, it was pleasant enough then ; but I should try it in the winter, when there was no fire in the grate and nothing in the cupboard. And so on, all over again. There was the man at the end there, with six children, and the biggest not older than that boy of ten or eleven there, and, taking it throughout last year, they didn't average eight shillings a week. There were eight of 'em, and a shilling apiece ! And that's how people lived. "Ah," broke in a rugged, gaunt-looking fellow, taking out his short pipe from his mouth, " and t' other day when a colt kicked my boy's brains out and I went to the parish to ask 'em to bury 'im, they told me as I ought to have money enough to do it myself." Up here in this delightful borderland between Buckinghamshire and Oxfordshire there were just the same stories as I have found almost everywhere else, and these men seemed quite eager to discuss things. Nowhere there about their homes could they get a bit of allotment. One of them had been down in the direction of Marlow, and he declared—I don't know how truly—that some of the people down there had got bits of ground at a shilling a pole, or eight pounds an acre. But up round their cottages they couldn't get it at any price. The most intelligent of the party was a man who had lived some years in Newcastle. He had seen shiploads of coffins come in ready made from foreign parts, and doors and window-sashes and chairs. That was the reason trade had been so bad all round there, because things that ought to be made at home were made abroad and imported. He was for putting a tax on ready-made imports, while admitting raw material free. I am afraid this man's view is typical of that of a large number of countrymen, who sit on fences on Sunday afternoons and brood over their troubles and the causes of them. No ripple of the late proceedings at Newcastle had apparently reached this little colony.

Away again through the lanes and highways, past orchards and broad expanses of stubble, and by wayside grass plots where the gipsies are encamped—looking so delightfully picturesque in the distance, and so disgustingly dirty and degraded close at hand—and I presently turn in for a bit of lunch into a village inn, where I find the landlord's face somehow curiously familiar. He is a countryman who years ago went to London, got enrolled in the City Police, where he served up till a year or two back, and has now settled here with a pension of something over a pound a week. Put this object-lesson against the other poor man whom I have described as sticking to his plough, and now when his best days are over with the winter and the workhouse staring him in the face, and we have a good illustration of what is continually drawing away Hodge from the land. Out again and along the gleaming white road, past the open cottage doors where babies in their best bibs and tuckers are seated on the mat, while father sits on guard just outside with his pipe. Doors are open back and front, and one can see through across the red-brick floor into the garden behind, still gay with dahlias and geraniums, Michaelmas daisies and marigolds, with here and there a well-laden apple-tree. Rest—in perfect rest and quiet—that is the best way to express the manner in which all the villagers seem to be spending the beautiful autumn Sunday. Mother in her Sunday clothes sits just inside the house or out in the little front garden, and father is leading the youngest little toddler up and down the road holding to one of his fingers. Here and there a book or a newspaper may be seen in hand, and as the bells tinkle out for afternoon church or chapel the harmonium begins again to drone out upon the breeze, fathers and mothers and children saunter quietly out over the green with books under their arms, past the flocks of grey geese that strut and cackle as boldly as though Michaelmas had quite gone, and as though the big shining holly-

trees were not already furbishing up their berries for Christmas. Not a wheel in the roadway disturbs the quiet; old
horses and skittish ponies put their velvet noses over the
glistening blackberry-bushes and sniff at the passer-by as
though they know it is the day of rest, and can afford a
little impudence; and sunburnt young rustics, in black coats
and with flowers in their button-holes, are wooing buxom
lasses by the roadside. How lovely the country is as the
sun sinks and the shadows lengthen. Look at that little
hamlet there, nestling in the hollow, with the furze bushes
scrambling about the broken slopes. The whole place
looks to have grown there as naturally as the fungus growth
about an old tree trunk, and out beyond it the russeting
woods stretch away to the blue hills. And presently comes
the journey's end, and Stokenchurch, just within the boun-
daries of Oxfordshire, is reached in time for a cup of tea
and a stroll into the queer little church before service begins. The bell ropes hang down from the odd little slated
tower into the nave below, and while I am looking round
and the sexton is trimming the oil lamps, the discordant old
bells ding-dong-ding their call to worship, and a large congregation—as large, at least, as the church will hold—comes
streaming from all quarters, while the Salvation Army and
two or three chapels are also gathering their people together.
I have gone out of the church for a short time, and when I
return the vicar and choir are moving up to the nave, and a
processional hymn is being sung heartily by the whole congregation. I have observed the notice board in the porch of
the church, and I have been struck by the signs of vigorous
church life in this out-of-the-way village—mothers' meetings
and Dorcas meetings, and guilds and societies and bands of
hope, and many other movements are indicated here, and
I am not surprised at the bright and hearty way in which
the service goes, though some of it is not to my own taste.
But what a prig one must be if because he couldn't admire

the way in which the vicar intones the prayers, he failed to recognise the evident earnestness and kindly feeling and practical good sense of his sermon.   He talked about helping one another, and a right cheery, stirring, and helpful sermon it was.   And then he got out of the pulpit, and—as he had done all through the service—sat down to the organ and led his people in their singing of two hymns, in which everybody sang.   The vicar here seems to be greatly liked.

But what about the drink on Sunday?   Well, I am describing what comes under my own observation, and to-day I have seen nothing of its evils.   I have had my cup of tea at an inn at which I was assured they did the best business, and I was curious to see what would be going on there in the evening.   I came out of church, therefore, and betook myself to the tap-room to await the vehicle that was presently coming for me.   There were four or five people quietly smoking their pipes and with their mugs of beer before them ; but they were chatting in the most orderly and peaceful way, and if I may judge of them by what occurred at another village inn at which I presently arrived for the night, they would in an hour or so finish their chat and their beer, and go quietly home, and before ten o'clock the village would have come to the close of an autumn Sunday, so beautiful in its peace and pleasantness, and invigorating restfulness, that it couldn't but intensify one's feeling of regret that this rural population here, as everywhere else, dwindles year by year.

LETTER XX.

DEATH IN THE VILLAGE.

October 9.

MORE rustic cottages, more flowery gardens, more laden orchards, and grassy slopes and smiling meadows and bubbling springs and carolling larks, and blue skies and playful breezes. Surely life in yonder little place is healthy and happy and prosperous! How charmingly it is situated on that swelling hill! How beautiful its handsome church beams down in the brilliant afternoon sun from its slight eminence amid the trees! How prettily the neighbouring rectory peeps out in its garb of dark-green ivy and crimson Virginia creeper from amid its shrubs and tall trees and trimly kept turf! Away yonder towards the setting sun is some of the finest pasture land in England, and though the River Thame has overflowed its banks and flashes along now a great swelling flood across the verdant meadows, it does but give life and added beauty to the scene. What could be prettier or pleasanter, more peaceful, more smilingly contented?

Alas! alas! look at that churchyard. There are three little newly-made graves side by side, and dotted about the ground are three or four others, and up yonder in the chapel graveyard at the top of the village are two or three more. And in ever so many of those picturesque cottages are hapless little mortals smitten for death and lying feverishly tossing there in an atmosphere foul and pest-laden, for all the health-giving breezes that are gambolling about the mossy roofs and tossing the hollyhocks and Michaelmas daisies outside. The rector's children have been hurried off, and so have the curate's, for the village is smitten with a virulent plague, and already a dozen deaths have darkened the homes here, and in all probability many more must follow. Two hospital nurses have been brought down by Baron Rothschild, whose estate is in the neighbourhood, and who has another village, to which the outbreak may easily spread, close to his gates. But one of them has been stricken down with the disease, and the other seemed in such peril of it that both have had to be withdrawn. As I set out from Aylesbury this afternoon, however, two others were there only awaiting the medical officer's orders to go and step into the deadly breach and bravely grapple with the dread malady. Ever since the spring there have been symptoms of virulent blood poisoning among the villagers, old and young, and at length diphtheria broke out in its worst form. The rector, the Rev. P. L. Cautley, whom many will know and greatly respect as formerly the Vicar of Southwold, has been here only a short time, and is only just recovering from a serious illness, and I found him to-day still feeble and suffering and full of anxiety. He may well be so. I went through the village in company with the gentleman who has been acting as curate during the rector's illness, the Rev. P. H. Case, and I found really a very painful state of things. In one cottage a woman, who looked herself almost too ill and exhausted to stand, and the hard, dry, stony look of whose eyes told a terrible tale of anguish and suffering, came out of a little stifling den of a room adjoining her living room, and told us that one child was lying dead in there and another one ill. There was another child about, and the watchfulness and care necessary to keep this other little one out of harm's way evidently bore heavily on the poor woman's heart. How is it possible for these people to isolate cases of infectious illness in such houses as theirs? A large proportion of the cottages in this village are ruinous and filthy and ought to be swept away. Some of them have no sort of ventilation in their bed-rooms. Windows are fixtures, and will not open, and some of the bed-rooms that have these fixed windows have no fire-places, so that when three or four or five people go to bed in them they soon become insupportably foul. I went into one room in which there was only one bed, and in this I was assured had lain a woman who had been confined only a fortnight, and she had had with her in bed the baby and two other children, one of them ill with diphtheria. A month ago, she told us with quivering lip, she had four children. The only one left was the newly-born child. Three had been taken. Of course the people themselves are excessively foolish—almost as foolish as we all were about matters of infection a generation ago. Even where isolation is practicable they cannot be made to understand the necessity for it, and those of them who might be supposed to know better seem capable of great folly. One of the children belonging to the Baptist Sunday-school died, and they actually brought down some of the other children to the infected cottage, and if it hadn't been peremptorily forbidden would have had them carry the coffin out to the grave. In this village of Quainton there are probably five or six hundred people. Looking round the place I should say a good half of them are housed in ill-constructed ramshackle cottages, utterly unsatisfactory in times of health. When sickness of an infectious or contagious character breaks out, the wonder is that it doesn't sweep the village. Ay, and worse than that. The fact is we are all so linked together, town and village, in one way and another, and every year becoming more so, that it is difficult to assign any limit to an outbreak of this kind. To say nothing of the commercial interests between London and this particular district, I was informed by a highly-placed official on the railway here that something like fifty children had this summer been sent down into this very village for their summer holiday from London. One of the fifty—so at least I was credibly informed—was on Monday last carried back to town in a coffin hermetically sealed. I give

these statements as I received them, and they appear to me
to be probably true; but circumstances did not permit of
my verifying them.   If they are true, there must certainly
have been the grossest carelessness somewhere, for this
village has been known to be in a suspicious and unhealthy
condition since the spring.   Quite certainly one little victim
was sent home to London in his coffin; whether he was one
of the visitors sent down for a holiday I cannot say
positively, nor do I feel confident about the number, but
there were unquestionably some there this summer, and an
attempt has been made to attribute to these little strangers
the outbreak of diphtheria.   The responsibility for it, however, cannot be shirked in this way.

The fact is this village of five or six hundred people is in
a scandalously filthy condition.   The cottages are old and
badly constructed, and some of them are packed together in
a way suggestive of London slums.   Numbers of these ought
to be pulled down, and their materials carted out into an
open space and burnt.   They are said to be alive with
vermin; and the description I had of the condition of some
of the poor children when they came to be laid out for
burial is too sad to be given here.   The village seems to
have a good water supply from the springs on the hill
behind it; but even this seems to want some scientific
attention.   I was struck by the number of cases in which
women to whom I spoke were suffering from goître.   I am
informed that it is extremely common in the village, and
that it is probably attributable to something in the nature of
the water supply.   It is now, I understand, under analysis.
But whatever may be said of the water, there can be no
doubt that the site of the village is literally saturated with
sewage.   The position of the place on the hillside would
render it the easiest thing in the world to drain it most
effectually, and with good water and efficient drainage, and
comfortable cottages, Quainton might be, and ought to be,

one of the prettiest and healthiest villages in the kingdom, as one day, with a good village council to look after its own affairs, it undoubtedly will be. At present the place can scarcely be said to have any drainage at all. There is something in the nature of a drain running down through the place, but it was probably never intended for anything but surface water ; into this, however, the house drains seem to have been conducted, and I suspect that if it were opened it would be found in many points to be a festering mass of sewage enough to poison an army. The people say that the smell from this straggling drain has all the summer been dreadful, and the first case of diphtheria broke out in a house under which this pestilential little channel passed, while the others, one after the other, have been dotted along its course. The outpourings from it stagnate down on the lower fringe of the village.

Who is responsible for this state of things, and for the deaths that have resulted from it, and will result from it? The Aylesbury Board of Guardians, unhesitatingly. Guardians, forsooth ! Of whom or of what have they been the guardians ? Why, of the pockets of the farmers and squires of their own class. Have they taken any reasonable interest in these five or six hundred unhappy villagers committed to their guardianship ? I have a positive assurance that when some time ago a letter was sent to them calling attention to the dreadful state of some of these cottages they didn't so much as read it. I am credibly informed that they have some sort of a standing order by which all such letters are not to be read at the Board but to be taken as read, and passed over to their district sanitary inspector — to the officer, that is, whose action—or inaction—may very likely be impugned. But what about the Board's medical officer? Well, they have a medical officer, a clever, and, I hear, a very popular young practitioner of Aylesbury. On the death of his predecessor a few months ago he took to his large practice and succeeded to his official post. He would do, there cannot be the least reason to doubt, all that a medical man in extensive private practice can do, and all that can reasonably be expected for the emoluments of his office. He seems to be now working with great zeal and energy and no little anxiety to grapple with the legacy of mischief left him in Quainton. But the rational and satisfactory course is, as I pointed out early in this series of articles, such as the combined boards of Chelmsford and Maldon have adopted. They have appointed a thoroughly well-qualified man to the charge of the sanitary condition of their districts, giving him such a salary as will enable him to devote his whole time and attention to his duties. Quite apart from the direct action of such an officer, his educational influence with the people is immense. They say these people in Quainton are stupid and ignorant. Why, of course they are. How can modern ideas of infection, of germs and molecules, and the diffusion of gases, and that kind of knowledge, percolate down to these poor cottagers ? Nothing struck me more forcibly when I was the other day going a round from house to house with Dr. Thresh, of Chelmsford, than the instruction he was giving and the intelligence he was awakening on the importance of pure water and fresh air, and careful drainage, and such matters. It is just what these people want—someone continually moving about among them pointing out what is wrong, and explaining why it is wrong, and authoritatively insisting on its being put right for the sake of the community if not for themselves. Most of these boards of guardians are wretched failures for every purpose but that of protecting themselves against any increase of rates, and it is quite time that at least many of their functions were handed over to popularly-elected councils. Another illustration of the need of such bodies to deal with purely local affairs was afforded in the course of the efforts that were yesterday being made to obtain some sort of hospital to which these poor suffering children might be removed, and the plague be stayed by isolation. The village school had, of course, been broken up, and the schoolroom could have been converted into a convenient and comfortable hospital ward. Application was made to the Education Department, and after I forget how many days of deadly delay, there came the curt reply to the effect that my Lords of the Privy Council had no power to grant the permission. It was feared at Quainton that if the schoolroom were taken for the purpose without permission, they might permanently lose their grant or be compelled to put up another school, and when I left them yesterday they were anxiously endeavouring to elicit by letter and telegram from " My Lords " in Whitehall a statement as to whether they would by-and-by consent that the room should again be used as a school if care were taken properly to disinfect it. With a village council, this purely local matter could have been settled in an hour, and probably would have been settled weeks ago and many a life saved. The village schoolmistress, Mrs. Reeves, made heroic efforts to nurse the stricken children before the arrival of the nurses ; and Mrs. Cautley, the vicar's wife, has had an extremely hard and anxious time. The most unselfish and ungrudging assistance has also been given by the local squire, Captain Pigott, and Mrs. Pigott. Infinite trouble and expense and worry, besides suffering and death, brought into many a poor home ; and all might have been avoided if, when the people complained that they were being choked with foul smells, and their complaints were forwarded to their precious guardians, those guardians had paid as much attention as they would have done if they had had a hint that some poor hungry wretch had been snaring their rabbits. We want village councils badly, and we'll have them, too, before the world is much older.

J

LETTER XXI.

VILLAGE HOUSE-MOVING.

October 15.

THIS series of articles must shortly be closed. It is not
that the subject is by any means exhausted.   There are two
or three considerations which render it unadvisable to
prolong it much further, else there are many other points in
connection with village life that might be touched on.   I
am not sure, for instance, that it might not be well worth
while to inquire a little more closely than I have been able
to do into the possible effect of a further development of
our postal system in ameliorating village life.   There seem
to me to be many ways in which some of that huge profit
made by the Post Office every year might be advantageously
employed in bringing town and country into closer touch
with each other.   Then again there is a wide subject for
inquiry presented in the provision made for the medical
needs of the village.   I have heard some piteous stories of
the difficulty of getting the doctor in times of extremity and
even in cases of ordinary sickness.   I know one poor fellow
who lay on a bed of sickness and suffering for ten days
before they could get a doctor to see him, all this time his
family around him being on the brink of starvation.   Country
doctors, as a body, seem to me to be among the most heroic
and self-sacrificing of men.   Many of them could scarcely
lead the lives they do if they were not actuated by a great
pity for human sorrows, at least as much as by any hope of
payment.   If they are willing to sacrifice time and strength
and comfort in attendance on patients from whom there is
scarcely even a remote chance of ever getting a shilling, all
honour to them.   But I do not know what right we have to
blame them if they are not willing.   Why should doctors be
expected to work for nothing any more than lawyers or

tradesmen ? It will of course be said that for the poor of our villages there is the parish doctor. A great deal might be said about this. In one of the most wretched places I have met with I found a poor woman lying at death's door from a most agonising malady, for which the parish doctor was visiting her once a week. It was true, probably, that nothing could be done for her ; but who doesn't know the relief and satisfaction of having a call from the doctor, even though the case may be hopeless ? This poor creature lay in pitiable suffering, her husband out of health and out of work, and she would have been without nurse, as well as doctor, but for the charity of another almost as poor as herself, who, in much anxiety for the family of children she herself had left at home, was, when I called, hobbling about the cottage on a crutch, ministering as well as she could to the comfort of the dying woman and her children. But it is by no means to be assumed that the parish doctor is always available even once a week. What may be the rule with Poor Law Guardians generally I do not know, but I was assured in one village that a man who had not less than ten shillings a week, and more than five children to support out of it, was not deemed to be entitled to the parish doctor. He must pay for his own medical attendance ; and a respectable mother of a family I talked with seemed half crazy with anxiety over a bill of two pounds for medical attendance that had thus been incurred, and for which the doctor had warned her he could only give her a month's credit. She had four or five children. Her husband had regular work at ten shillings a week, and might have done pretty well only that the arbitrary and inconsiderate treat-ment of his employer had prevented him working a little extra at harvest time this year.

Another phase of rural life has presented itself to me during the past week or so. You cannot go far along country roads just now without meeting waggons piled up

with the goods and chattels of farm hands changing quarters.
They are carters and shepherds mainly who are exchanging
one master for another.   They have been to some Michaelmas hiring fair, and have got fresh places, and here they are
jogging about the country with their tables and chairs, and
beds and boxes, and wives and children heaped up on the
new master's waggon.   I don't know whether it is another
indication of agrarian unrest and unsettlement, but I am
told that this autumn there is a very unusual number of such
changes.   Carters and shepherds are among the rather
better paid of farm hands, and in some districts I hear that
masters have been trying to lower their wages, while the
men themselves have not only resisted any such attempts,
but have been demanding some improvement, and in some
localities I hear that they have been successful.   In some
parts of Oxfordshire, for instance, where the unionist emis-
saries have been stirring up the people, I hear that there
has been a decided advance.   It is about there that I found
the greatest number of removals.   Some of these little
family cavalcades, with their pots and kettles, and cradles
and hen coops, have looked forlorn and desolate enough—
more so, perhaps, than they really were.   One unlucky
wight in the neighbourhood I was in yesterday had had a
dire disaster.   He had stuffed the family wardrobe and all
the bed linen into a sack, and as they had gone bumping
and jolting along the country roads it had somehow tumbled
off, and they had lost it all.   Search and inquiries were
alike fruitless, and he had been going all round the neighbourhood trying to buy postage stamps enough to send on
for an advertisement in a local paper.   The postal authorities, by the way, had fixed up a letter box conveniently
enough, but had ingeniously made no provision for the sale
of stamps except at the post office, which had evidently
been located for the special convenience of the squire and
the clergyman, right at the far end of the village.   This was

at Minster Lovel, the scene of Feargus O'Connor's famous experiment in land settlement, and I was assured that many of the people for whom the wall box had been fixed, if they wanted stamps, found it most convenient to go down into Witney, somewhere about three miles off. Such removals as I have been describing are of course common enough in town as well as country. Neither in town nor country, however, is any exceptional disturbance of the kind a healthy or satisfactory sign of the times. It means political disfranchisement, social uprooting, a certain demoralisation, and a good deal of discomfort. These people whom one meets about the country roads just now are, almost all of them, occupants of their employers' houses, and are liable any week to be turned out neck and crop from home and employment if they do not please their masters. Beyond the power themselves to turn out and find another place, and jog off as these people are doing now, they have absolutely no independence in any shape or form. One man told me that not only did his master insist on his being up by a certain time in the morning, but did his best to compel him to go to bed at a certain time at night. Another said that he and his master had fallen out because his—the labourer's—wife seemed likely to be affecting the next census returns to an extent the farmer didn't approve of. As an intelligent country woman said to me, in reference to these waggon loads of furniture : How can people take any pleasure in their homes, or their gardens, or their employment, when they are always liable to be turned out at a week's notice? It is of no use to offer them allotments and security in their tenure of them unless they can also have some security in the occupancy of their homes. But, then again, what is the use of security in their homes unless they have some sort of certainty about employment?

And, talking of homes, I am reminded how very inadequately I have been able to convey the truth as to large

numbers of them.   Last week I was in one of the pleasantest
and prettiest villages I ever saw.   Its gardens and trees and
babbling brook, spanned by little bridges, its open greensward stretching up the hillside, and its creeper-covered
cottages together formed a sweet little picture ; while the
church and the parsonage at the hill foot was suggestive of
intelligent oversight and friendly care for the people.   Yet
those people were wretchedly poor.   As to the cottages,
some of them I was shown by the people occupying them
were ruinous to the last degree.   They were saturated by
rain, the winds blew through and through them, and one at
least was in such a perilous condition that the lad who had
to sleep in the back bedroom didn't like going to bed there.
He couldn't keep warm, and he was afraid the roof would
fall in upon him.   One hole in the thatch the woman had
stopped by thrusting in a great bundle of old clothes and
rags, but the rain poured in, and the winds whistled through
the cracks in its walls, its timbers looked to be parting, and
how in the world it can have stood—if indeed it has stood
—through the gale of the past few hours, I am sure I do
not understand.   Why, then, hasn't the sanitary authority
condemned the structure ?   Well, the sanitary authority,
such as it is, has condemned it.   But what is the good?
There is not another house of any kind that this respectable
working-man's family can creep into.   If there were, they
would only be too eager to get into it without any
"authority."   One gets sick of talking about these rural
boards and all their ways and works.   The whole business
of sanitary management and medical supervision is a hideous
farce. I showed in my last article how one of these precious
boards dealt with a letter calling attention to a state of
things that ought to have had instant attention, and how at
least a dozen deaths have resulted from their inaction.
Here is another "Sanitary Authority" under which this
pretty village and its tumble-down cottages are placed.

They have a district twelve miles broad and fifteen miles long, and comprising twenty-nine villages. To look after this great rural district the Local Board of Guardians pay a medical officer forty pounds a year! And they themselves devote every month half-an-hour to sanitary matters—just six hours a year! If, in seeking to be elected to the office of Guardian, they had any sense of the responsibility they were incurring, or any humanitarian intention whatever, how could they trifle in this ridiculous fashion?

Another word or two as to the drink question. I set out with the expectation of finding that drink played a very prominent part in the social affairs of the village. I had no sooner begun this series of articles than I got letter after letter giving some very painful evidences of it. I have been very agreeably surprised to find practically none. Let me again remind the readers of the *Daily News*, many of whom I know feel very strongly on this subject, that I am referring simply and solely to those parts of the country through which I have been moving, and that I am speaking only of what has come under my own observation. Judging by that, it is certainly difficult to entertain any reasonable doubt that the temperance propaganda has in many ways, direct and indirect, been more successful than is commonly supposed, and that combined with the general rise in intelligence and education, which is invariably allowed to be the main cause of the exodus from the country to the town, it has really effected a great change in the habits of our peasantry. Take one simple fact. I have now for over two months been moving continuously through the rural parts of Essex, Suffolk, Norfolk, Oxfordshire, Berkshire, and Buckinghamshire. It has been during harvest time, when the people have a little more money in their pockets than at other times of the year, and in a great many cases I have mingled with the company in the bars and taprooms of village inns and beerhouses. Yet I have seen only one

solitary case of drunkenness among them. That they drink
far too much to be good for them, and that they injure and
impoverish themselves and their families, is only too apparent, but they do not get drunk as they did. On Sunday
evenings I certainly expected to find the public-houses in
the villages full and noisy. I am bound to say—and I am
heartily glad to be able to believe it—that the village drink
trade presents many indications of rapid decay. In Stokenchurch I was told by the men idling on the village green on
Sunday evening that there were seventeen or eighteen
hundred people in the parish and sixteen public-houses, but
I heard on all hands that they were none of them doing the
business they did, and a good many of them might as well
shut up. On the Sunday evening I was there I did not see
or hear the least indication of drunkenness. I did not, it
is true, stay there till closing time, but I drove on to
another village, where also the supply of public-houses was
ridiculously out of proportion to any possible need ; there
was equal quiet and good order. In the taproom of the inn
I stayed at for the night they were sitting enveloped in the
usual cloud of smoke discussing the size of their potatoes
and the temperature of the previous night, and when closing
time came they quietly bade each other good-night, and in
ten minutes the whole place seemed to be asleep.

Talking of closing time, I was very forcibly reminded of
the foolish people who are so apt to prate about the impos-
sibility of making people sober by Act of Parliament, one
night when in the midst of a laughing, swearing, guzzling,
chorus-singing company of perhaps thirty or forty men.
There was not one of them giving any sign of drunkenness,
but filthy-looking pots of beer—for one of which I was
compelled to pay, on penalty of having to pledge the company in the vile stuff they had three or four of them been
slobbering into—pots of beer kept looming through the
smoke in so rapid a series that it seemed impossible that

it could go on much longer without such signs, when the landlord put his head in and said, "Closing time, please." I had forgotten the earlier hour of the closing for the country, and could not doubt that by eleven o'clock that taproom must have become a pandemonium, and half the company must have gone reeling home. But ten o'clock had come, and the blessed Act of Parliament put a stopper on those quart pots and bade the company clear out. There wasn't a word of objection—not a murmur. It was merely that bedtime had come. They finished their song, swallowed off their beer, bade each other good-night, and in a quarter of an hour the whole place was as still as death. I went to bed that night musing on the practicability of still further curtailing the hours of sale. Ten o'clock is at least an hour later in the villages than eleven is in London; and, if the publics could be closed at nine, which is fully late for going to bed when villagers are at home, another important step would have been taken in the moral and material elevation of the people. I am reminded by the singing of the Salvationists under the window of the room in which I am writing, that wherever I have been I have found these people strenuously battling against drink and degradation, and I am strongly inclined to attribute to them and their efforts much of the improvement to which I have been testifying.

LETTER XXII.

CONCLUSION.

October 19.

AFTER two months of continuous movement about the country, the one dominant, all-significant fact appears to me to be the evolution of large farming. Of this tendency I could have given any number of illustrations only that it seemed unnecessary to keep on accumulating evidence as to a fact which nobody seems to dispute. Of course the agglomeration of small farms into large ones is not universally the case. Here and there I have come across localities where there seemed to be some tendency the other way. But I can confidently say that wherever I have been such cases are quite the exception, and that the general movement is from small farms to large ones.

How is this to be regarded? Is it an outcome of the times likely to be permanent, or is it merely a passing phase of agriculture, due to temporary causes which two or three good seasons and certain changes in our land laws may remove? In studying this question of the land and the labourer, it surely must be important to come to a right decision on this point. If some modification of law and a general reduction of rents, and perhaps a little better luck in the seasons, may be expected to break up these large farms again and re-establish the middle-class farmer in prosperity, then possibly the labour question may right itself. If rents go down and capital is made more secure, and farms multiply, labour may be in greater demand, wages will tend to rise ; and, with lower rents and better markets, higher wages would be easily given, while some amendment in the Acts relating to cottages and allotments may do all that is really requisite in promoting the comfort and prosperity of the agricultural working-man. If, on the other hand, this large-scale farming is not due merely to temporary causes, but is really attributable to the operation of those same economic forces which are producing gigantic businesses in every other department of commerce, then it may be— indeed it must be—that under existing circumstances this depopulation of the land will go on and accelerate, and if we mean to check it, nothing short of a total change of our agricultural system will avail us. Modifications of laws and reductions of rent may for a time stave off the necessity for such a change, but cannot finally avert it. What are the

probabilities of the future? " You must remember," said a
shrewd country solicitor to me the other day, "that these
big farmers, although they are at some disadvantage as
compared with smaller men, can do with a profit that a
small farmer couldn't live upon.   Many of them don't do
with their land as well as they might do, but they get
something out of it, and if they can farm on a sufficiently
large scale they can make an income." The large agriculturists are doing, in fact, exactly what the large houses of
business in all the towns of the kingdom are doing—doing
a "cutting trade," making small profits on a large turnover.
Turn to almost any trade you please in London, and you
will be told that profits are not what they were ; that if you
want to make the same income you made a few years ago
you must do three or four times as much business.   Great
concerns are the order of the day everywhere.   A small man
is rapidly finding his position becoming more and more
difficult, and in business circles nobody appears to have the
slightest expectation that these great concerns will ever again
give place to small ones.   You will be told in the City that
this is due to the stress of increased competition, and that
is just what I am everywhere told in the country.   A few
years ago the farmers were so thriving that the margin of
cultivation was extended.   Incomes could be made out of
very inferior land.   But our agriculturists are in competition
with all the world, and profits are not what they were.
Nobody, so far as I am aware, predicts that this stress of
competition is likely to slacken ; on the contrary, the general
apprehension is that as communication opens up and trading
facilities develop it will become constantly keener.   There
will be fluctuations of course, and farming is peculiarly liable
to them ; but the general drift of things will tend to reduce
profits, to make everything cheaper and cheaper for the
consumer.   Farmers will require the benefit of the best laws
and ample capital, and the best methods.   But competition

will go on and profits will go down, and operations will be larger and larger.   So, at least, I hear it contended.

Now, if that is really the fact, it will be just as well to recognise it, and not to waste our time in endeavouring to put back the tide with our mops. - In those sleepy hollows in which I have been roaming, one cannot help occasionally doing a little day-dreaming.   I have been specially inclined to it sometimes when lingering about the old churches with their crumbling walls and ivy-mantled towers and slumbering grave-yards—

"Where heaves the turf in many a mouldering heap."

Again and again, from some such resting-place, I have found myself looking out over the harvest fields, pondering on the marvellous social and industrial developments that have taken place since those old churches first gathered the peasantry into their quaint shadows.   One looks back on those primitive folk in their total isolation from foreign lands, with their small clearings, their simple husbandry, their rude implements, their ignorance of science, and their crops scantier and punier than we are very well able to realise.   The centuries have crept on; the light of science has been kindled, and has burnt brighter and clearer.   The whirr and the rattle of mechanism have risen higher and higher, and one's thoughts wander away yonder to the land of the setting sun, where so much of our corn is now grown. At harvest tide it is no longer the local peasantry who are called into action, but great cavalcades of men and horses and machinery sweep over the vast yellow plains, clearing all before them like great flights of devouring locusts. Everything is done by machinery—ploughing, sowing, reap-ing, binding, carrying, threshing, grinding, or storing in granaries—all is a matter of mechanism.   Musing on this farthest development of agricultural enterprise, and looking backward and forward and all around—-reflecting on the momentous fact that in our own country farming seems to

be moving on towards something of the same gigantic scale
—listening to the whirr of the very same machines rising
higher and higher from our own fields, and knowing that
every year men are obliged to move off into the towns to
make way for them, one can only stand silent and awe-
stricken under the sweep of forces as calm as the midnight
stars, as irresistible as the tide, and as regards all our prejudices and prepossessions, as pitiless as the tempest. Looking backward and forward and around, one would fain hope
that the gradual unfoldings of our social system may show
us how we may bring science and mechanical invention to
bear, not for the accumulation of useless wealth in the hands
of the few, but for the good of the many and for the eman-
cipation of all the toiling sons of men. Who knows, I
have sometimes thought, but that that way lies our path, and
that these perplexing changes and movements are but the
loosenings of the old and the worn out in the grasp of
that—

> " Divinity that shapes our ends,
> Rough hew them how we will."

But, after all, there is the undoubted fact that large
farming is not in all respects advantageous farming. Acre
for acre, as at present conducted, it will not produce from
the land what the allotment-holder and the very small
farmer can fetch out of it, while it has the utterly disastrous
effect of driving our rural population into the slums of the
towns. In truth, neither the very large farm nor the very
small one is altogether satisfactory, while the medium-sized
farm—apparently having some of the disadvantages of both,
and not all the advantages of either—is disappearing. The
ideal system would be one which combined the large capital,
the fine machinery, the scientific methods and business-like
management of the great farmers, with the thoroughness
and personal devotion of the small ones. It would, in fact,
be a large farm under the best possible management; in

which everybody upon it took a personal interest and had a
personal share.   There are many who believe that co-
operation in some form or other, and that alone, will fulfil
these conditions.   I have talked with a great many who are
looking in this direction for a solution of the agricultural
problem.   On the other hand co-operative farming is held
by some to be impracticable.   It is certainly true that the
result of the one extensive experiment of which I have any
direct knowledge, appears on the face of it to support this
view.   I went down into a midland county the other day to
inquire a little into the circumstances under which a bold
and promising enterprise of the kind had failed.   The net
result of the experiment had been the loss of some thousands
of pounds, and what seemed to be a demonstration of the
futility of such schemes.   For one or two reasons I cannot
give particulars of this enterprise.   If I could, I think I
could show that it really demonstrated nothing of the kind.
One or two conditions absolutely essential to success were
altogether wanting, and failure under the circumstances
must have resulted under any system.

Yesterday I was at Chipping Norton, where I had understood the co-operative society had been engaged in
farming arable land for the supply of their own business.
This I find has been going on for six years, and the last
report upon the farm is " This department shows very satisfactory results for 1890."   It is true that it is on quite a
small scale—only 112 acres—and it has not yet been deemed
expedient to devote the profits to dividend, but there is the
principle successfully applied, and I was assured that there
would certainly be considerable advantage in working the
concern on more extensive proportions.   This society is, of
course, but a small one in a small country town, only it
happens to be one of the very few that have tried farming.
In combination with it the members of the society are supplied with provisions and grocery, ironmongery, boots and

shoes, bread, meat, and coals, and there is also a building department to enable members to build or purchase houses. Now, imagine a scheme of this sort developed to the proportions of Lord Wantage's estate in Berkshire. Imagine those two villages I described the other day with their beautiful little homes and pleasant gardens, the finely timbered park, the schools, and workshops, and reading-rooms, and stores, and the great farm lands all around—every bit owned by the people and worked by the people for the sole benefit of the people, who elect their own officers and share all the profits. Think of every man in such an agricultural and industrial community absolutely fearless of everything but public opinion and the law he lives under, cringing to nobody, dependent on nobody, working for himself and the public good, hailing with hearty satisfaction every new machine, every advance of science, every economy in method, since these things no longer tend to throw him out of employment and keep down earnings, but rather to promote his wealth and lessen his toil.

My function in this series of articles has been mainly to record facts, leaving the significance of them to the readers of the *Daily News.* I should, however, be doing this with little discretion or intelligence if in moving about the country I failed to note the ideas and speculations I find occupying the minds and stirring the hearts of many of the most thoughtful and far-seeing of those I have met. There are many who find in this collective action a most fascinating conception of the method by which the people will by-and-by be got back on to the land under the most favourable conditions, and under the strongest possible incentive to effort. Nothing has struck me more impressively than the evidence I have met with, that even where the exactly opposite method is adopted, and men are put down into small holdings to work in total independence of each other, one of the very first fruits of their experience, where the men are fairly intelligent or under intelligent guidance, is a co-operative movement. I was in a neighbourhood the other day where almost everybody seemed to have a plot of ground for corn-growing. The whole landscape seemed dotted about with Liliputian ricks that you might almost have played leap-frog over. It looked quite ridiculous. "Can this pettifogging little business possibly be in the line of progress?" I asked myself, "or," as I have asked before, "are we really going back to the thirteenth century?" "You see," said in effect a gentleman in the neighbourhood with whom I afterwards talked, a philanthropist who had himself done much to promote this small culture, "You see, these men are in this way learning to co-operate." They had in fact been discovering that their isolated efforts were made under all sorts of disadvantages, and they were forming committees among themselves for the hiring of a plough and a threshing-machine, and a cart for manure and so forth. It would obviously be quite in the line of natural and probable development if by-and-by these men should club together to buy a co-operative plough, to build a co-operative barn, or to set up a co-operative cart to take the produce home or send it to market. Already, I was informed, the collective idea had made such advances in that neighbourhood that three villages were between them spending £17,000 a year at their stores; and here in addition is the germ of co-operative farming.

Let this sort of thing go on and what would be more reasonable than that the local Council, which very shortly these people will take part in electing, should acquire the ownership of the land they are renting, and be entrusted with the management of the ploughs and carts and threshing-machines and barns for the common use? What is more likely than that, by-and-by, the Council should decide to lay down a free tramway connecting the village with the nearest town, thus mitigating that sense of isolation which renders

village life distasteful to many, while promoting general prosperity and giving to the whole community the benefit of produce such as, to my certain knowledge, is now lying in numbers of villages quite out of the reach of our markets? Whether the cultivators of the soil should still continue, each working on his own little plot, subject to such general rules as might be found necessary for the good of the community, or whether it would be better to work as an organised whole and on a grand scale, would be a detail that time and experience might determine. Very possibly it might be found that some crops—such as the great staples of food—would be more advantageously cultivated on a large scale; while some vegetables, and fruits and flowers generally, would be best grown on a smaller system. There really seems no inherent improbability that by this pathway of joint harmonious working—not necessarily beginning in the very elementary way just described, because it is not all men who need such rudimentary lessons, but in some such pathway of joint harmonious working—we may arrive at the ideal village life, prosperous, intelligent, healthy, free, and as happy as life can well be in a world like this. As for those who croak about the character of the people, and pretend to believe that this, that, and the other desirable thing cannot be attained because the "labouring man" is so lazy and so drunken, so ungrateful, so ignorant, so short-sighted—out upon them! What can be expected of people who know little but penury and privation and hardship, and almost entire exclusion from the many influences that have placed these superior croakers themselves so high above all human frailties and foibles? I have no patience with people who, as the Vicar of Ixworth says, appear to regard the "labourer" as of a different order of being. Character, of course, is a fundamental matter, and all who are labouring to elevate and purify and dignify home life, to let in light and knowledge, and make men sober and self-restraining, are working

K

at the very foundations on which the social fabric of the future must be based. To do this is the great work of the Church, and the school, and the platform, and the printing-press. To prate as though it cannot be done is to betray, not merely a want of faith in God or man, but a want of common-sense.

I have now come to the end of the task I undertook, though I have not visited all the localities I had marked down. I have drawn some dark pictures of village life, but in looking backward on my two months' ramble, it is not the darkness that has most impressed itself upon me, but the peace and beauty and fruitfulness of it all. My wanderings have deepened my love for the land I live in; have heightened my respect for the lowly virtues of its people; and —because I see the first tremors of a mighty movement upwards and onwards—I have tenfold firmer faith in a glorious future.

APPENDIX I.

——◆◆——

LIFE IN OUR VILLAGES.

Some deductions from, and reflections and suggestions upon, the correspondence on this subject.

THE present relationship of landlord and tenant has failed to produce, or to continue to produce, as a whole, owners who contribute to the success of the farming industry in the manner they should do, tenants with enterprise and confidence to make the best of the land, and labourers content with their lot.

The ownership of land is a dignified source from which to draw an income to spend in town and in the luxuries of life and in travel. A due proportion of the rents is not spent in that constant and careful development of the land which is necessary if farming is not, alone, to stand still among the constantly-improving industries and ever-multiplying competition of the times ; nor are rents now spent to the extent they used to be in the maintenance of the owner and his family upon the estate.

Family settlements are largely to blame. How great a proportion of the land is owned for life only, and heavily charged with family provisions, so that the life-owner cannot afford to do other than extract all he can during his all too short tenure ! Hence the owner does not contribute his share of the capital of the farm in the shape of buildings fitted for scientific farming, and of improvements the fruits of which are to wait for. Facilities for land transfer and simplification of titles are all very well and desirable, and landowners naturally do not object to add to the value of their property at the expense of the lawyers' fees. But it is clearly not near the root of the evil. And facility of transfer will be equally impossible and useless unless the power of settlement is once for all entirely put an end to, so that life-estates and complicated titles may be impossible. The present much-vaunted powers of sale by tenants-for-life do not help the free working of natural cause and effect with regard to the dispersion of estates. The suggested abolition of tithes and the relief of local taxation from imperial sources are both steps in an absolutely wrong direction. They add to the rental value of the land at the cost of the tenant as a certain contributor to the imperial taxes, and as a possible supporter of the Church.

The tenant lacks enterprise and confidence to farm in a manner to pay. He holds too tenaciously to producing the low-priced commodity of corn, instead of constantly seeking crops of higher intrinsic value, such as the best fruits, vegetables, poultry and dairy produce, live stock of the highest quality. Crops of higher value entail improved appliances, greater cost in labour, and much and minute care. From these the farmer shrinks—from lack of capital, lack of experience or knowledge with regard to them, and lack of a satisfactory law of tenant-right.

It is said that large farms, scientifically cultivated, pay; and the order and promptitude on Lord Wantage's farm in hand is instanced. But it must be recollected that few who have the very large capital requisite for so extensive an undertaking care to embark it in farming; and though we admire the way in which such owners manage their land, we know little of the financial results; and farming on such a scale, except under some co-operative or social scheme, seems altogether beside the question.

Medium-sized farms are at a discount. The farm which pays, and which attracts the right kind of tenant, is that of about sixty acres, on which a man and his family take part in the work. But in these days of scientific dairy-farming such farmers are under some disadvantages in the manufacture of butter and cheese, and in the carriage of milk to station or market. These disadvantages disappear before local co-operative cheese and butter factories. Such works might fitly be carried out by the parish under Parish Councils (as local authorities supply gas and water), the profits being divided between those using them, after payment of the low interest at which the parish could borrow the necessary capital, and of the working expenses. And by a little co-operation of the simplest kind between farmers, a great saving could be effected in carrying milk and other produce to station or the neighbouring town or factory. In numerous villages may be seen, any day, half a dozen carts, each carrying a fraction of a load of milk, when one good common-property waggon could collect and carry the whole at a tithe of the cost to each farmer.

Fruit and vegetable culture should be taught in the village schools. The training necessary for the acquisition of any knowledge is an education. The acquisition of practical knowledge is surely as much a cultivation of the mental powers as the acquisition of a smattering of knowledge beyond that which is rudimentary, and it is more congenial and profitable to the country boy and girl. The State gives the start

in education ; the average boy would learn reading, writing, and arithmetic, and acquire some slight knowledge of history and geography,
and would acquire thoroughly the practical knowledge which would be
of such use to him in life. What the clever boy acquires is simply the
foundation of future learning, the lever by which the world of knowledge and his future are opened.

What the labourer wants is higher wages and, most especially, more
constant employment. Consider the loss involved in fitful employment—even suppose wages, when earned, to be fairly high, quite as
high as the farmer under present circumstances can afford. The farmer
is at the cost of a high wage for the work performed, but to the
labourer the advantage of the wage is minimised by the fact that it is
only occasional.

The value of allotments insufficient for a livelihood is doubtful.
If a labourer has constant employment, he has neither the time nor the
inclination for the work necessary to cultivate an allotment. And,
except under favourable circumstances as to market, there is no sale for
much of the produce he would raise ; whilst for him to raise corn on a
small scale at the usual prices of flour ill repays his labour. His work
on his allotment frequently coincides with the period of his most constant and profitable employment by the farmer ; and there is always the
danger that, if he eke out a subsistence by aid of his allotment, he
simply earns a higher wage by double toil. That he should have
garden ground to his cottage, on which to raise vegetables and fruit for
his family, goes without saying. Such he can manage without infring-
ing upon his time and wage-earning powers.

At present everyone is intent on growing something to sell to someone else. If a few were to think of growing what their own families, or
even their own district, required, there would be some saving in the
destructive cost of transit. You will be given American cheese and
Dutch eggs at an inn in a remote rural district—not because they cannot be produced cheaper on the spot, but because every farmer in the
district is striving to produce something by which he can benefit the
railway companies, and has no time or thought for the production of
what is consumed in his house or at his door.

But how to provide the garden, the small fruit-farm, the small dairy
and general farm (every general farm should of course include fruit-
trees) with protection to the cultivator for his improvements ? Not by
purchase. That consumes in a low-paying investment the capital the
farmer requires for his work. But while the landowner must receive
every consideration for his vested interests so far as they are not detri-
mental to the general welfare, the cultivator must have land at a fair

rent, have ample security of tenure, liberty of cultivation and of sale for his improvements. It is to the aid of a local authority we must look, and a properly representative local authority. Let the Parish Council have power to acquire at a fair rent suitable land—say, (*a*) For a cow pasture, in which it will let gaits ; (*b*) for garden plots and the erection of cottages ; (*c*) for small fruit and poultry farms, of a size sufficient, when highly cultivated, to maintain a family ; (*d*) for small mixed farms. Give the authority power to take such lands at agricultural prices, with a discount on account of the safety of the rent and the reduction of cost of stewardship. Let a statement be drawn up of the condition of the land and buildings, and let all improvements upon that condition and in buildings, roads, fruit-trees, &c., belong to the local authority. Provide a tribunal (the County Court) to determine the rent and condition, and settle the statement when not agreed upon. The local authority sub-lets without profit other than the necessary expenses. It plants, builds, and improves, charging interest ; or the tenant does the planting, building, and improving, or some of them, and has of course free sale of his tenant-rights. Let the local authority have power to establish centrally in the parish such of the following as may meet the particular local requirements :—(*e*) A butter and cheese factory ; (*f*) a factory for making fruit cans and packages for fruit, vegetable, and dairy produce ; (*g*) a jam or fruit canning factory ; (*h*) a threshing and grist mill ; (*i*) a public bath and washhouse ; (*j*) reading, refreshment, and amusement rooms ; (*k*) workrooms for local industries. Give the local authority the care of the sanitation, the roads, the commons, the schools.

In a village with such of these institutions as were suitable to its soil and situation, every appliance for small culture might be produced on the spot ; the villagers would almost maintain, and maintain well, their families from their own land—they, or their neighbours, producing flour, oatmeal, beans, fruit, vegetables, milk, butter and cheese, poultry and eggs, beef and mutton ; they would pack and send off for sale to the luxurious townsman the most perfect samples of their productions at high prices ; and they would carry on such industries as the locality was fitted for.

Although the great landlord-and-peasant idea, carried out with good-sense and good-feeling, as it is in very many—nay, most—instances to-day, is in some respects excellent, picturesque, and pleasant to contemplate, it is not congenial with the spirit of the times, nor is it a stimulant of the only kind of real improvement—self-improvement. With an intelligent interest in his work, with his local parliament, his free library, with his club-rooms for social intercourse and under his own management, with his recreation ground, with cricket and football, with constant employment for his labour in the requirements of the high cultivation around him, the dweller in Arcady would no longer seek the delusive advantages of a town life.

But with every effort the result will be disappointing unless we can have lower railway rates. I believe one of the greatest boons the country could have would be the adaption of the penny-post system to the carriage of inland goods—uniform low rates, irrespective of distance. The result would be to bring the market to the land of the producer, the commodity to the door of the consumer; all land would produce that for which it was most fitted, and the value of land close to and remote from the large towns would approximate. And I believe this could be done without loss to the railway companies ; for instead of seeing, as at present, goods trains capable of carrying two or three hundred tons running with forty or fifty, at the same cost to the company, we should see the trains laden to their utmost capacity—a fact that would recompense the companies for the greatly-reduced rates.

And again, cultivators must constantly seek to produce the highest qualities of fruit, butter, and cheese—qualities which will command higher prices than foreign produce. How frequent in the market reports of the *Daily News* is that of "Fruit cheap, but the better qualities command a high price"! Consider the high percentage of difference between the prices of the best and of common fruit—three or four hundred per cent.—and the importance of producing the best qualities is seen at once. The difference between the prices of common fruit and dairy produce and of the best affords a margin of profit which will account for failure or success.

A. H. JACKSON.

Eastbourne, Oct. 15, 1891.

APPENDIX · II.

— ◦◦ —

CORRESPONDENCE.

Many letters of special value and interest have necessarily been omitted. From the great mass of correspondence it has been found practicable to give only a selection.

SIR,—I have carefully read the interesting accounts of your Special Commissioner of "Life in Our Villages." Perhaps a few lines from this part of the kingdom may not be uninteresting to your readers. I am a farmer in South Leicestershire, occupying a small dairy farm. Living in the heart of the Midlands, we have many industries around us—collieries, ironworks, and various kinds of factories. The wage paid to our agricultural labourers is considerably higher than in the more southern parts. I pay my waggoner 19s. per week, my cowman 18s., labourers 16s. and 17s. all the year round, exclusive of overtime in harvest. A lad who lives in the house has £9 10s. per annum and his board. The hours of work are from half-past five morning to six at night. These wages would be considered excessive in some counties, but I am quite sure that for good wages men will give good honest work, and I can say that my men take as much interest in and are as anxious about my stock and crops as I am myself. I always discuss any important work to be done on the farm freely with them, and often profit by their sound experience. I do find that they are ever to the minute with regard to time—freely rising at any hour of the night, or sitting up all night sometimes with a sick animal, &c. I always try to treat them with the same courtesy and respect as they do me. I think my neighbours pay rather less than I do for the winter months and more for the summer, often setting piecework, which I do not approve of. My cowman also hires a pasture field of about four acres in the village, and keeps two cows and some pigs. He has also a large garden. The waggoner also has a very good garden, with a large and productive orchard. I believe they are content and happy. Now I come to the younger generation. Although our villages are not deserted to anything like the same extent to which they appear to be in the south and east, yet the pick of our young men do go off to other employments which offer higher wages and many advantages which we have not in the country, especially society and free libraries, and they also escape the patronage and attention of the parson (meant in all good-will) and the parson's wife, and the weariness of attending services at church which they do not understand. The old country parson is gone. The Dissenting chapels do not attract as they once did. Perhaps this migration has its advantages, bringing fresh blood and vigour and muscles into the towns. I am convinced that by paying wages on which a man can live and bring up a family respectably, farmers will always obtain all the help they require. Farmers complain that times are bad, and that they cannot afford more wages. Times are bad, very bad, but why are wages-always to be attacked? What about rents? Are those who toil not nor spin to bear no share of the bad times except a paltry return of 10 per cent.? Are those who have borne the heat of the day alone to be the sufferers, and their hard lot made still harder? But landlords cannot afford to reduce rents; in numberless cases they are receiving not more than 2 or 3 per cent. on the money invested. Well, those men have speculated in land. Some speculate in brewery shares. They must take the consequences of having paid too much. But few landlords are in this case. I know a village not many miles from here where the average rent 70 years ago was 20s. per acre. It is now 45s. per acre. Why do farmers persistently and stubbornly support that party in the State which never yet as a party did anything for them, or anybody else, unless compelled, except themselves?—the party which upholds the Game Laws, and is now doing its best to make the Ground Game Act a nullity? Why do they not (recognising the red herring of a duty on wheat), shoulder to shoulder with their workpeople, send up representatives who will uphold agriculture, reform the land laws, and establish where necessary land courts with power to fix fair rents, with fixity of tenure, &c.? The time was when they did so, and the farmers who fought at Naseby and Marston Moor "never were beaten," and I am proud to trace my descent from one of these.—Yours, &c.,

A LEICESTERSHIRE FARMER.

SIR,—I trust you will pardon me for wishing to join in the interesting correspondence which is now going on in respect to the life of our labouring population, because I have been a Tory member of Parliament, and therefore opposed to many of the views expressed in your journal on other subjects. When the late Lord Tollemache was living he honoured me with his acquaintance, and we were in very frequent correspondence; and in the autumn of 1885 we issued, above our joint signature, some rules for a suggested land scheme, which was published at the time in most of the newspapers, and I have very little doubt that it appeared in yours. The words were as follows :—

LAND SCHEME ASSOCIATION.

We, the undersigned, intend to take the following steps, or similar steps, according to special requirements :

1. To offer to any agricultural labourer residing on our estates in a dairy district, land sufficient to keep a cow, or, in an arable district, half an acre attached like a garden to his cottage.

2. All agricultural labourers when once admitted to a cottage on the recommendation of a neighbouring farmer, will become at once the tenant of the landlord, and not of the farmer.

3. The number of small farms and buildings on our estates shall be double the number of farms above 100 acres, provided tenants can be procured for them,

4. In future all applicants for small farms and holdings under 30 acres must show that they have some additional occupation from which to derive profits besides farming, to support them and their families.

5. Any respectable person with sufficient means can have on our estates half an acre on a lease of 99 years, or for ever, as a site for a good and comfortable house, to which will be added, if required, land at a rack rent.

6. With respect to farms above 100 acres all respectable tenants will, on application, be given a lease of 20 years, on condition that they will secure to the landlord a good system of husbandry, and to the tenant a comfortable and convenient farmhouse, with suitable buildings attached.

7. The foregoing rules to be carried out on our respective estates without any unnecessary loss of time.

(Signed)   TOLLEMACHE OF HELMINGHAM.
            W. J. HARRIS.

————

A special note follows in Lord Tollemache's handwriting, but which was not then published, as follows : "A year's notice should be given to the owners of land to enable them to commence managing their estates so that they may escape altogether from the compulsory powers." I have many letters from Lord Tollemache showing the deep regret he experienced at the landowners of England not responding to the appeal, but it is only right that I should add that he was not altogether without encouragement from one or two of the very largest landowners (I hardly feel at liberty to mention the names). Lord Tollemache's success is well known, and if any of your correspondents wish to see the measure of my success, they have only to purchase a copy of the " Land Agents' Record," under date July 18 last. To sum up the results very briefly : when I came into possession of this estate 20 years ago, the population was about 240, now it is over 430. Most of the parishes around have either stood still or decreased in population. Twenty years ago a large part of the parish was moorland, now the cultivation is extending in all directions, and there is hardly any land that remains unused for farming purposes except that which has been planted with fir-trees. No very great outlay has been incurred. New cottages have been built in a plain but substantial manner, and the old cottages have been strengthened and repaired, while cow-houses and pig-styes have been put up as the tenants have required them, and a moderate rate of interest has been charged on the outlay. The well-understood agreement between my small tenants and myself has been that I shall never raise their rents so long as they live, unless the rates and taxes—which I pay for them—are raised, and then only to that extent. They could all have leases if they wished it, but they have none of them gone to the expense. The rent is about what it would be valued at by a land surveyor acquainted with the capabilities of the district, and if the improvements made are of a substantial nature I give assistance—such, for

instance, as in draining, where I give the pipes. The village public-house, which used to be a great nuisance, has been turned into a farmhouse, and there is not a single labourer in this parish who has been seen the worse for drink for many years. I consider that I have gained by my policy. The larger farmers can always get labourers to come and help them when they have extra work in hand, and I am by my policy manufacturing "true Conservatives." Not those who wish to vote against the progress that you advocate, but those who are fairly satisfied with their lot, and who have no wish to see a general upheaval of society. If landowners generally would understand that their true policy is to use every effort to satisfy the thrifty and industriously inclined people they would save themselves from attacks which must unsettle the security of their investments. They are either great benefactors or the reverse. No one has so much power of doing good as they have, and many of them do a great deal of good. Let them study what Lord Tollemache did, and what he advised others to do, and a drastic policy may be averted. If not, I, for one, shall not object to see a drastic policy adopted if it be honestly applied.—Yours faithfully, WILLIAM J. HARRIS.
Halwill Manor, Beaworthy.

SIR,—I have read with great interest the accounts by your Commissioner and the letters of various correspondents anent life in our villages. It seems to me quite evident, according to these sources of information, that the youth of the villages are drifting fast to the large towns, with a view to, and because they really do, obtain better wages and chances of improving their position generally. It also seems clear that it is chiefly owing to this cause that the country is suffering through lack of sufficient labour for its proper cultivation. It is no less apparent that all efforts at present directed with a view to prevent this general exodus by granting allotments and providing instruction and amusement for the people, in order to make the country life more attractive, have hitherto failed in their object, and tend to increase rather than diminish the steady flow townwards. Now all this is (at least, as far as we can see at present) unalterable, and appears to be regulated by the law of supply and demand. For there is a demand for strong and intelligent young men to engage in various occupations in the towns, and the town is able and willing to pay well for the labour of the country. Moreover, the latter do not go to swell the great army of clerks and those of kindred occupations, but, as your Commissioner states, the employment they obtain is generally partly of a manual or mechanical character—such as taking round carts of milk or grocery, and work on the railway. Taking these facts into consideration, it seems hard to try and prevent Hodge from getting a good wage in return for good work. No, some other plan must be tried to procure labour for cultivation. I suppose there is no back-flow from the over-populated town into the country. The unemployed in large centres, though they would welcome an escape from the crowding and smoke into the purer air and larger space of the country, yet, perhaps, have

neither the knowledge nor the requisite strength for manual outdoor labour. In my opinion it is here that the waste goes on, and yet it is difficult to see a way of bringing the workers on to the land again. It remains to be seen whether General Booth's scheme, which has been so largely supported, will meet with the expected success. There is, however, a certain class, like the others, composed of youths, who would be able, and many of whom are specially trained, for an outdoor life. I refer to the boys in the industrial homes and in institutions such as Dr. Barnardo's. Instead of sending off by the shipload to other shores such useful material on which so much of the money of the country has been spent, why, may I ask, should they not be taught and encouraged to cultivate the soil of Old England, and be placed in a position to become patriotic Englishmen, with the true interests of their country at heart? We have already seen, when abroad, how well they repay the trouble spent in their training. Perhaps it would be said that land in England would be too dear for them to have much of their own. But they could begin with small holdings, and gradually grow to be the small farmers, who would work their land themselves, and with their habits of economy would not waste their profits in needless expenditure. They might keep pigs, rabbits, and poultry, and by this means we should not be obliged to purchase such large quantities of eggs and rabbits from France and Belgium, where they are produced, not on the large farms, but by the industry of the small but independent landholder. Thanking you by anticipation, and hoping you will pardon my trespassing so much on your space, I am yours truly,   P. B. W.
Hereford.

Sir,—The problem " How to retain country men on farm lands " is hardly to be settled by a smart article, nor likely to be accomplished by tenant farmers. Here, in the West of England, a slight improvement in the conditions under which farm workfolks live would keep a full supply of "hands" on the land. Any number of workmen could be retained if the men could get half-a-crown or three shillings a day all the year round, and could get cottages to live in by paying rent for them. That is to say, cottages not under the control of their employers, but so held that the tenancy might be continuous, though the men should change masters. I have lived in Somerset for nearly forty years, and have never known a crop injured for want of workfolk where there was a fair proportion of cottage homes held independently of the employers. The demand among country workmen is for homes with gardens, from which they cannot be evicted at the will of their employers. Wages would rise but to a very moderate extent, because the number of workmen would increase, and competition check extravagant demands. The low rate of wages on farms, which surprises town-trained economists, is made endurable in the country by many ameliorating influences. House-rent is very low, potatoes and other garden stuffs are to be had for the growing. Coal clubs and clothing clubs are helpful; strong rough clothes are sufficient in the sweet air; while the clergy, the farmers, and fellow workfolk are kindly and helpful in

illness or misfortune to an extent impossible in towns. A trace of feudal serfdom often hangs around the isolated hamlets ; but, thanks to fifty years of steady growth in Liberal principles, it is like ivy round an old ruin, an added grace, and not much in the way.—Yours faithfully,
Pylle.   JOHN HIGGINS.

———

SIR,—As a country man in a rural district I am delighted with the letters of your Commissioner. They show a quick grasp of the subject at issue, and all he says could be said of my county, Beds. I do hope he will favour us with a visit. He will find in nearly every village (except on or near the M.R.) a decrease in the population, which may be accounted for in two or three ways, viz., failure in the staple work—straw-plaiting—the better wages paid in the towns, and the increased facilities of obtaining employment in the towns when a situation is lost. Formerly, when the straw work "went well," it mattered little to the labourer whether the day was wet or not, as he could earn as much at home by plaiting, and he and his family could in the evenings considerably add to his wages. Now the case is quite altered. It is now a rarity to see a man plaiting. The Canton plait being made of rice straw, and a better colour and cheaper than the home-made material, it has driven the latter out of the market. A Conservative candidate during a contest in "South Beds" some years ago promised the villagers when addressing them that he would go in for taxing the Canton plaits. But when he went to Luton, where the plaits are made into hats and bonnets, his friends, the Tory manufacturers, soon told him that he had made a mistake, and nothing more was heard of taxing Canton plaits. The wages given here are 12s. per week and loss of wet time, with often five or six whole weeks unemployed in the winter. Cattle men, who work nearly half the Sunday, get one or two shillings more per week. There are a few farmers who keep a quantity of cows, and who send their milk to London ; these give their men 14s. or 15s. per week, Sunday work included. During harvest £1 per week is the wages paid men working from four or five o'clock until eight p.m. Some men have to walk two miles to and from work. How can we improve the lot of these men, who, I contend, are as clever at their work as many an artisan at his? The man that can plough, drill, mow, thatch, thresh corn, or drain, ought to have an income of more than 12s. per week. We can improve their lot by giving them an opportunity of working for themselves on the land that the farmers say does not pay. I heard a farmer say at a public meeting not six months ago that the question was not what percentage on the outlay did the land pay, for it did not pay anything ; and this farmer holds about 700 acres of land. The wonder is why on earth they don't give it up and let the men have a try. Some of your correspondents seem to think that a reduction of rent would enable the farmer to give more wages. Well, sir, on one of my rounds the landlord gave back 50 per cent., but, from all I could learn, not an extra labourer was employed, nor an additional shilling given to the labourer. What is required is not a reduction in rent but a part of the labour bill borne by the landlord, who would thus see what number of labourers were employed on his estate, and would also improve his farms. I consider it would be beneficial to the agricultural labourers greatly to add to the number of small holders, as this would also tend to raise the wages on the farms. But for men wholly employed on the farm a good garden attached to his cottage is better than half an acre a mile away.—I am, Sir,

"A SOUTH BEDS MAN."

———

Sir,—I have watched with much interest the correspondence on village life in your paper, and the efforts some have made to prove that farming is unprofitable. When I was a boy in receipt of 1s. 6d. a week, and my widowed mother made an effort to keep house on a few shillings a week, with bread at 11d. the four-pound loaf, the dinner of the agricultural labourer and his family was often yellow swedes with a little salt. Then it was the same cry, "Farming don't pay." When I became a young man and courted a nice girl, my master said farming did not pay; at wheat only fetching 70s. a quarter he could not afford above 10s. a week; so I said, "My sweetheart is too nice a girl to keep in a hovel on 10s. a week, so I must seek a warmer clime, for English charity is too cold for me to thrive on." It is the same old tale—"Farming don't pay." I have had three years of voluntary inspection of the agricultural districts, and am certain farming can pay. Farmers have not yet learned their business. Let farming become a scientific profession. Farmers are driving away all the best men and women out of the village. Landlords, the cry is against you now. Farmers say the rents are too high. They are not. Raise the rents. If a house becomes dilapidated, the owner is compelled to pull it down or else make it tenantable; if the latter, he raises the rent. If land becomes impoverished, the owner ought to be compelled to make it into good heart or sell it; it ought not to lie idle in a little country teeming with millions of people requiring food to eat. Raise the rent, but make the farm worth the money first. Then let it to a man that understands his business; for a good farm deserves a good farmer, and a good farmer requires good men, not drones and fools; and a good man will want a good wife, and a good home for her. Therefore see that the cottage accommodation is ample for the farm; and if the best men are to be kept from leaving the villages, there must be something done to keep them on the land. Many of the cottages I have inspected are a disgrace to a civilised country. In the county of Bucks 10,000,000 fruit-trees could be planted without injury to the permanent pastures or cornfields—I can prove this—and the profit on these ought to pay the rent of all the farms.—Respectfully yours, GEORGE GINGER.
Buckinghamshire Labour Bureau, Aylesbury,
September 12.

———

Sir,— As one who has been until lately a country parson in Dorsetshire, I have taken the deepest interest in your timely and accurate articles on "Life in Our Villages." The great evil of the agricultural labourer's life is that it is a life without hope. Between the labourer and the classes above him a great gulf is fixed. In old age he can only look forward to the workhouse. To remedy this sad state of things nothing is more necessary than more small holdings, which men with small capital could take, and become, in a certain measure, independent. Let me give two cases which lately came under my notice in the same village. Not long ago a young man came to me to arrange about his wedding. He had put off marriage until he was about thirty, and had always lived with his parents and been of a saving disposition. He told me that on his marriage he intended to invest his savings, about £100, in taking a small beer-house with a few acres of land attached to it. I expressed regret at this. He answered, "Well, it is the only way I can get a bit of land," and I had to acknowledge that his plea was true. Another case. An agricultural labourer some years ago was given a little heifer in lieu of wages owed him by a semi-bankrupt farmer. The heifer for some time was fed by his wife at the wayside. It became a cow, and, in due time, the parent of other cows. The labourer took a field. Now he is a small holder. He cultivates about 20 acres of land under every possible disadvantage. It is situated in the next parish to that in which his own cottage stands. He pays a very high rent for it. He has to go more than a mile twice a day with his pony-cart to milk his cows. He has no proper buildings; but he makes his little bit of land pay. He is far more independent than the ordinary labourer, and has no reason to fear the workhouse in his old age. The question of "Life in Our Villages" will not be solved by small holdings, but they will go some way towards it. Small holdings will also in an indirect way have a beneficial effect on the physique of the labouring population. They will make it possible for the poor to get milk readily and cheaply for their children. The small holders will sell milk in small quantities. It is too much trouble for the large farmers to do so. Ordinarily, the children of the rural poor are brought up without milk from the time they are weaned. The effect on the growth and health of the children is very bad. Again, the agricultural labourers need union. They are the most disunited of all the battalions of the great army of labour. They are helpless in the hands of their employers. More and more, I regret to say, it is becoming the custom to turn men off during winter, on the plea that there is no work for them to do. If the rent is to be paid, the labour bill must be kept down. I have come home from an afternoon's visiting, during which I have again and again come across instances of the breadwinner being thrown out of work for six or eight weeks in the midst of a bitter winter, and have marvelled at the heroic patience of the agricultural labourer. He suffers in silence. If he was violent, politicians would at once recognise that something must be done. A strong agricultural labourers' union, a multiplication of small holdings, and something in the shape of a national pension fund for old age, would transform the hard and dreary lot of the rural labourer.— I am, &c., W. S. SWAYNE.

SIR,—In common with many thousands of your readers whose early associations were " truly rural," I have followed the correspondence which has appeared in your columns lately with considerable interest. My old friend Hodge appears to me in some danger now of being over-coddled. Time was when his "friends were few." A couple of decades back the *Daily News* stood out very conspicuously as the champion of his cause, and I could almost fancy that the same gifted pen that is now portraying his vicissitudes in Essex lifted the veil then, to the astonishment of those who wondered what the agitator Joseph Arch was about. A good many things have happened since then, and the most important, as far as the labourer is concerned, has been the opening-up to him of a new world in the shape of the British Colonies. The whilom English village encumbrance has become the eagerly-sought-for-and-amply-remunerated necessity of the Canadian and Australian farmer. It has been my great felicity to see the men who were treated as criminals by their besotted British employers for daring to question the adequacy of an eighteenpence a day wage, receiving from their New Zealand masters seven and eight shillings for a two hours shorter day's work. I am unable any longer to pity men whom I have thus seen so amply remunerated when they have had the pluck to avail themselves of the circumstances of life. There is not a British colony at this moment that would not gladly welcome any number of good field-workers. Why, then, should I be called upon to waste my sympathy on such valued members of society? If any of them are still underpaid, it is surely their own fault. I have never seen a poor farm labourer abroad. He is ever master of the position. Hundreds of the Berkshire, Oxford-shire, Wiltshire, and Warwickshire men, whose severe hardships your Correspondent of 1872-3 so graphically narrated, are to-day prosperous colonial farmers, and there is nothing to hinder hundreds more from becoming such. I therefore venture to enter a protest against any longer regarding Hodge as an object of pity. If we have any pity to spare, let it be displayed towards the unfortunate London clerks and other genteel fraternity whom no one wants and whom every colony spurns from its door. I shrewdly suspect that it is the British farmer rather than his labourer who is to-day " up a tree." The low price of produce generally, while it has spelt ruin to the master, has meant a twenty-five per cent. increase of the purchasing power of the labourer's wage. I am glad to find that Mr. George Loosley, who knows rural life as well as most men, endorses this view of the labourers' present case. "They work shorter hours, have more money, and are very independent," he told us lately in his letter. I hope, however, he is incorrect in saying that "the average agricultural labourer is less trusty and efficient " than he used to be. I am afraid this is only a stingy employer's estimate of the case. Certainly the higher colonial wage and shorter hours of work have no such result. One of the most striking revelations of my extensive travels during the last decade has been the vast improvement in the morale of the workmen consequent on their improved circumstances. The slouching, obsequious, shuffling fellow of the English village I have met in New Zealand transformed into a smart, self-reliant, energetic citizen, full of "go," and not wanting in political enthusiasm. The conclusion of the whole matter, therefore, appears to me to be somewhat thus : there must be no more coddling of the farm labourer. If he cannot stand up, let him fall down. If, with the world before him, he elects to vegetate in such vile quarters as your Correspondent has described, let him do so. No maudlin sympathy can permanently help those who will not help themselves.—I am, &c.,   ARTHUR CLAYDEN.

SIR,—There seems to be much doubt as to the efficacy of the allotment system, even if it were thoroughly carried out, as a means of retaining labourers in the country. I believe myself in allotments as a temporary stopgap, but to that extent only. They are a help if certain conditions of convenience, fair rent and so forth are present ; but much more is needed. To put the matter into a nutshell—it is the prospects (or the absence of them) of the labourer that present the difficulty. The skilful, energetic worker in any other line "gets on," his prospects improve, he has something to look forward to. The labourer has nothing of the kind. Be he as skilful and industrious as he may, he is only worth the more to his employer ; his own wages remain the same. It is the prospect of reaping some increasing reward for industry and skill, as life goes on, that is the attraction in the towns. Can the labourer be given some such hope in his own particular business? Certainly ; if he can be given access to the land on fair terms, and with security that he will be allowed to reap all the fruits of his own industry thereon. There are in my own parish men who afford examples of this. They rent land on which their predecessors (generally their fathers or other relations) had "squatted" before the enclosure of the commons. The excellent cottages (in comparison with many others about the place) in which they live, the fruitful, well-drained gardens which they cultivate, are the product of their own and their predecessors' spare labour through many years. They pay rent to the parish ; rent which even now is double that of the average rent of the whole parish. I say "even now" because I had a hard fight soon after my arrival in the parish against a proposed large increase of the rentals of these plots, and succeeded in preventing it. I need not enter into details, but the fight was obstinate. I only succeeded by adopting the "Plan of Campaign." The point is : Do these men leave the place? No, sir, they don't. They stick like limpets to their base, and it would take a good deal to move them now. Where there is one such holding there ought to be fifty. Yet these men have no real security—only such security as the common-sense and justice of the parish officials may give them. Notice they are tenants, not freeholders. The great objection to a peasant proprietary is the constant temptation to mortgage the land. By means of these expensive mortgages the petty local money-lender gets hold of plot after plot, he grows into a landowner and his son into a squire—perhaps a defender of the Church and a Primrose "knight" or whatever they call themselves. If parish councils are to be any good you must abolish the property vote. It is that which has

L

rendered the vestry a nullity as a means of expressing the popular will. There is a great deal more to be said and done. The Liberals must take it in hand in downright earnest. For myself, I am sick of half-measures and counsels of expediency. We want village councils, with one man one vote ; we want village co-operative stores, in which every villager should be a shareholder, so that the poor man need not pay more than anyone else for his tea and sugar ; we want an improved system of houses of public refreshment and amusement, under parochial management, and served by salaried officials, the profits going towards public improvements ; we want a good system of intermediate schools to which our cleverest boys can go free of expense to their parents ; we want technical education in every parish ; we want—oh ! lots of things ; and more power to the elbows of the men who will try to get them for us !—Your obedient servant,

ARNOLD D. TAYLOR.

Churchstanton Rectory, Honiton, August 31.

––––––

SIR,—I, in common with thousands of others, am extremely glad at the prominence you are giving to "Life in Our Villages" in your valuable columns. The district where this is written is a model for the system of small holdings and allotments, having several hundred acres unenclosed and in plots varying from one rood to two acres, each plot a separate freehold or copyhold property, the plough furrow being the boundary in each case, which gives great facilities for a poor man to acquire small lots either as owner or tenant. Many of our farm labourers occupy one to three acres, and keep one cow and feed two or three pigs, they and their families doing the necessary hand labour at times when it does not interfere with their ordinary employment, except an occasional day in harvest. I don't know one man in ten in this and the adjoining parish of Belton that is now farming from thirty to one hundred acres that either they or their fathers have not been farm servants or farm labourers in their early life, and all, or nearly all, rising step by step through this system of small holdings, commencing with one, or at most a few acres, and gradually adding to or exchanging their holdings as their means increased. There are in the district a number of men holding from ten to twenty acres who, in addition to cow and pig, keep one horse, and for the heavy part of the work on their land two will yoke together, which effectually gets over the difficulty of one-horse farming. This parish contains near 6,000 acres, occupied as follows :—Only two occupying over 200 acres ; from 100 to 200, twelve ; from 50 acres to 100, fourteen ; from 20 acres to 50, thirty-one ; from 10 acres to 20, forty ; from 2 acres to 10, one hundred and fifteen ; and from 2 roods to 2 acres there are eighty occupiers. A fair question to ask would be : Under such a system of small holdings would as large an amount of food be raised as on an equal quantity of land in large farms? I have no hesitation in saying that there is a larger amount of grain, at least an equal amount of beef, a much larger quantity of pork or bacon and vegetables, but a smaller quantity of mutton, very small holdings not being adapted to sheep-walks. Some two years ago I was summoned to give evidence before a Committee of the House of Commons, under the chairmanship of Mr. J. Chamberlain, sitting to inquire into this question of small holdings, and to ascertain whether there was any general desire for its extension. From the cross-questioning by Mr. Chaplin and some others I concluded that the Tory members of the Committee were dead against any compulsory clause, whilst such men as Mr. Halley Stewart and Sir Walter Foster were the men who were anxious for powers to place the land in a great many more hands than any voluntary system is likely to accomplish. Before leaving home to attend the Committee I called together at least a dozen men that I knew had been in possession of from one to two acres each for a few years only, and after some conversation with them, I suggested that they should strengthen my hands by signing a paper expressing their experience, as given me then, to which they gave a ready consent. It was to this effect: that before having their allotments they had a great dread of a long frost in each winter as they came round, feeling that a few weeks out of work would mean either being thrown on the parish for support, or they and their families would be on the verge of starvation. But since they had had the land they had grown a half-acre each of wheat, barley, and potatoes, which had given them bread, bacon, and potatoes for the winter, and in some cases for the greater part of the year, at but little cost, they having done the work required when not otherwise employed. And now, they said with one voice, we can face the severest winter without any fear of either hunger or of being pauperised.—Yours, &c.,

Epworth, Doncaster.   J. STANDRING.

Sir,—After forty years' experience in agriculture, allow me to say that under existing circumstances farming can be made to pay only on very large occupations of one thousand acres and upwards, and on small tenancies of thirty to forty acres. Medium-sized farms of two to five hundred acres are surely doomed, by the fact of not being able to compete successfully with the larger and smaller occupiers in the important matter of labour. Obviously the small farmer does not need much extra help, and on very large farms the use of the best modern machinery materially economises the labour account, and the land is also efficiently cultivated.—Yours faithfully,   BREVITY.

Brighton.

Sir,—Will you allow an ignorant man, a man from the dung-hill, to make a few remarks upon the great question which your correspondent has so ably put before the public during the last few days? I know something about the cultivation of the land; for years I worked at the roughest work done on the land, cleaning out pig-sties, turning manure, digging; and to-day, after twenty years of laborious work, I occupy the land I worked on and employ fifty hands. And, sir, if I had to start life again as poor as I was twenty years ago, with only 5s. in my pocket, I would choose the land. If I had to start afresh to-morrow with a balance of £1,000 at my banker's, I would choose the land. Nothing is so grateful for care and intelligent management as the land. Look upon the cultivation of the land as men look upon any other business or profession, put into it the same intelligence and determination, and I have not the least doubt the same favourable results will follow. Many of the present occupiers of the land are ignorant of their work ; they do not grow the right thing, and if they discovered the right thing they do not know how to grow it. Farmers (if they hoe), and also market gardeners, hoe to kill the weeds, and if there are no weeds they do not hoe. They are ignorant of the need of hoeing and why they should hoe. They are too slovenly, untidy, wanting in trimness, thoroughness ; and yet, sir, they are not altogether to blame. They are the product of a bad and vicious system. If the land is to be cultivated profitably and the villagers are to be prosperous and contented, the present occupiers of the land must be got rid of ; there is no other remedy. The intelligent and enterprising man avoids the land, and it has been handed over to the incompetent. How could any industry compete with the foreigner if all the best men were driven out of it ? If a man takes land to cultivate he wants security. When I asked an agent to give me a lease and compensation for necessary buildings and improvements, he simply laughed at me and said, " We do not want such tenants as you are ; we should never get rid of you ; you would spend so much on the land, we could never buy you out." Just so, sir, and that is why the land is a failure, they do not want intelligent and independent tenants. An Act of Parliament is wanted that will enable a man to buy land as simply as he would buy anything else ; he should not have to run the risk of a heavy lawyer's bill, and perhaps a long delay before he takes possession, the only cost should be the cost of a stamp for the benefit of the revenue ; this would bring about a revolution in our land, and the revolution would be gradual. Thriftless land-owners would soon be rid of their land, and other landowners would soon find it an advantage to part with their land, and thrifty labourers and small occupiers would soon become owners, and the revolution would be complete. Men of intelligence, men of will, would soon discover that the cultivation of land was profitable ; it is profitable now, where the men are the right men. A remark was made to me the other day that Mr. Smith was a good and successful farmer. I replied, "Yes, he was a clock-maker till he was thirty years of age." "So-and-so is a good farmer." "Yes, he was a draper up to thirty-five." These two men brought business ability into their work. They had not the prejudice of the farmer, and what they did they did with all their might. If, sir, it pays men living in Russia and America to grow food to send into our markets, surely it will pay men at home to grow the same thing. We have become so used to foreign produce that we think there is nothing strange in having it ; but, sir, it shows on our part incompetency and ignorance. Why buy eggs from abroad? Why buy apples ? No country is better suited to growing them than ours.

Allow me to give one illustration to show the stupidity of many

English growers. A London herb dealer wanted twenty to thirty tons of marjoram to dry, also other herbs. He says to the English grower : " Will you cut these herbs off close to the ground, and not pull them up by the roots, and dry the herbs for me ? " The grower says : " No, our way is to bunch them up for the London market with the roots ; if that does not suit, you can go without." Our London man is a man of business, and will not be played with, so he goes to Germany, and the German gives him what he wants, and the bottled herbs and packet herbs the grocer and green-grocer supply mainly come from Germany. I could give endless illustrations of the ignorance and stupidity of the English grower, also his prejudice against properly packing fruit ; but I have done. Allow me to thank you for bringing public attention to so important a matter. There are men in England with brains and energy to restore to England that prosperity in her agricultural districts which she so much needs if our Parliament has only the wisdom to spend a little time in framing an Act that will give security to the occupier.—I am, Sir, yours respectfully, HODGE.

The Rev. J. Denny Gedge, Methwold Vicarage, Norfolk, observes :— " The explanations of the exodus of the labourer with which your Commissioner has been plied are most of them but subsidiary causes ; and, Liberal though I am, I am constrained to own that the Tory Vicar held up to ridicule in your Saturday's issue has, instinctively if unphilosophically, come nearest to the right explanation, unpleasant as it may be to some of us to have to confess this. Increased information is the main cause of the trouble. For the chief trial of country life is its monotony. The Vicar is right—they have lost that blessed ignorance which enabled them to be happy in their condition, and much that was available and satisfied their forefathers is too coarse and rude for them. There are not wanting in every village those of a nobler and sweeter disposition who have turned their increased information to the account of personal culture and considerable refinement ; but such tempers are equally rare in all classes, and the greater number, especially of the young, have, as a knowledge of human nature should have led us to expect, simply become unsettled, and crave after a variety of experience and interest such as the country can never afford. For those whom necessity or prudent acquiescence retains in the country charity should teach us to provide all the recreation possible. It is simply terrible, when, as in my own place, ground cannot be had even for cricket and other suitable sports. Every village should have its cricket ground, its fives-court, and its apparatus for athletics ; every village schoolmaster should be capable to train for a cantata ; and no better gifts than that of a piano for the village platform, or of instruments for a village band, can be made to a village by its wealthier neighbours. It is sad indeed when almost the only excitement, even for the young, is to be found in the society of the village alehouse. Dancing should be encouraged and, if possible, taught in every schoolroom. Nothing refines more the relations of the sexes under proper management. One will always welcome the political meetings of either party, which are always largely attended, and find most considerate and patient hearers in our labourers, unless the speakers insult them by turning firm, conscientious, and reasonable argument to rude invective, which, I am glad to say, is largely condemned from whatever side it comes. Everything in the way of wholesome sport and interest is to be encouraged. In Imperial days Rome had to work her farms by slave colonies, and the working of our farms has become difficult because we no longer have either ignorance or serfdom. Enormous is the difficulty that lies on the country landlord, still more on the impoverished clergyman, who can rarely escape his surroundings, to find variety sufficient to satisfy the craving interests of to-day, especially in the case of the young. For the elder man many of us hope that some relief will be found when, through village councils and suchlike, he has to do the work that has hitherto been done for him ; in which case, after a little period of disturbance, I, for one, do not fear but that the labourer, once settled in his harness, and face to face with realities, will show the same good business sense and moderation in office as other Englishmen, and take a pride in being sensible."

Sir,—Every Liberal is indebted to you for the admirable articles and correspondence in your columns on this question. The exodus of the rural population is a fact which everyone professes to deplore. The causes which produce the evil have been at work for centuries, and only by a variety of remedies will a cure be obtained. The result to be secured is the re-peopling of our country districts, and this can only be done by making it worth the while of the people to live there. This you will not do unless it is possible for a labourer to make up his income to £1 a week. An ordinary allotment will not do this. South of the River Trent, it is doubtful if the income of the labourer averages 12s. a week throughout the year, and it is a total mistake to suppose that the extension of large farms, with improved machinery, will be any help to him. The valuable letter of your correspondent "A Leicestershire Farmer" conclusively shows how much more likely small farmers are than large to pay good wages, from the fact that they work amongst their men, and, nothing being wasted, they have a much larger surplus out of which wages can be paid.

What is wanted is that farms should be cultivated by labourers in the prime of life, looking forward by means of hard work and thrift to occupying small holdings on their own account as they get older. They cannot get the means of doing this unless in addition to their work they have an acre of land and upwards at a fair rent and with security of tenure—in fact, roughly speaking, the three F's of Ulster fame. The advocates of large farms will tell you that this system will prevent their getting labourers. What it will doubtless do will be to secure for the labourers the alternative of either getting work all the year round and a livelihood of £1 a week, or of spending their time partly on their own land and partly on the farmer's. I venture to say it will be better for both farmer and labourer when this is the case. Everyone is familiar with the complaint of farmers that labourers do not work now as they used to. Other employers, I believe, do not make similar complaints. The fact is a man does not see why he should for twelve shillings a week be giving as much hard work as he can get £1 for if he sold it in the town market. Where the men are well paid you can secure a good day's work without great grumbling.

Far-reaching reforms will be needed to bring this state of things about. The power of preventing the sale of land by settlement must be abolished. Village Councils, with one man one vote, will have to be created, with compulsory powers for hiring land for allotments subject to the approval of a supervising authority, and, if needs be, for afterwards providing land for the purpose of small holdings. A good system of allotments followed by the abolition of the Law of Settlement, together with a system of land transfer based on the example of our Colonies, would speedily provide an outlet for the energies and hopes of the working people of our rural districts. The South Division of Worcestershire, where I am fighting the Liberal battle, would furnish numbers of instances where men have made good progress by means of small cultivation, but where, owing to our land laws, their further progress is impossible. So long as the prejudices of the few are allowed to prevail over the interests of the majority, and the House of Lords and the great landowners and the lawyers are permitted to uphold our present ridiculous semi-feudal land system, our villages will be deserted and poverty-stricken. There is nothing which the good of our countrymen more imperatively calls for than the sweeping away of our present land system and the building up of a more righteous and popular law in its place. This work the Liberal party must strenuously enter upon or forfeit the confidence of the rural population.—Yours, &c., FREDERICK IMPEY,
Hon. Sec. Allotments and Small Holdings Association.
Longbridge, Worcestershire, Sept. 4.

" A Solicitor " says :—" The changes I advocate are these : 1, Disestablishment and disendowment of the Church ; 2, Abolition of the law of primogeniture, with the consequent abolition of the distinction between real and personal property, and the vesting of all property in the executors or administrators of a deceased owner for the benefit of all his family. This would require that the representatives of a deceased owner should have absolute power conferred by statute to sell land and houses, just as executors may now sell leaseholds ; 3, Abolition of entail and the right to settle land and houses—that is, the present law relating to settlement of estates. Nearly all the landed property of the great landowners is tied down by settlement, and it is possible to settle property by one instrument for a hundred years, and so keep it out of the market. Until a hundred years ago a man had power to settle his property in perpetuity ; but at the end of last century an Act was passed forbidding a settlement of property for more than a 'life in being and twenty-one years beyond.' By the operation of this law a man may by his will settle his property on his eldest son for life, and afterwards until his eldest son's eldest son attains 21. Suppose the testator's eldest son be only a year old, and lives to 80 or 90, the property is tied up and kept out of the market for nearly a century. This power of settlement, so far as relates to land and houses, should be abolished, and with the abolition should be enacted a power for all trustees of all settlements (whether they be wills or deeds) to sell the real estate without the consent of any Court.   4, Enfranchisement of Leaseholds.—The power to purchase the freehold should be conferred upon every leaseholder for 21 years and upwards. Consider, sir, what would result if the half of London which consists of leaseholds all tied down by settlements executed by the great landowners of London for the aggrandisement of their families were set free from the present restraints. The throwing of so much property into the market would be such an enormous increase of business for 'all sorts and conditions of men' that London pauperism would be sensibly diminished. The half of London has been built by tradesmen and other business men, whose families have lost all their outlay because the houses built by them have fallen into the ownership of their landlords, who have never spent a sixpence either in building or improving the property, or in rates and taxes, and this landlord class has been enriched to an untold degree at the expense of the general community."

SIR,—Our land laws are bad enough, but to make them out worse than they are is surely to put an obstacle in the way of their amendment. One cannot help suspecting that there is in "A Solicitor's" mind some notion of an indissoluble relation between the abolition of primogeniture and the compulsory division of property amongst the family—the establishment of the *légitime* of the French law. Of course there is no such connection; primogeniture will soon be swept away along with a good many other anomalies, but rather because it is an anomaly than because of any special importance in itself, or any good its abolition is likely to confer. How much land in the country does your correspondent suppose the succession is unprovided for by will or settlement, for it is to such land alone that the law of primogeniture, which is entirely a law of intestate succession, can apply. The very prevalence of settlements serves to minimise the chance of the law applying. As to compulsory division, that may or may not lie in the future, but its time is not yet. And the abolition of primogeniture will not have for its consequence "the abolition of the distinction between real and personal property," nor is it desirable that it should. The tendency of modern legislation has been to emphasise this distinction in one respect at any rate, viz., to secure that publicity in dealings with land which it was the object of our earliest conveyance—the feoffment with livery of seisin—to secure, and which the *nimia subtilitas* of our mediæval lawyers successfully evaded. Registration of title and registration of transfers of land, the desire for securing publicity at the present day have, for reasons too many and too intricate to discuss here, not been very successful, but everything points to their being made compulsory as the next step towards simplifying and cheapening dealings with land. Possibly it may be necessary to make the step a bold one, and here I would make a suggestion. For centuries it was possible by levying a fine to bar all claims not put forward within five years, and the fine was frequently resorted to by landowners as a means of strengthening their title. Why should not some such short term of prescription be set to all claims after the compilation of the new Domesday Book which a compulsory Act would necessitate? Such a provision would, there is little doubt, turn away the wrath of the landowners, which at present stands in the way of enforced registration. "A Solicitor," taking up "the abolition of entail, and the right to settle land and houses," goes on to speak of settlements "tying up" land and "keeping estates out of the market" for a hundred years, accompanying these statements with some historical information which is at least curious, if not peculiar. At what time could a man settle his property in perpetuity, and how will "A Solicitor" cite in Court or out of it the statute which abolished this power? Is it for nothing that we read of the common law rule against the abeyance of freeholds, and was it vain imagining that moved Lord Nottingham long before 1700 to declare that though the *ultimum quod sit* was not then plainly determined, it would soon be found out if men should set their wits to contrive that which the law had so long laboured against. So far from the rule against perpetuities being a restriction new-hatched by a statute of last century, it has taken shape from a series of judicial decisions, closing with the great case of Cadell *v.* Palmer in 1833; and, be it noted, the course of those decisions was in the direction not of tightening but of relaxing the rule. However, "A Solicitor" is right in this— that the rule as it now stands forbids a settlement for more than a life or lives in being, and 21 years afterwards. But to say that this may keep the land out of the market for a century is simply to state the thing which is not. Let us for a moment consider what is the usual form of settlement. A. purchases the fee simple of land, and so becomes, as we may say here, the absolute owner. He has a family, and proposes to make a settlement. It is, I am assured on the authority of the conveyancers, quite an unusual thing for the settlor to "make an eldest son," as it is called; in general he conveys the land in fee simple to trustees to pay out of the rents and profits portions to the children, with sometimes, but not so often as is supposed, a rather larger share to sons than daughters. In such a case there is nothing whatever to prevent the trustees selling the land or leasing it, or otherwise dealing with it as might a bonus paterfamilias. If it be an eldest son settlement, then the settlor and his son become tenants for life in succession, and the eldest son of such eldest son is named tenant in tail. This, it is true, ties up the property in one sense, but hardly in the sense which is likely to be understood by those who read "A Solicitor's" letter. By the Settled Estates Acts the tenant for life can at any time sell the property as freely as if he were absolute owner, and the proceeds then become subject to the trusts of the settlement. And as soon as any tenant in tail comes of age every limitation of the settlement taking effect after the estate tail may be destroyed by a deed executed by the tenant in tail with the consent of the tenant for life. Surely then this is a very different thing from keeping land out of the market for a century.

I have entered at this length into the questions raised by your correspondent's letter, not out of hostility to land reform, but because of a very keen appreciation of the rule that if a man would do a thing, it is necessary that he should first find exactly what he has to do. There are sufficient difficulties in the road without our friends stepping in and setting up bogies in our way. Such action can only discredit the cause. The law of settlement, I admit, is in a bad way, and much will have to be done to simplify it—very much before an effective registration of title is practicable. The estate tail will, of course, disappear, though, as I have pointed out, and as one hoped most people understood, entail does not mean the perpetual tying up of land. Settlements are objectionable because they are complicated, and hence make dealings with land expensive. To consider them directly responsible for high rents and bad landlords is a mistake. True, no doubt, it is that land is hampered with portions and charges of one kind and another; but is there any likelihood of improvement under a system of family division which would substitute a large number of small landlords for a small number of large ones? What experience we have does not encourage us. It is the feeling that little is to be gained for the man who works the soil by merely breaking up large estates that has driven so many of us to think that in the nationalisation of the land alone shall we find any great amelioration of the condition of the labourer. One word in regard to leasehold enfranchisement. Do not let us be carried away by any sentimental regard for the urban leaseholder. He is not in the beginning of things a particularly depressed person, and for my own part I see no more reason for giving him any unearned increment there may be than for putting it into the pocket of his landlord. The great curse which our leasehold system has brought upon us is the jerry-built house, and the remembrance that this system is in no small degree responsible for the state of things revealed by every inquiry into the housing of the poor should be our principal reason for placing leasehold enfranchisement among the first articles of the Liberal creed.—Yours very truly,

Temple, September 19.   ᴇ COLL. REG.

Sɪʀ,—The prices paid by the labourers at the village shops are higher than many would imagine. The labourer gets lower wages than the artisan, but pays far higher for his groceries than anyone in the towns. In the village the labourer has no choice of shops, and he must give 2s. a lb. for inferior tea, 9½d. for bad cheese, or go without. The town shopkeepers are forced to supply good things reasonably or their shops would be forsaken for one of the many others. The village shopkeeper is able to demand almost any price he likes; he knows the people are at his mercy, and the most they can do is to grumble at the prices. It is an injustice that a family living on 12s. a week should pay more for everything than I do, but it is a fact that they do. I am able to buy in larger quantities from the nearest town ; they have barely enough money to buy a week's supply, and cannot afford to pay train fares to the towns. A few days ago, a woman better off than most of her neighbours told me that by going to a town ten miles away and buying enough for a month she can pay her ticket and save 1s. a week on what she would give for the same things at the village shop. The really poor cannot afford a month's supply, simply because the money is not there to buy with, and therefore are forced to buy from a shop which would be forsaken in a town. Much can be done to help the poor in our villages by starting co-operative societies or keeping a few things to sell them one's self. I believe we save them a good deal by our little "store," by selling tea, cheese, candles, soap, oil, calicoes, shirtings, flannels, Salvation Army matches, and so on. We buy in large quantities, sell at a slight profit, but considerably lower than the shop. The profits are divided in proportion to the amount spent. Some receive as much as 5s. or 6s. back, and at the same time are buying really good tea at 1s. 4d., instead of paying 2s. for bad with no profit. One of the worst evils of village life is the high prices the labourer must pay. "High prices and poor stuff" is the general rule.

Odsey, near Royston, September 12. A RADICAL WOMAN.

———

SIR,—I read your articles on Village Life as they appear to my labourers, and we discuss the various questions raised. The result of our talk seems to be that the deplorable state of agriculture in Essex may also be seen here in Oxfordshire on the numerous farms which of late years have been neglected from want of capital or otherwise ; that the condition of the small farmer was never worse, but that the condition of the labouring man was never better than it is at present. The more people that go to the towns the better for those who are left behind. The only drawback is the distant view of the workhouse, for however great wages the labourer may receive, he puts by not a single farthing for old age. This prospect, however, might easily be averted if the enormous sum of money raised by the poor law in the village was kept in the village, instead of being sent away, who knows where ? I believe, however, that the workhouse contains no one from this village. The only remedy I can think of in order to keep all the land in cultivation is for joint-stock companies to find capital and work the neglected farms, and utilise capital which might otherwise go to such places as Chili and the Argentine Republic. I have during the past two years taken to farming for amusement, certainly not for profit ; and take great interest in agriculture. The rector your correspondent mentions ought to know that an allotment is of the greatest value to the labourer, and amply repays the labour expended on it. I have turned the fifth part of an acre of my farm to garden ground. This repays me 10 per cent., whilst the rest of my farm pays nothing.—Yours, &c.,

AN OXFORDSHIRE LANDLORD.

SIR,—Your correspondent " A Radical Woman," in calling attention to the high prices charged at the little shops in remote country villages, has indicated one of the reasons why a proper provision of allotment ground is so important to the agricultural labourer's well-being. From the small population resident within a walking distance, if the rural shopkeeper is to obtain a reasonable livelihood he must charge a large percentage of profit on the small quantities he is able to sell. A fair-sized allotment will enable the labourer to obtain all the flour, potatoes, and bacon required for use in his family at no further outlay than the rent of the land, for as the great difficulty felt by the country worker is the want of continuous employment, much of the time spent on the allotment would otherwise be wasted in enforced idleness, and consequently can hardly be said to have any money value to him. Not only is the whole of the retailer's profit saved on the food so produced, but a much more wholesome and nourishing quality obtained. This of course is only the case where the people have energy enough to bake at home, as upon this baking at home much of the serviceableness of large allotments depends. A supply of wheat straw is generally considered requisite for obtaining a proper provision of manure, while the bran and sharps left in making the wheat into flour serve to feed the pigs; but as wheat does not pay to grow on a small scale except when consumed by the grower, wherever this is not the practice then we hear great complaints of the deterioration of allotment land from want of manure. Moreover, the bread made from English wheat flour is of a quality much more suited to rearing a healthy family than that sold by the ordinary baker. Seeing that large allotments enable the labourer himself to produce the larger part of the food required in his household, as these become general we may hope to see his dependence upon the village shopkeeper at an early date much lessened.—Yours truly,

Birmingham, Sept. 16.   C. D. STURGE.

SIR,—I have read with much interest the graphic and incisive letters of your Commissioner, and have followed him mentally through many of the villages which he has described. Yet he "makes the poor crushed worm to turn" with some of his assertions about the clergy. Poverty is, as a rule, what we pay for belonging to the order, and how, it may well be asked, can we with our scanty incomes build model cottages and increase the wages of the labourer? By some mysterious process of reasoning which has taken deep root and ineradicable hold of the public mind, we are credited with "having plenty to get and little to do," as Serjeant Buzfuz observed to Sam Weller in the celebrated trial of " Bardell *v.* Pickwick." Let me say a few words in self-defence of myself and my order. I have been more than 35 years in the ministry, and was for many years a Liberal in politics, but always carefully abstained from in any way, either in public or private, influencing my people. I am now neutral, and do not intend to vote either one way or the other at the coming election. For the last nineteen years my lot has been cast in a small remote village in Suffolk, where there are no gentry either in the parish or neighbourhood, not even a retired tradesman, and where the position of a clergyman is positively nothing. The benefice may perhaps be 150*l.* in net value. I have given away all that I could, never charged even one sixpence for burials, marriages, or churchings, and allowed gravestones to be erected in the churchyard without fee. Sometimes I have taken off my coat or hat and given them away ; sometimes taken a share of my dinner to some poor person, subscribed to schools, clubs, and helped those who were in arrears with their rent. I have gone in and out among the people, and regarded all, whether Churchmen or Dissenters, as my friends and parishioners. This is no more than what is done by many clergymen in many parishes in England. Surely, sir, it is hard for us to be informed that " we are not worth our salt," and the more particularly as many of us have endured for many years thankless toil and may almost say, "What more could have been done to my vine- yard ?" In many instances, very little "salt" falls to our lot. Sydney Smith speaks of the poor clergyman endeavouring to preserve the heart of a gentleman, the spirit of a Christian, and the kindness of a pastor. He needs, verily, to pose in these characters, and he may say with Horace—

> " Virtute me involvo, probamque
> Pauperiem sine dote quæro "

—I am, &c.,

PRESBYTER OXONIENSIS SEXAGENARIUS.

SIR,—In his delightful article last Friday, your Special Commissioner writes as follows : " Away to the left, the pretty cottages with their thatched roofs, their steps of unhewn rock, their windows full of geraniums and fuchsias, and their porches overgrown with autumn roses and canariensis, are hobbling down the broken pathway in a picturesque irregular line, their red chimney-stacks gently streaming out into the trees above the soft blue smoke of the wood-fires." Compare this charming picture of an old English village—many of which still exist in every part of our country—with the modern cottages built by the farmer or speculator to pay five or seven per cent. interest. These are usually square brick boxes, built by contract in pairs or rows, and roofed with cold blue slates. The bricks are soft and porous, and the walls thin, so that these houses are cold and damp in winter, while to save timber and slates in the roof the eaves project only a few inches, giving an aspect of bareness and meanness that is absolutely oppressive. Such houses as these, which are spreading over the country by thousands yearly, destroy the charm of many a rural landscape ; and so long as we act on the erroneous principle of providing dwellings for the people instead of allowing them to build for themselves in the manner most convenient for themselves, these ugly, inconvenient, and unhealthy productions of the jerry-builder will continue to increase.

In order to find the true remedy for this evil let us ask ourselves, Why are the old cottages so invariably picturesque, so harmonious with the surrounding landscape in form and colour as to be a constant delight to the artist and lover of nature? The answer, I believe, is, because they were the natural product of the time and locality, being built by the very people who were to live in them, with materials found in the district, and in the style which experience had shown to be at once the most convenient and the most economical. The first owners of these old cottages, the men who built them, were either freeholders or copyholders, or those who had obtained land on lease for several lives, and they were actually erected in part by the men themselves, with the assistance of their neighbours, the village carpenter and mason. The materials were obtained either from their own land or from the moors, wastes, and woodlands, which were then open for the use of all the inhabitants of the manor. The walls were of rough stone or of brick, or timber-framed with rough-hewn wood in the upper storey, forming those charming wood-framed houses of Surrey, Sussex, Hereford, and some other counties. In Dorset and Devon the walls were often of clay mixed with straw, called "cobble," and this makes a far warmer, drier, and altogether more desirable dwelling than the modern brick, as many of the old cottages, which have lasted for centuries, prove. The roof, framed with rough posts, and with poles for rafters, has a slight irregularity of outline very pleasing to the eye when compared with the rigid straightness, flatness, and angularity of roofs built with machine-cut timber; while the thick covering of thatch, broken by the small rounded dormer windows and with the broadly-overhanging eaves, is not only far warmer in winter and cooler in summer than any tiled or slated roof, but has the inestimable advantage to the labourer that he can repair it himself without having to pay a skilled mechanic.

Of course, so long as our labourers and country mechanics have no land they can build no houses ; but if we so arrange that every labourer, young or old, can obtain an acre or two of land on a permanent tenure, the cottage problem, which so much disturbs our legislators and philan-thropists, will solve itself far better than they can solve it by legislative action. It will prove as easy as the three-acres-and-a-cow problem. A friend of mine was once talking to a labourer, and, having heard it stated over and over again that even if the labourer had the land he would in most cases have no money to buy the cow, he asked this man how he supposed it could be done, and received this answer, accom-panied by a smile at the questioner's ignorance of such a very simple matter—"Why, sir, we usually gets a calf, and her grows into a cow." Just in the same way the labourer will get a house. He will first build a hut or cabin of the rudest description, and this by continual additions will grow into a comfortable cottage. An unmarried labourer could put up a hut with walls of turf or clay and roof of sods or heather-thatch, which would shelter him till he got his land into cultivation and could invest his profits in materials to add to or build his cottage. Your correspondent "Agricola," who has lived for twenty years and saved money on a two-acre holding, shows how this may be done even while paying a high rent. The result of this system of letting the people provide their own houses would be that we should have, as of old, individuality and variety in our rural cottages, with that harmony and picturesqueness which results from the use of local materials and hand-work in place of machine-work. We should have stone, or brick, or clay, or timber walls, thatched or tiled or stone-slabbed roofs, one-storey or two-storey houses, porches or verandahs, fantastic gables and chimneys, and those pleasing irregularities which result either from individual taste or the growth of a small house into a larger one by repeated additions; the whole set in a groundwork of shrubs and fruit-trees, and a foreground of vegetables and flowers.

The man who had built such a cottage for his permanent home would love it as we all love our own handiwork, and would spend much of his time and savings in adding to its convenience, comfort, and beauty. With such houses of their own, and with their garden and orchard, their cow, pigs, and poultry to attend to, the labourer would have constant interest and occupation at home, the public-house would remain empty, and the great drink question would perhaps cease to be so serious as it is now. Everyone admires the cottages of past centuries, and regrets their rapid disappearance. If we give our labourers and village residents of all kinds a secure tenure of land suitable to their respective needs, there seems no reason why they should not build for themselves as cosily and picturesquely as did their ancestors. There are many and cogent reasons why we should do this as speedily as possible. By this means alone we shall be able to re-populate the rural districts and relieve the terrible pressure of competi-tion in our towns. By this means also we may hope to destroy that deadly curse of poverty, the increasing amount of which may be estimated by the terrible statement of the Registrar-General that the deaths which occur in English workhouses have steadily increased from 5·6 per cent. of the total deaths in 1875 to 6·9 of the total in 1888. By this great reform we shall give our workers the best incentive to sobriety and industry—the sure prospect of a homestead of their own in which they may live in comfort and security, relieved from the dread of ending their days in the workhouse. This, too, will enable our cottagers to grow for their own use, or for sale, abundance of bacon, butter, poultry, eggs, and fruit, in the place of the many millions, worth of these articles we now import from abroad. And, lastly, this will perhaps save us from the crowning disgrace of covering our beautiful land with the very ugliest of houses for our labourers' use, and of thus destroying, for some generations to come, much of the picturesque charm of rural England.—Yours, &c., ALFRED R. WALLACE.
Parkstone, Dorset.

———

SIR,—If the Liberals really wish to ameliorate the lot of our labourers and not merely to catch a few votes at the next general election by vague and vain promises, the first thing to be done is to break down the combination of squire and parson. Until this is done, village councils and all other proposals of a like nature are mere foolishness. The parson and the squire may be the best men alive, but their beneficent tyranny is apt to treat the labourer "like a horse or mule which hath no understanding, whose mouth must be held with bit and bridle." This was an ideal of the past, when it was thought that the masses were sent into the world to supply the needs of a favoured few. Nowadays, all this is changed. Hodge is beginning to find out his importance, and at the same time he is beginning to discover his own misery. Very soon he will have to learn two more things—freedom and responsibility ; but I venture to say he will never know what these words mean till the baneful influence of the squire and parson is minimised. Let all Liberals face the great problem of Disestablishment and Disendowment.

I am a minister of the Established Church, but I own with regret that in our Church the power of the purse is greater than the power of the Cross. Vast as are the revenues of the Church, they have to be supplemented by private resources just as vast, for one of the surest means to episcopal favour is the possession of a long purse and good banking account, and much of this enormous power is used in the country for the subjugation of poor Hodge. If the agricultural labourers want to live like men and not like domestic animals without either freedom or responsibility, they must repudiate clerical tyranny and claim a just share in the administration of their own Church. By means of disestablishment and disendowment the revenues of the Church would be more equitably used, the power of the Bishops lessened, and the power of the laity increased. If the villagers wanted a parson, they could have the man of their choice, and throughout the length and breadth of the land we should find ministers in sympathy with the people, and devoted to their social and moral welfare. If the Liberals are wise, they will put Disestablishment on their agenda paper at once. It will not only get rid of a mass of corruption and thinly veiled simony, it will do more than anything else to make a man of Hodge, and instead of a broken-down, miserable slave, we shall have a free and independent labourer with plenty of work and plenty of hope. Whenever the Liberals let us see that they seriously mean to take in hand this great and necessary reform they will have the help and sympathy of many　　　　A CURATE.

Mr. Josiah Godden, of Woodstock, writes:—" Cobden once said the English people in their dislike of change were almost Chinese, and it would seem so on this very question of Life in Our Villages. Fifty years ago Feargus O'Connor, and twenty years ago Joseph Arch told this same story, and yet it has again to be told and enforced with all the power and influence of the *Daily News*. The bottom word of the whole matter is land nationalisation. Yes, sir, this is a big word, and alarms by its strangeness, but it will be familiar enough to the people of England before long. You cannot, try how you will, get to a final settlement of this matter unless you give to every occupier of land absolute security, so that he may not be subject to the caprice, passion, or greed of any individual, but rest upon the solid basis of national right and power."

PRINTED BY CASSELL & COMPANY, LIMITED, LA BELLE SAUVAGE, LONDON, E.C.

Illustrated, Fine-Art, and other Volumes.

Abbeys and Churches of England and Wales, The: Descriptive, Historical, Pictorial. Two Series. 21s. each.

Adventure, The World of. Fully Illustrated. Complete in Three Vols. 9s. each.

American Library of Fiction. Crown 8vo, cloth, 3s. 6d. each.

> A Latin-Quarter Courtship. By Henry Harland (Sidney Luska).
> "89." By Edgar Henry.
> Karmel the Scout. By Sylvanus Cobb, Junr.
> Grandison Mather. By Henry Harland (Sidney Luska).

Anglomaniacs, The: A Story of New York Life of To-day. By Mrs. BURTON-HARRISON. 3s. 6d.

Arabian Nights Entertainments, Cassell's Pictorial. 10s. 6d.

Architectural Drawing. By PHENÉ SPIERS. Illustrated. 10s. 6d.

Art, The Magazine of. Yearly Vol. With 12 Photogravures, Etchings, &c., and several hundred choice Engravings. 16s.

Artistic Anatomy. By Prof. M. DUVAL. Translated by F. E. FENTON. 5s.

Bashkirtseff, Marie, The Journal of. *Cheap Edition.* 7s. 6d. *Library Edition,* in Two Vols., 24s.

Bashkirtseff, Marie, The Letters of. Translated by MARY J. SERRANO. 7s. 6d.

Birds' Nests, Eggs, and Egg-Collecting. By R. KEARTON. Illustrated with 16 Coloured Plates. 5s.

Black America. A Study of the Ex-slave and his late Master. By W. LAIRD CLOWES. 6s.

Black Arrow, The. A Tale of the Two Roses. By R. L. STEVENSON. Illustrated. 3s. 6d.

British Ballads. With 275 Original Illustrations. In Two Vols. 15s.

British Battles on Land and Sea. By JAMES GRANT. With about 600 Illustrations. Three Vols., 4to, £1 7s.; *Library Edition,* £1 10s.

British Battles, Recent. Illustrated. 4to, 9s.; *Library Edition,* 10s.

Browning, An Introduction to the Study of. By A. SYMONS. 2s. 6d.

Bunyan's Pilgrim's Progress and The Holy War, Cassell's Illustrated Edition of. With 200 Original Illustrations. Cloth, 16s.

Butterflies and Moths, European. With 61 Coloured Plates. 35s.

Canaries and Cage-Birds, The Illustrated Book of. With 56 Facsimile Coloured Plates, 35s. Half-morocco, £2 5s.

Cassell's Family Magazine. Yearly Vol. Illustrated. 9s.

Cathedrals, Abbeys, and Churches of England and Wales. Descriptive, Historical, Pictorial. *Popular Edition.* Two Vols. 25s.

Celebrities of the Century. *Cheap Edition.* 10s. 6d.

Choice Dishes at Small Cost. By A. G. PAYNE. 1s.

Cities of the World. Four Vols. Illustrated. 7s. 6d. each.

Civil Service, Guide to Employment in the. 3s. 6d.

Civil Service.—Guide to Female Employment in Government Offices. 1s.

Climate and Health Resorts. By Dr. BURNEY YEO. *New and Cheaper Edition.* 7s. 6d.

Clinical Manuals for Practitioners and Students of Medicine. A List of Volumes forwarded post free on application to the Publishers.

Clothing, The Influence of, on Health. By F. TREVES, F.R.C.S. 2s.

Colonist's Medical Handbook, The. By E. A. BARTON, M.R.C.S. 2s. 6d.

Colour. By Prof. A. H. CHURCH. With Coloured Plates. 3s. 6d.

Commerce, The Year-Book of. Third Year's Issue. 5s.

Commercial Botany of the Nineteenth Century. By J. R. JACKSON, A.L.S. Cloth gilt, 3s. 6d.

Conning Tower, In a. By H. O. ARNOLD-FORSTER. 1s.

Cookery, A Year's. By PHYLLIS BROWNE. *New and Enlarged Edition.* 3s. 6d.

Cookery, Cassell's Dictionary of. Containing about Nine Thousand Recipes, 7s. 6d.; Roxburgh, 10s. 6d.

Cookery, Cassell's Popular. With Four Coloured Plates. Cloth gilt, 2s.

Cookery, Cassell's Shilling. 384 pages, limp cloth, 1s.

Cookery, Vegetarian. By A. G. PAYNE. 1s. 6d.

Cooking by Gas, The Art of. By MARIE J. SUGG. Illustrated. Cloth, 3s. 6d.

Copyright, The Law of Musical and Dramatic. By EDWARD CUTLER, THOMAS EUSTACE SMITH, and FREDERIC E. WEATHERLY, Esquires, Barristers-at-Law. 3s. 6d.

Countries of the World, The. By ROBERT BROWN, M.A., Ph.D., &c. Complete in Six Vols., with about 750 Illustrations. 4to, 7s. 6d. each.

Cromwell, Oliver. By J. ALLANSON PICTON, M.P. 5s.

Culmshire Folk. By the Author of "John Orlebar," &c. 3s. 6d.

Cyclopædia, Cassell's Concise. Brought down to the latest date. With about 600 Illustrations. *Cheap Edition.* 7s. 6d.

Cyclopædia, Cassell's Miniature. Containing 30,000 subjects. 3s. 6d.

Dairy Farming. By Prof. J. P. SHELDON. With 25 Coloured Plates. 21s.

David Todd. By DAVID MACLURE. 5s.

Dickens, Character Sketches from. FIRST, SECOND, and THIRD SERIES. With Six Original Drawings in each by F. BARNARD. 21s. each.

Disraeli, Benjamin, Personal Reminiscences of. By HENRY LAKE. 3s. 6d.

Disraeli in Outline. By F. CARROLL BREWSTER, LL.D. 7s. 6d.

Dog, Illustrated Book of the. By VERO SHAW, B.A. With 28 Coloured Plates. Cloth bevelled, 35s.; half-morocco, 45s.

Dog, The. By IDSTONE. Illustrated. 2s. 6d.

Domestic Dictionary, The. Illustrated. Cloth, 7s. 6d.

Doré Gallery, The. With 250 Illustrations by DORÉ. 4to, 42s.

Doré's Dante's Inferno. Illustrated by GUSTAVE DORÉ. 21s.

Doré's Milton's Paradise Lost. Illustrated by DORÉ. 4to, 21s.

Dr. Dumány's Wife. A Novel. By MAURUS JÓKAI. Translated from the Hungarian by F. STEINITZ. 7s. 6d. net.

Earth, Our, and its Story. By Dr. ROBERT BROWN, F.L.S. With Coloured Plates and numerous Wood Engravings. Three Vols. 9s. each.

Edinburgh, Old and New. With 600 Illustrations. Three Vols. 9s. each.

Egypt: Descriptive, Historical, and Picturesque. By Prof. G. EBERS. With 800 Original Engravings. *Popular Edition.* In Two Vols. 42s.

Electricity in the Service of Man. With nearly 850 Illustrations. *Cheap Edition.* 9s.

Electricity, Age of. By PARK BENJAMIN, Ph.D. 7s. 6d.

Electricity, Practical. By Prof. W. E. AYRTON. 7s. 6d.

Employment for Boys on Leaving School, Guide to. By W. S. Beard, F.R.G.S. 1s. 6d.

Encyclopædic Dictionary, The. Complete in Fourteen Divisional Vols., 10s. 6d. each; or Seven Vols., half-morocco, 21s. each; half-russia, 25s.

England, Cassell's Illustrated History of. With 2,000 Illustrations. Ten Vols., 4to, 9s. each. *Revised Edition.* Vols. I., II., III., and IV., 9s. each.

English Dictionary, Cassell's. Giving definitions of more than 100,000 words and phrases. 7s. 6d.

English History, The Dictionary of. *Cheap Edition.* 10s. 6d.

English Literature, Dictionary of. By W. DAVENPORT ADAMS. *Cheap Edition,* 7s. 6d.; Roxburgh, 10s. 6d.

English Literature, Library of. By Prof. HENRY MORLEY.
  VOL. I.—SHORTER ENGLISH POEMS. 7s. 6d.
  VOL. II.—ILLUSTRATIONS OF ENGLISH RELIGION. 7s. 6d.
  VOL. III.—ENGLISH PLAYS. 7s. 6d.
  VOL. IV.—SHORTER WORKS IN ENGLISH PROSE. 7s. 6d.
  VOL. V.—SKETCHES OF LONGER WORKS IN ENGLISH VERSE AND PROSE. 7s. 6d.

English Literature, Morley's First Sketch of. *Revised Edition,* 7s. 6d.
English Literature, The Story of. By ANNA BUCKLAND. 3s. 6d.
English Writers. By Prof. HENRY MORLEY. Vols. I. to VIII. 5s. each.
Æsop's Fables. Illustrated by ERNEST GRISET. Cloth, 3s. 6d.
Etiquette of Good Society. 1s.; cloth, 1s. 6d.
Eye, Ear, and Throat, The Management of the. 3s. 6d.
Faith Doctor, The. A Novel. By EDWARD EGGLESTON. 7s. 6d. net.
Family Physician, The. By Eminent PHYSICIANS and SURGEONS. *New and Revised Edition.* Cloth, 21s.; Roxburgh, 25s.
Father Stafford. A Novel. By ANTHONY HOPE. 6s.
Fenn, G. Manville, Works by. Boards, 2s. each; cloth, 2s. 6d. each.
POVERTY CORNER. | DUTCH THE DIVER. Boards only.
MY PATIENTS. Being the Notes of a Navy Surgeon. | THE VICAR'S PEOPLE. Cloth only.
THE PARSON O' DUMFORD. Boards only.
Field Naturalist's Handbook, The. By the Rev. J. G. WOOD and Rev. THEODORE WOOD. 5s.
Figuier's Popular Scientific Works. With Several Hundred Illustrations in each. 3s. 6d. each.
THE HUMAN RACE. | MAMMALIA. | OCEAN WORLD.
WORLD BEFORE THE DELUGE. Revised.
Flora's Feast. A Masque of Flowers. Penned and Pictured by WALTER CRANE. With 40 Pages in Colours. 5s.
Flower de Hundred, The Story of a Virginia Plantation. By Mrs. BURTON HARRISON, Author of the "Anglomaniacs," &c. 3s. 6d.
Flower Painting in Water Colours. With Coloured Plates. First and Second Series. 5s. each.
Flower Painting, Elementary. With Eight Coloured Plates. 3s.
Flowers, and How to Paint Them. By MAUD NAFTEL. With Coloured Plates. 5s.
Fossil Reptiles, A History of British. By Sir RICHARD OWEN, K.C.B., F.R.S., &c. With 268 Plates. In Four Vols., £12 12s.
Four Years in Parliament with Hard Labour. By C. W. RADCLIFFE COOKE, M.P. *Third Edition.*
France as It Is. By ANDRÉ LEBON and PAUL PELET. With Three Maps. Crown 8vo, cloth, 7s. 6d.
Garden Flowers, Familiar. By SHIRLEY HIBBERD. With Coloured Plates by F. E. HULME, F.L.S. Complete in Five Series. 12s. 6d. each.
Gardening, Cassell's Popular. Illustrated. Four Vols. 5s. each.
Geometrical Drawing for Army Candidates. By H. T. LILLEY, M.A. 2s.
Geometry, First Elements of Experimental. By PAUL BERT. 1s. 6d.
Geometry, Practical Solid. By MAJOR ROSS. 2s.
Gilbert, Elizabeth, and her Work for the Blind. By FRANCES MARTIN. 2s. 6d.
Gleanings from Popular Authors. Two Vols. With Original Illustrations. 4to, 9s. each. Two Vols. in One, 15s.
Gulliver's Travels. With 88 Engravings by MORTEN. *Cheap Edition.* Cloth, 3s. 6d.; cloth gilt, 5s.
Gun and its Development, The. By W. W. GREENER. With 500 Illustrations. 10s. 6d.
Guns, Modern Shot. By W. W. GREENER. Illustrated. 5s.
Health at School. By CLEMENT DUKES, M.D., B.S. 7s. 6d.
Health, The Book of. By Eminent Physicians and Surgeons. 21s.
Health, The Influence of Clothing on. By F. TREVES, F.R.G.S. 2s.

Heavens, The Story of the. By Sir ROBERT STAWELL BALL, LL.D.,
F.R.S., F.R.A.S. With Coloured Plates. *Popular Edition.* 12s. 6d.
Heroes of Britain in Peace and War. With 300 Original Illus-
trations. *Cheap Edition.* Vol. I. 3s. 6d.
Holiday Studies of Wordsworth. By Rev. F. A. MALLESON, M.A. 5s.
Horse, The Book of the. By SAMUEL SIDNEY. With 28 Fac-simile
Coloured Plates. *Enlarged Edition.* Demy 4to, 35s.; half-morocco, 45s.
Houghton, Lord: The Life, Letters, and Friendships of Richard
Monckton Milnes, First Lord Houghton. By T. WEMYSS
REID. In Two Vols., with Two Portraits. 32s.
Household, Cassell's Book of the. Complete in Four Vols. 5s. each.
How Women may Earn a Living. By MERCY GROGAN. 6d.
Hygiene and Public Health. By B. ARTHUR WHITELEGGE, M.D. 7s. 6d.
India, Cassell's History of. By JAMES GRANT. With about 400
Illustrations. Library binding. One Vol. 15s.
In-door Amusements, Card Games, and Fireside Fun, Cassell's
Book of. *Cheap Edition.* 2s.
Irish Union, The; Before and After. By A. K. CONNELL, M.A. 2s. 6d.
Italy from the Fall of Napoleon I. in 1815 to 1890. By J. W. PROBYN.
New and Cheaper Edition. 3s. 6d.
"Japanese" Library of Popular Works, Cassell's. Consisting of
Twelve Popular Works, printed on thin paper. 1s. 3d. each net.

> Handy Andy. — Oliver Twist. — Ivanhoe. — Ingoldsby Legends.—
> The Last of the Mohicans. — The Last Days of Pompeii.—The
> Yellowplush Papers. — The Last Days of Palmyra. — Jack
> Hinton, the Guardsman. — Selections from Hood's Works.—
> American Humour.—The Tower of London.

John Orlebar, Clk. By the Author of "Culmshire Folk." 2s.
John Parmelee's Curse. By JULIAN HAWTHORNE. 2s. 6d.
Kennel Guide, The Practical. By Dr. GORDON STABLES. 1s.
Khiva, A Ride to. By Col. FRED. BURNABY. 1s. 6d.
Kidnapped. By R. L. STEVENSON. Illustrated. 3s. 6d.
King Solomon's Mines. By H. RIDER HAGGARD. Illustrated. 3s. 6d.
Ladies' Physician, The. By a London Physician. 6s.
Lake Dwellings of Europe. By ROBERT MUNRO, M.D., M.A.
Cloth, 31s. 6d. ; Roxburgh, £2 2s.
Law, How to Avoid. By A. J. WILLIAMS, M.P. 1s. *Cheap Edition.*
Legends for Lionel. By WALTER CRANE. Coloured Illustrations. 5s.
Letts's Diaries and other Time-saving Publications published
exclusively by CASSELL & COMPANY. (*A list free on application.*)
Life Assurance, Medical Handbook of. 7s. 6d.
Little Minister, The. By J. M. BARRIE. Three Vols. 31s. 6d.
Loans Manual. By CHARLES P. COTTON. 5s.
Local Government in England and Germany. By the Right Hon.
Sir ROBERT MORIER, G.C.B., &c. 1s.
Local Option in Norway. By THOMAS M. WILSON, C.E. 1s.
Locomotive Engine, The Biography of a. By HENRY FRITH. 5s.
London, Greater. By EDWARD WALFORD. Two Vols. With about
400 Illustrations. 9s. each.
London, Old and New. Six Vols., each containing about 200
Illustrations and Maps. Cloth, 9s. each.
London Street Arabs. By Mrs. H. M. STANLEY (DOROTHY TENNANT).
A Collection of Pictures. Descriptive Text by the Artist. 5s.
Master of Ballantrae, The. By R. L. STEVENSON. Illustrated. 3s. 6d.
Mathew, Father, His Life and Times. By F. J. MATHEW, a Grand-
nephew. 2s. 6d.
Mechanics, The Practical Dictionary of. Containing 15,000 Draw-
ings. Four Vols. 21s. each.
Medicine, Manuals for Students of. (*A List forwarded post free.*)
Metropolitan Year-Book, The, for 1892. Paper, 1s. ; cloth, 2s.

Metzerott, Shoemaker. Cr. 8vo, 5s.

Modern Europe, A History of. By C. A. FYFFE, M.A. Complete in Three Vols. 12s. each.

Music, Illustrated History of. By EMIL NAUMANN. Edited by the Rev. Sir F. A. GORE OUSELEY, Bart. Illustrated. Two Vols. 31s. 6d.

National Library, Cassell's. In Volumes. Paper covers, 3d.; cloth, 6d. (*A Complete List of the Volumes post free on application.*)

Natural History, Cassell's Concise. By E. PERCEVAL WRIGHT, M.A., M.D., F.L.S. With several Hundred Illustrations. 7s. 6d.

Natural History, Cassell's New. Edited by Prof. P. MARTIN DUNCAN, M.B., F.R.S., F.G.S. Complete in Six Vols. With about 2,000 Illustrations. Cloth, 9s. each.

Nature's Wonder Workers. By KATE R. LOVELL. Illustrated. 5s.

Naval War, The Last Great. By A. NELSON SEAFORTH. One Vol., with Maps and Plans. 2s.

Navy, Royal, All About The. By W. LAIRD CLOWES. Illustrated. 1s.

Nelson, The Life of. By ROBERT SOUTHEY. Illustrated with Eight Plates. 3s. 6d. An Edition of Southey's "Nelson" is published as a Volume of the National Library, price 3d. Cloth, 6d.

Nursing for the Home and for the Hospital, A Handbook of. By CATHERINE J. WOOD. *Cheap Edition.* 1s. 6d.; cloth, 2s.

Nursing of Sick Children, A Handbook for the. By CATHERINE J. WOOD. 2s. 6d.

Oil Painting, A Manual of. By the Hon. JOHN COLLIER. 2s. 6d.

Our Own Country. Six Vols. With 1,200 Illustrations. 7s. 6d. each.

Pactolus Prime. A Novel. By ALBION W. TOURGÉE. 5s.

Painting, The English School of. By ERNEST CHESNEAU. 5s.

Painting, Practical Guides to. With Coloured Plates:—

MARINE PAINTING. 5s.	TREE PAINTING. 5s.
ANIMAL PAINTING. 5s.	WATER-COLOUR PAINTING. 5s.
CHINA PAINTING. 5s.	NEUTRAL TINT. 5s.
FIGURE PAINTING. 7s. 6d.	SEPIA, in Two Vols., 3s. each; or in One Vol., 5s.
ELEMENTARY FLOWER PAINTING. 3s.	
FLOWER PAINTING, Two Books, 5s. each.	FLOWERS, AND HOW TO PAINT THEM. 5s.

Paxton's Flower Garden. By Sir JOSEPH PAXTON and Prof. LINDLEY. With 100 Coloured Plates. *Price on application.*

People I've Smiled with. By MARSHALL P. WILDER. 2s.; cloth, 2s. 6d.

Peoples of the World, The. In Six Vols. By Dr. ROBERT BROWN. Illustrated. 7s. 6d. each.

Phantom City, The. By W. WESTALL. 5s.

Phillips, Watts, Artist and Playwright. By Miss E. WATTS PHILLIPS. With 32 Plates. 10s. 6d.

Photography for Amateurs. By T. C. HEPWORTH. Illustrated. 1s.; or cloth, 1s. 6d.

Phrase and Fable, Dictionary of. By the Rev. Dr. BREWER. *Cheap Edition, Enlarged,* cloth, 3s. 6d.; or with leather back, 4s. 6d.

Picturesque America. Complete in Four Vols., with 48 Exquisite Steel Plates and about 800 Original Wood Engravings. £2 2s. each.

Picturesque Australasia, Cassell's. With upwards of 1,000 Illustrations. Complete in Four Vols. 7s. 6d. each.

Picturesque Canada. With 600 Original Illustrations. 2 Vols. £3 3s. each.

Picturesque Europe. Complete in Five Vols. Each containing 13 Exquisite Steel Plates, from Original Drawings, and nearly 200 Original Illustrations. ORIGINAL EDITION. Cloth, £21; half-morocco, £31 10s.; morocco gilt, £52 10s. The POPULAR EDITION is published in Five Vols., 18s. each.

Picturesque Mediterranean. With Magnificent Original Illustrations by the leading Artists of the Day. Complete in Two Vols. £2 2s. each.

Pigeon Keeper, The Practical. By LEWIS WRIGHT. Illustrated. 3s. 6d.

Pigeons, The Book of. By ROBERT FULTON. Edited and Arranged by L. WRIGHT. With 50 Coloured Plates, 31s. 6d.; half-morocco, £2 2s.

Poems, Aubrey de Vere's. A Selection. Edited by J. DENNIS. 3s. 6d.

Poets, Cassell's Miniature Library of the :—

BURNS. Two Vols. 2s. 6d.	MILTON. Two Vols. 2s. 6d.
BYRON. Two Vols. 2s. 6d.	SCOTT. Two Vols. 2s. 6d. [2s. 6d.
HOOD. Two Vols. 2s. 6d.	SHERIDAN and GOLDSMITH. 2 Vols.
LONGFELLOW. Two Vols. 2s. 6d.	WORDSWORTH. Two Vols. 2s. 6d.

SHAKESPEARE. Illustrated. In 12 Vols., in Case, 12s.

Police Code, and Manual of the Criminal Law. By C. E. HOWARD VINCENT, M.P. 2s.

Polytechnic Series, The.

Forty Lessons in Carpentry Workshop Practice. Cloth gilt, 1s.

Practical Plane and Solid Geometry, including Graphic Arithmetic. Vol. I., Elementary Stage. Cloth gilt, 3s.

Forty Lessons in Engineering Workshop Practice. 1s. 6d.

Technical Scales. Set of Ten in cloth case, 1s. Also on Celluloid in Case, 10s. 6d. the set.

Elementary Chemistry for Science Schools and Classes. Crown 8vo, 1s. 6d.

Building Construction Plates. A Series of 40 Drawings. Royal folio size. 1½d. each.

Portrait Gallery, The Cabinet. First and Second Series, each containing 36 Cabinet Photographs of Eminent Men and Women. With Biographical Sketches. 15s. each.

Poultry Keeper, The Practical. By L. WRIGHT. Illustrated. 3s. 6d.

Poultry, The Book of. By LEWIS WRIGHT. *Popular Edition.* 10s. 6d.

Poultry, The Illustrated Book of. By LEWIS WRIGHT. With Fifty Coloured Plates. *New and Revised Edition.* Cloth, 31s. 6d.

Queen Summer ; or, The Tourney of the Lily and the Rose. Penned and Portrayed by WALTER CRANE. With Forty Pages of Designs in Colours. 6s. *Large Paper Edition,* 21s. net.

Queen Victoria, The Life and Times of. By ROBERT WILSON. Complete in Two Vols. With numerous Illustrations. 9s. each.

Rabbit-Keeper, The Practical. By CUNICULUS. Illustrated. 3s. 6d.

Railway Guides, Official Illustrated. With Illustrations, Maps, &c. Price 1s. each; or in cloth, 2s. each.

GREAT WESTERN RAILWAY.	LONDON AND SOUTH-WESTERN RAILWAY.
GREAT NORTHERN RAILWAY.	
LONDON, BRIGHTON AND SOUTH COAST RAILWAY.	MIDLAND RAILWAY.
	SOUTH-EASTERN RAILWAY.
LONDON AND NORTH-WESTERN RAILWAY.	GREAT EASTERN RAILWAY.

Railway Library, Cassell's. Crown 8vo, boards, 2s. each.

THE ASTONISHING HISTORY OF TROY TOWN. By Q.	JACK GORDON, KNIGHT ERRANT, GOTHAM, 1883. By BARCLAY NORTH.
THE ADMIRABLE LADY BIDDY FANE. By FRANK BARRETT.	THE DIAMOND BUTTON. By BARCLAY NORTH.
COMMODORE JUNK. By G. MANVILLE FENN.	ANOTHER'S CRIME. By JULIAN HAWTHORNE.
ST. CUTHBERT'S TOWER. By FLORENCE WARDEN.	THE YOKE OF THE THORAH. By SIDNEY LUSKA.
THE MAN WITH A THUMB. By BARCLAY NORTH.	WHO IS JOHN NOMAN? By CHARLES HENRY BECKETT.
BY RIGHT NOT LAW. By R. SHERARD.	THE TRAGEDY OF BRINKWATER. By MARTHA L. MOODEY.
WITHIN SOUND OF THE WEIR. By THOMAS ST. E. HAKE.	AN AMERICAN PENMAN. By JULIAN HAWTHORNE.
UNDER A STRANGE MASK. By FRANK BARRETT.	SECTION 558; or, THE FATAL LETTER. By JULIAN HAWTHORNE.
THE COOMBSBERROW MYSTERY. By JAMES COLWALL.	THE BROWN STONE BOY. By W. H. BISHOP.
DEAD MAN'S ROCK. By Q.	A TRAGIC MYSTERY. By JULIAN HAWTHORNE.
A QUEER RACE. By W. WESTALL.	THE GREAT BANK ROBBERY. By JULIAN HAWTHORNE.
CAPTAIN TRAFALGAR. By WESTALL and LAURIE.	
THE PHANTOM CITY. By W. WESTALL.	

Redgrave, Richard, C.B., R.A. Memoir. Compiled from his Diary. By F. M. REDGRAVE. 10s. 6d.

Richard, Henry, M.P. A Biography. By CHARLES S. MIALL. 7s. 6d.

Rivers of Great Britain: Descriptive, Historical, Pictorial. RIVERS OF THE EAST COAST. 42s.

Rivers of Great Britain: The Royal River: The Thames, from Source to Sea. With Descriptive Text and a Series of beautiful Engravings. *Original Edition*, £2 2s.; *Popular Edition*, 16s.

Robinson Crusoe, Cassell's New Fine-Art Edition of. With upwards of 100 Original Illustrations. 7s. 6d.

Rossetti, Dante Gabriel, as Designer and Writer. Notes by WILLIAM MICHAEL ROSSETTI. 7s. 6d.

Russia, Through, on a Mustang. By THOMAS STEVENS. 7s. 6d.

Russo-Turkish War, Cassell's History of. With about 500 Illustrations. Two Vols. 9s. each.

Saturday Journal, Cassell's. Yearly Volume, cloth, 7s. 6d.

Science for All. Edited by Dr. ROBERT BROWN. *Revised Edition.* Illustrated. Five Vols. 9s. each.

Sculpture, A Primer of. By E. ROSCOE MULLINS. With Illustrations. 2s. 6d.

Sea, The: Its Stirring Story of Adventure, Peril, and Heroism. By F. WHYMPER. With 400 Illustrations. Four Vols. 7s. 6d. each.

Secret of the Lamas, The. A Tale of Thibet. Crown 8vo, 5s.

Shaftesbury, The Seventh Earl of, K.G., The Life and Work of. By EDWIN HODDER. Three Vols., 36s. *Popular Edition*, One Vol., 7s. 6d.

Shakespeare, The Plays of. Edited by Professor HENRY MORLEY. Complete in 13 Vols., cloth, 21s.; half-morocco, cloth sides, 42s.

Shakespeare, Cassell's Quarto Edition. Containing about 600 Illustrations by H. C. SELOUS. Complete in Three Vols., cloth gilt, £3 3s.

Shakespeare, Miniature. Illustrated. In Twelve Vols., in box, 12s.; or in Red Paste Grain (box to match), with spring catch, 21s.

Shakespeare, The England of. By E. GOADBY. Illustrated. 2s. 6d.

Shakspere, The International. *Édition de Luxe.*
   "OTHELLO." Illustrated by FRANK DICKSEE, R.A. £3 10s.
   "KING HENRY IV." Illustrated by EDUARD GRÜTZNER, £3 10s.
   "AS YOU LIKE IT." Illustrated by ÉMILE BAYARD, £3 10s.
   "ROMEO AND JULIET." Illustrated by F. DICKSEE, R.A. Is now out of print, and scarce.

Shakspere, The Leopold. With 400 Illustrations. *Cheap Edition.* 3s. 6d. Cloth gilt, gilt edges, 5s.; Roxburgh, 7s. 6d.

Shakspere, The Royal. With Steel Plates and Wood Engravings. Three Vols. 15s. each.

Social Welfare, Subjects of. By Sir LYON PLAYFAIR, K.C.B. 7s. 6d.

Splendid Spur, The. Edited by Q. Illustrated. 3s. 6d.

Standard Library, Cassell's. Stiff covers, 1s. each; cloth, 2s. each.

Coningsby.	Adventures of Mr. Ledbury.	Eugene Aram.
Mary Barton.		Jack Hinton.
The Antiquary.	Ivanhoe.	Poe's Works.
Nicholas Nickleby (Two Vols.).	Oliver Twist.	Old Mortality.
	Selections from Hood's Works.	The Hour and the Man.
Jane Eyre.		Handy Andy.
Wuthering Heights.	Longfellow's Prose Works.	Scarlet Letter.
Dombey and Son (Two Vols.)		Pickwick (Two Vols.).
	Sense and Sensibility.	Last of the Mohicans.
The Prairie.	Lytton's Plays.	Pride and Prejudice.
Night and Morning.	Tales, Poems, and Sketches. Bret Harte.	Yellowplush Papers.
Kenilworth.		Tales of the Borders.
Ingoldsby Legends.	Martin Chuzzlewit (Two Vols.).	Last Days of Palmyra.
Tower of London.		Washington Irving's Sketch-Book.
The Pioneers.	The Prince of the House of David.	The Talisman.
Charles O'Malley.	Sheridan's Plays.	Rienzi.
Barnaby Rudge.	Uncle Tom's Cabin.	Old Curiosity Shop.
Cakes and Ale.	Deerslayer.	Heart of Midlothian.
The King's Own.	Rome and the Early Christians.	Last Days of Pompeii.
People I have Met.		American Humour.
The Pathfinder.	The Trials of Margaret Lyndsay.	Sketches by Boz.
Evelina.		Macaulay's Lays and Essays.
Scott's Poems.	Harry Lorrequer.	
Last of the Barons.		

Sports and Pastimes, Cassell's Complete Book of. *Cheap Edition.* With more than 900 Illustrations. Medium 8vo, 992 pages, cloth, 3s. 6d.

Stanley in East Africa, Scouting for. By T. STEVENS. With 14 Illustrations. Cloth, 7s. 6d.

Star-Land. By Sir ROBERT STAWELL BALL, LL.D., F.R S., F.R.A.S. Illustrated. Crown 8vo, 6s.

Steam Engine, The. By W. H. NORTHCOTT, C.E. 3s. 6d.

Storehouse of General Information, Cassell's. With Wood Engravings, Maps, and Coloured Plates. In Vols., 5s. each.

Story of Francis Cludde, The. A Novel. By STANLEY J. WEYMAN. 7s. 6d. net.

Story Poems. For Young and Old. Edited by Miss E. DAVENPORT ADAMS. 6s.

Strange Doings in Strange Places. Complete Sensational Stories. 5s.

Teaching in Three Continents. Personal Notes on the Educational Systems of the World. By W. C. GRASBY. 6s.

Technical Education. By F. C. MONTAGUE. 6d.

Thackeray, Character Sketches from. Six New and Original Drawings by FREDERICK BARNARD, reproduced in Photogravure. 21s.

The "Short Story" Library.

Noughts and Crosses. By Q. 5s. | **Eleven Possible Cases.** By Various Authors. 6s.
Otto the Knight, &c. By OCTAVE THANET. 5s. | **Felicia.** By Miss FANNY MURFREE. 5s.
Fourteen to One. &c. By ELIZA-BETH STUART PHELPS. 5s. | **The Poet's Audience, and Delilah.** By CLARA SAVILE CLARKE. 5s.

Treasure Island. By R. L. STEVENSON. Illustrated. 3s. 6d.

Trees, Familiar. By G. S. BOULGER, F.L.S. Two Series. With 40 full-page Coloured Plates by W. H. J. BOOT. 12s. 6d. each.

"Unicode": the Universal Telegraphic Phrase Book. *Desk or Pocket Edition.* 2s. 6d.

United States, Cassell's History of the. By the late EDMUND OLLIER. With 600 Illustrations. Three Vols. 9s. each.

Universal History, Cassell's Illustrated. Four Vols. 9s. each.

Vicar of Wakefield and other Works by OLIVER GOLDSMITH. Illustrated. 3s. 6d.; cloth, gilt edges, 5s.

Vision of Saints, A. *Edition de Luxe.* By LEWIS MORRIS. With 20 Full-Page Illustrations. 21s.

Waterloo Letters. Edited by MAJOR-GENERAL H. T. SIBORNE, late Colonel R.E. With numerous Plans of the Battlefield. 21s.

Web of Gold, A. By KATHARINE PEARSON WOODS. Crown 8vo, 6s.

What Girls Can Do. By PHYLLIS BROWNE. 2s. 6d.

Wild Birds, Familiar. By W. SWAYSLAND. Four Series. With 40 Coloured Plates in each. 12s. 6d. each.

Wild Flowers, Familiar. By F. E. HULME, F.L.S., F.S.A. Five Series. With 40 Coloured Plates in each. 12s. 6d. each.

Wood, Rev. J. G., Life of the. By the Rev. THEODORE WOOD. Extra crown 8vo, cloth. *Cheap Edition.* 5s.

Work. An Illustrated Magazine for all Workmen. Yearly Vol., 7s. 6d.

World of Wit and Humour, The. With 400 Illustrations. 7s. 6d.

World of Wonders. Two Vols. With 400 Illustrations. 7s. 6d. each.

Yule Tide. Cassell's Christmas Annual. 1s.

ILLUSTRATED MAGAZINES.

The Quiver. ENLARGED SERIES. Monthly, 6d.
Cassell's Family Magazine. Monthly, 7d.
"Little Folks" Magazine. Monthly, 6d.
The Magazine of Art. Monthly, 1s.
Cassell's Saturday Journal. Weekly, 1d.; Monthly, 6d.
Work. Weekly, 1d.; Monthly, 6d.

CASSELL'S COMPLETE CATALOGUE, containing particulars of upwards of One Thousand Volumes, will be sent post free on application.

CASSELL & COMPANY, LIMITED, *Ludgate Hill, London.*

Bibles and Religious Works.

Bible, Cassell's Illustrated Family. With 900 Illustrations. Leather, gilt edges, £2 10s.

Bible Dictionary, Cassell's. With nearly 600 Illustrations. 7s. 6d.

Bible Educator, The. Edited by the Very Rev. Dean PLUMPTRE, D.D., Wells. With Illustrations, Maps, &c. Four Vols., cloth, 6s. each.

Bible Student in the British Museum, The. By the Rev. J. G. KITCHIN, M.A. 1s.

Biblewomen and Nurses. Yearly Volume. Illustrated. 3s.

Bunyan's Pilgrim's Progress and Holy War. With 200 Illustrations. With a New Life of Bunyan by the Rev. JOHN BROWN, B.A., D.D. Cloth, 16s.

Bunyan's Pilgrim's Progress (Cassell's Illustrated). 4to. 7s. 6d.

Bunyan's Pilgrim's Progress. With Illustrations. Cloth, 2s. 6d.

Child's Bible, The. With 200 Illustrations. *150th Thousand.* 7s. 6d.

Child's Life of Christ, The. With 200 Illustrations. 7s. 6d.

"Come, ye Children." Illustrated. By Rev. BENJAMIN WAUGH. 5s.

Conquests of the Cross. With numerous Illustrations. Complete in Three Vols. 9s. each.

Doré Bible. With 238 Illustrations by GUSTAVE DORÉ. Small folio, best morocco, gilt edges, £15.

Early Days of Christianity, The. By the Ven. Archdeacon FARRAR, D.D., F.R.S. LIBRARY EDITION. Two Vols., 24s. ; morocco, £2 2s. POPULAR EDITION. Complete in One Volume, cloth, 6s. ; cloth, gilt edges, 7s. 6d. ; Persian morocco, 10s. 6d. ; tree-calf, 15s.

Family Prayer-Book, The. Edited by Rev. Canon GARBETT, M.A., and Rev. S. MARTIN. Extra crown 4to, cloth, 5s. ; morocco, 18s.

Gleanings after Harvest. Studies and Sketches by the Rev. JOHN R. VERNON, M.A. 6s.

"Graven in the Rock." By the Rev. Dr. SAMUEL KINNS, F.R.A.S., Author of "Moses and Geology." Illustrated. 12s. 6d.

"Heart Chords." A Series of Works by Eminent Divines. Bound in cloth, red edges, One Shilling each.

MY BIBLE. By the Right Rev. W. BOYD CARPENTER, Bishop of Ripon.

MY FATHER. By the Right Rev. ASHTON OXENDEN, late Bishop of Montreal.

MY WORK FOR GOD. By the Right Rev. Bishop COTTERILL.

MY OBJECT IN LIFE. By the Ven. Archdeacon FARRAR, D.D.

MY ASPIRATIONS. By the Rev. G. MATHESON, D.D.

MY EMOTIONAL LIFE. By the Rev. Preb. CHADWICK, D.D.

MY BODY. By the Rev. Prof. W. G. BLAIKIE, D.D.

MY GROWTH IN DIVINE LIFE. By the Rev. Preb. REYNOLDS, M.A.

MY SOUL. By the Rev. P. B. POWER, M.A.

MY HEREAFTER. By the Very Rev. Dean BICKERSTETH.

MY WALK WITH GOD. By the Very Rev. Dean MONTGOMERY.

MY AIDS TO THE DIVINE LIFE. By the Very Rev. Dean BOYLE.

MY SOURCES OF STRENGTH. By the Rev. E. E. JENKINS, M.A., Secretary of Wesleyan Missionary Society.

Helps to Belief. A Series of Helpful Manuals on the Religious Difficulties of the Day. Edited by the Rev. TEIGNMOUTH SHORE, M.A., Canon of Worcester, and Chaplain-in-Ordinary to the Queen. Cloth, 1s. each.

CREATION. By the Lord Bishop of Carlisle.

THE DIVINITY OF OUR LORD. By the Lord Bishop of Derry.

THE MORALITY OF THE OLD TESTAMENT. By the Rev. Newman Smyth, D.D.

MIRACLES. By the Rev. Brownlow Maitland, M.A.

PRAYER. By the Rev. T. Teignmouth Shore, M.A.

THE ATONEMENT. By William Connor Magee, D.D., Late Archbishop of York.

Holy Land and the Bible, The. By the Rev. CUNNINGHAM GEIKIE, D.D. Two Vols., with Map, 24s. *Illustrated Edition,* One Vol., 21s.

Lectures on Christianity and Socialism. By the Right Rev. ALFRED BARRY, D.D. Cloth, 3s. 6d.

Life of Christ, The. By the Ven. Archdeacon FARRAR, D.D., F.R.S. ILLUSTRATED EDITION, morocco antique, 42s. CHEAP ILLUSTRATED EDITION. Cloth, 7s. 6d. ; cloth, full gilt, gilt edges, 10s. 6d. LIBRARY EDITION. Two Vols. Cloth, 24s. ; morocco, 42s. POPULAR EDITION, in One Vol., 8vo, cloth, 6s. ; cloth, gilt edges, 7s. 6d. ; Persian morocco, gilt edges, 10s. 6d. ; tree-calf, 15s.

Marriage Ring, The. By WILLIAM LANDELS, D.D. *New and Cheaper Edition.* 3s. 6d.

Moses and Geology ; or, The Harmony of the Bible with Science. By the Rev. SAMUEL KINNS, Ph.D., F.R.A.S. Illustrated. *Cheap Edition,* 6s.

My Comfort in Sorrow. By HUGH MACMILLAN, D.D., LL.D., F.R.S.E., &c. Cloth, 1s.

New Testament Commentary for English Readers, The. Edited by the Rt. Rev. C. J. ELLICOTT, D.D., Lord Bishop of Gloucester and Bristol. In Three Volumes. 21s. each. Vol. I.—The Four Gospels. Vol. II.—The Acts, Romans, Corinthians, Galatians. Vol. III.—The remaining Books of the New Testament.

New Testament Commentary. Edited by Bishop ELLICOTT. Handy Volume Edition. St. Matthew, 3s. 6d. St. Mark, 3s. 6d. St. Luke, 3s. 6d. St. John, 3s. 6d. The Acts of the Apostles, 3s. 6d. Romans, 2s. 6d. Corinthians I. and II., 3s. Galatians, Ephesians, and Philippians, 3s. Colossians, Thessalonians, and Timothy, 3s. Titus, Philemon, Hebrews, and James, 3s. Peter, Jude, and John, 3s. The Revelation, 3s. An Introduction to the New Testament, 3s. 6d.

Old Testament Commentary for English Readers, The. Edited by the Right Rev. C. J. ELLICOTT, D.D., Lord Bishop of Gloucester and Bristol. Complete in Five Vols. 21s. each. Vol. I.—Genesis to Numbers. Vol. II.—Deuteronomy to Samuel II. Vol. III.—Kings I. to Esther. Vol. IV.—Job to Isaiah. Vol. V.—Jeremiah to Malachi.

Old Testament Commentary. Edited by Bishop ELLICOTT. Handy Volume Edition. Genesis, 3s. 6d. Exodus, 3s. Leviticus, 3s. Numbers, 2s. 6d. Deuteronomy, 2s. 6d.

Protestantism, The History of. By the Rev. J. A. WYLIE, LL.D. Containing upwards of 600 Original Illustrations. Three Vols. 9s. each.

Quiver Yearly Volume, The. 250 high-class Illustrations. 7s. 6d.

Religion, The Dictionary of. By the Rev. W. BENHAM, B.D. *Cheap Edition.* 10s. 6d.

St. George for England ; and other Sermons preached to Children. By the Rev. T. TEIGNMOUTH SHORE, M.A., Canon of Worcester. 5s.

St. Paul, The Life and Work of. By the Ven. Archdeacon FARRAR, D.D., F.R.S., Chaplain-in-Ordinary to the Queen. LIBRARY EDITION. Two Vols., cloth, 24s. ; calf, 42s. ILLUSTRATED EDITION, complete in One Volume, with about 300 Illustrations, £1 1s. ; morocco, £2 2s. POPULAR EDITION. One Volume, 8vo, cloth, 6s. ; cloth, gilt edges, 7s. 6d. ; Persian morocco, 10s. 6d. ; tree-calf, 15s.

Shall We Know One Another in Heaven? By the Rt. Rev. J. C. RYLE, D.D., Bishop of Liverpool. *Cheap Edition.* Paper covers, 6d.

Signa Christi: Evidences of Christianity set forth in the Person and Work of Christ. By the Rev. JAMES AITCHISON. 5s.

"Sunday," Its Origin, History, and Present Obligation. By the Ven. Archdeacon HESSEY, D.C.L. *Fifth Edition.* 7s. 6d.

Twilight of Life, The. Words of Counsel and Comfort for the Aged. By the Rev. JOHN ELLERTON, M.A. 1s. 6d.

Educational Works and Students' Manuals.

Agricultural Series, Cassell's. Edited by JOHN WRIGHTSON, Professor of Agriculture.
   Crops. By Professor WRIGHTSON. **2s. 6d.**
   Soils and Manures. By J. M. H. MUNRO, D.Sc. (London), F.I.C., F.C.S. **2s. 6d.**
Alphabet, Cassell's Pictorial. 3s. 6d.
Arithmetics, The Modern School. By GEORGE RICKS, B.Sc. Lond. With Test Cards. (*List on application.*)
Atlas, Cassell's Popular. Containing 24 Coloured Maps. **3s. 6d.**
Book-Keeping. By THEODORE JONES. For Schools, **2s.**; cloth, **3s.** For the Million, **2s.**; cloth, **3s.** Books for Jones's System, **2s.**
Chemistry, The Public School. By J. H. ANDERSON, M.A. **2s. 6d.**
Classical Texts for Schools, Cassell's. (*A List post free on application.*)
Cookery for Schools. By LIZZIE HERITAGE. **6d.**
Copy-Books, Cassell's Graduated. *Eighteen Books.* **2d. each.**
Copy-Books, The Modern School. *Twelve Books.* **2d. each.**
Drawing Copies, Cassell's Modern School Freehand. First Grade, **1s.**; Second Grade, **2s.**
Drawing Copies, Cassell's "New Standard." *Complete in Fourteen Books.* **2d., 3d., and 4d. each.**
Electricity, Practical. By Prof. W. E. AYRTON. **7s. 6d.**
Energy and Motion. By WILLIAM PAICE, M.A. Illustrated. **1s. 6d.**
English Literature, First Sketch of. By Prof. MORLEY. **7s. 6d.**
English Literature, The Story of. By ANNA BUCKLAND. **3s. 6d.**
Euclid, Cassell's. Edited by Prof. WALLACE, M.A. **1s.**
Euclid, The First Four Books of. *New Edition.* In paper, **6d.**; cloth, **9d.**
Experimental Geometry. By PAUL BERT. Illustrated. **1s. 6d.**
French, Cassell's Lessons in. *New and Revised Edition.* Parts I. and II., each **2s. 6d.**; complete, **4s. 6d.** Key, **1s. 6d.**
French-English and English-French Dictionary. *Entirely New and Enlarged Edition.* 1,150 pages, 8vo, cloth, **3s. 6d.**
French Reader, Cassell's Public School. By G. S. CONRAD. **2s. 6d.**
Gaudeamus. Songs for Colleges and Schools. Edited by JOHN FARMER. **5s.** Words only, paper covers, **6d.**; cloth, **9d.**
German Dictionary, Cassell's New. German-English, English-German. *Cheap Edition.* Cloth, **3s. 6d.**
German of To-Day. By Dr. HEINEMANN. **1s. 6d.**
German Reading, First Lessons in. By A. JAGST. Illustrated. **1s.**
Hand-and-Eye Training. By G. RICKS, B.Sc. 2 Vols., with 16 Coloured Plates in each Vol. Cr. 4to, **6s. each.** Cards for Class Use, 5 sets, **1s. each.**
"Hand-and-Eye Training Cards." Five Sets in Case. **1s. each.**
Handbook of New Code of Regulations. By J. F. MOSS. **1s.**; cloth, **2s.**
Historical Cartoons, Cassell's Coloured. Size 45 in. × 35 in., **2s. each.** Mounted on canvas and varnished, with rollers, **5s. each.**
Historical Course for Schools, Cassell's. Illustrated throughout.
   I.—Stories from English History, **1s.** II.—The Simple Outline of English History, **1s. 3d.** III.—The Class History of England, **2s. 6d.**
Latin-English Dictionary, Cassell's. By J. R. V. MARCHANT, **3s. 6d.**
Latin Primer, The First. By Prof. POSTGATE. **1s.**
Latin Primer, The New. By Prof. J. P. POSTGATE. Crown 8vo, **2s. 6d.**
Latin Prose for Lower Forms. By M. A. BAYFIELD, M.A. **2s. 6d.**
Laundry Work (How to Teach It). By Mrs. E. LORD. **6d.**
Laws of Every-Day Life. By H. O. ARNOLD-FORSTER. **1s. 6d.**
Little Folks' History of England. Illustrated. **1s. 6d.**
Making of the Home, The. By Mrs. SAMUEL A. BARNETT. **1s. 6d.**
Map-Building Series, Cassell's. Outline Maps prepared by H. O. ARNOLD-FORSTER. Per Set of Twelve, **1s.**

Marlborough Books:—Arithmetic Examples, 3s. Arithmetic Rules, 1s. 6d. French Exercises, 3s. 6d. French Grammar, 2s. 6d. German do., 3s. 6d.

Mechanics for Young Beginners, A First Book of. By the Rev. J. G. EASTON, M.A. 4s. 6d.

Mechanics and Machine Design, Numerical Examples in Practical. By R. G. BLAINE, M.E. With Diagrams. Cloth, 2s. 6d.

"Model Joint" Wall Sheets, for Instruction in Manual Training. By S. BARTER. Eight Sheets, 2s. 6d. each.

Natural History Coloured Wall Sheets, Cassell's New. 18 Subjects. Size, 39 by 31 in. Mounted on rollers and varnished. 3s. each.

Object Lessons from Nature. By Prof. L. C. MIALL, F.L.S. 2s. 6d.

Physiology for Schools. By ALFRED T. SCHOFIELD, M.D., M.R.C.S. 1s. 9d. ; Three Parts, paper covers, 5d. each.

Poetry Readers, Cassell's New. Illustrated. 12 Books. 1d. each.

Popular Educator, Cassell's NEW. With Revised Text, New Maps, New Coloured Plates, New Type, &c. To be completed in 8 Vols. 5s. each.

Readers, Cassell's "Higher Class." (*List on application.*)

Readers, Cassell's Historical. Illustrated. (*List on application.*)

Readers, Cassell's Readable. Illustrated. (*List on application.*)

Readers for Infant Schools, Coloured. Three Books. 4d. each.

Reader, The Citizen. By H. O. ARNOLD-FORSTER. Illustrated. 1s. 6d.

Reader, The Empire. By G. R. PARKIN. 1s. 6d

Reader, The Temperance. By Rev. J. DENNIS HIRD. Cr. 8vo, 1s. 6d.

Readers, The "Modern School" Geographical. (*List on application.*)

Readers, The "Modern School." Illustrated. (*List on application.*)

Reckoning, Howard's Anglo-American Art of. By C. FRUSHER HOWARD. Paper covers, 1s. ; cloth, 2s. *Large Paper Edition*, 5s.

Round World, The. By H. O. ARNOLD-FORSTER. 3s. 6d.

School Certificates, Cassell's. Three Colours, 6¼ × 4¾ in., 1d. ; Five Colours, 11¾ × 9¼ in., 3d. ; Seven Colours and Gold, 9⅞ × 6¾ in., 3d.

Science Applied to Work. By J. A. BOWER. 1s.

Science of Everyday Life. By J. A. BOWER. Illustrated. 1s.

Shade from Models, Common Objects, and Casts of Ornament, How to. By W. E. SPARKES. With 25 Plates by the Author. 3s.

Shakspere's Plays for School Use. 5 Books. Illustrated. 6d. each.

Shakspere Reading Book, The. Illustrated. 3s. 6d.

Spelling, A Complete Manual of. By J. D. MORELL, LL.D. 1s.

Technical Manuals, Cassell's. Illustrated throughout :—
Handrailing and Staircasing, 3s. 6d.—Bricklayers, Drawing for, 3s.— Building Construction, 2s. — Cabinet-Makers, Drawing for, 3s. — Carpenters and Joiners, Drawing for, 3s. 6d.—Gothic Stonework, 3s. —Linear Drawing and Practical Geometry, 2s.—Linear Drawing and Projection. The Two Vols. in One, 3s. 6d.—Machinists and Engineers, Drawing for, 4s. 6d.—Metal-Plate Workers, Drawing for, 3s.—Model Drawing, 3s.—Orthographical and Isometrical Projection, 2s.—Practical Perspective, 3s.—Stonemasons, Drawing for, 3s.—Applied Mechanics, by Sir R. S. Ball, LL.D., 2s.—Systematic Drawing and Shading, 2s.

Technical Educator, Cassell's. *Revised Edition.* Four Vols. 5s. each.

Technology, Manuals of. Edited by Prof. AYRTON, F.R.S., and RICHARD WORMELL, D.Sc., M.A. Illustrated throughout :— The Dyeing of Textile Fabrics, by Prof. Hummel, 5s.—Watch and Clock Making, by D. Glasgow, Vice-President of the British Horological Institute, 4s. 6d.—Steel and Iron, by Prof. W. H. Greenwood, F.C.S., M.I.C.E., &c., 5s.—Spinning Woollen and Worsted, by W. S. B. McLaren, M.P., 4s. 6d.—Design in Textile Fabrics, by T. R. Ashenhurst, 4s. 6d.—Practical Mechanics, by Prof. Perry, M.E., 3s. 6d.— Cutting Tools Worked by Hand and Machine, by Prof. Smith, 3s. 6d. (*A Prospectus on application.*)

CASSELL & COMPANY, LIMITED, *Ludgate Hill, London.*

Books for Young People.

"Little Folks" Half-Yearly Volume. Containing 432 4to pages, with about 200 Illustrations, and Pictures in Colour. Boards, 3s. 6d.; cloth, 5s.

Bo-Peep. A Book for the Little Ones. With Original Stories and Verses. Illustrated throughout. Yearly Volume. Boards, 2s. 6d.; cloth, 3s. 6d.

Pleasant Work for Busy Fingers. By MAGGIE BROWNE. Illustrated. 5s.

Cassell's Pictorial Scrap Book, containing several thousand Pictures. Coloured boards, 15s.; cloth lettered, 21s. Also in Six Sectional Vols., 3s. 6d. each.

The Marvellous Budget: being 65,536 Stories of Jack and Jill. By the Rev. F. BENNETT. Illustrated. 2s. 6d.

Schoolroom and Home Theatricals. By ARTHUR WAUGH. Illustrated. 2s. 6d.

Magic at Home. By Prof. HOFFMAN. Illustrated. Cloth gilt, 5s.

"Little Folks" Painting Book, The New. Containing nearly 350 Outline Illustrations suitable for Colouring. 1s.

Little Mother Bunch. By Mrs. MOLESWORTH. Illustrated. Cloth, 3s. 6d.

Ships, Sailors, and the Sea. By R. J. CORNEWALL-JONES. *Cheap Edition.* Illustrated. Cloth, 2s. 6d.

Famous Sailors of Former Times. By CLEMENTS MARKHAM. Illustrated. 2s. 6d.

The Tales of the Sixty Mandarins. By P. V. RAMASWAMI RAJU. With an Introduction by Prof. HENRY MORLEY. Illustrated. 5s.

Pictures of School Life and Boyhood. Selected from the best Authors. Edited by PERCY FITZGERALD, M.A. 2s. 6d.

Heroes of Every-day Life. By LAURA LANE. With about 20 Full-page Illustrations. Cloth. 2s. 6d.

Books for Young People. Illustrated. Cloth gilt, 5s. each.

The Champion of Odin; or, Viking Life in the Days of Old. By J. Fred. Hodgetts.	Under Bayard's Banner. By Henry Frith.
The Romance of Invention. By James Burnley.	Bound by a Spell; or, The Hunted Witch of the Forest. By the Hon. Mrs. Greene.

Books for Young People. Illustrated. 3s. 6d. each.

The White House at Inch Gow. By Mrs. Pitt.	Polly: A New-Fashioned Girl. By L. T. Meade.
A Sweet Girl Graduate. By L. T. Meade.	"Follow My Leader." By Talbot Baines Reed. [Pitt.
The King's Command: A Story for Girls. By Maggie Symington.	The Cost of a Mistake. By Sarah
Lost in Samoa. A Tale of Adventure in the Navigator Islands. By Edward S. Ellis.	A World of Girls: The Story of a School. By L. T. Meade.
Tad; or, "Getting Even" with Him. By Edward S. Ellis.	Lost among White Africans. By David Ker.
For Fortune and Glory: A Story of the Soudan War. By Lewis Hough.	The Palace Beautiful. By L. T. Meade.
	On Board the "Esmeralda." By John C. Hutcheson.
	In Quest of Gold. By A. St. Johnston.

Crown 8vo Library. *Cheap Editions.* 2s. 6d. each.

Rambles Round London. By C. L. Matéaux. Illustrated.	Wild Adventures in Wild Places. By Dr. Gordon Stables, R.N. Illustrated.
Around and About Old England. By C. L. Matéaux. Illustrated.	Modern Explorers. By Thomas Frost. Illustrated. *New and Cheaper Edition.*
Paws and Claws. By one of the Authors of "Poems written for a Child." Illustrated.	Early Explorers. By Thomas Frost.
Decisive Events in History. By Thomas Archer. With Original Illustrations.	Home Chat with our Young Folks. Illustrated throughout.
The True Robinson Crusoes. Cloth gilt.	Jungle, Peak, and Plain. Illustrated throughout.
Peeps Abroad for Folks at Home. Illustrated throughout.	The England of Shakespeare. By E. Goadby. With Full-page Illustrations.

The "Cross and Crown" Series. Illustrated. 2s. 6d. each.

Freedom's Sword: A Story of the Days of Wallace and Bruce. By Annie S. Swan.
Strong to Suffer: A Story of the Jews. By E. Wynne.
Heroes of the Indian Empire; or, Stories of Valour and Victory. By Ernest Foster.
In Letters of Flame: A Story of the Waldenses. By C. L. Matéaux.

Through Trial to Triumph. By Madeline B. Hunt.
By Fire and Sword: A Story of the Huguenots. By Thomas Archer.
Adam Hepburn's Vow: A Tale of Kirk and Covenant. By Annie S. Swan.
No. XIII.; or, The Story of the Lost Vestal. A Tale of Early Christian Days. By Emma Marshall.

"Golden Mottoes" Series, The. Each Book containing 208 pages, with Four full-page Original Illustrations. Crown 8vo, cloth gilt, 2s. each.

"Nil Desperandum." By the Rev. F. Langbridge, M.A.
"Bear and Forbear." By Sarah Pitt.
"Foremost if I Can." By Helen Atteridge.

"Honour is my Guide." By Jeanie Hering (Mrs. Adams-Acton).
"Aim at a Sure End." By Emily Searchfield.
"He Conquers who Endures." By the Author of "May Cunningham's Trial." &c.

Cassell's Picture Story Books. Each containing about Sixty Pages of Pictures and Stories, &c. 6d. each.

Little Talks. | Daisy's Story Book. | Auntie's Stories.
Bright Stars. | Dot's Story Book. | Birdie's Story Book.
Nursery Toys. | A Nest of Stories. | Little Chimes.
Pet's Posy. | Good-Night Stories. | A Sheaf of Tales.
Tiny Tales. | Chats for Small Chatterers. | Dewdrop Stories.

Cassell's Sixpenny Story Books. All Illustrated, and containing Interesting Stories by well-known writers.

The Smuggler's Cave.
Little Lizzie.
Little Bird, Life and Adventures of.
Luke Barnicott.
The Delft Jug.

The Boat Club.
Little Pickles.
The Elchester College Boys.
My First Cruise.
The Little Peacemaker.

Cassell's Shilling Story Books. All Illustrated, and containing Interesting Stories.

Bunty and the Boys.
The Heir of Elmdale.
The Mystery at Shoncliff School.
Claimed at Last, and Roy's Reward.
Thorns and Tangles.
The Cuckoo in the Robin's Nest.
John's Mistake.
The History of Five Little Pitchers.
Diamonds in the Sand.

Surly Bob.
The Giant's Cradle.
Shag and Doll.
Aunt Lucia's Locket.
The Magic Mirror.
The Cost of Revenge.
Clever Frank.
Among the Redskins.
The Ferryman of Brill.
Harry Maxwell.
A Banished Monarch.
Seventeen Cats.

Illustrated Books for the Little Ones. Containing interesting Stories. All Illustrated. 1s. each; cloth gilt, 1s. 6d.

Scrambles and Scrapes.
Tittle Tattle Tales.
Up and Down the Garden.
All Sorts of Adventures.
Our Sunday Stories.
Our Holiday Hours.
Indoors and Out.
Some Farm Friends.

Wandering Ways.
Dumb Friends.
Those Golden Sands.
Little Mothers & their Children.
Our Pretty Pets.
Our Schoolday Hours.
Creatures Tame.
Creatures Wild.

Albums for Children. 3s. 6d. each.

The Album for Home, School, and Play. Containing Stories by Popular Authors. Illustrated.
My Own Album of Animals. With Full-page Illustrations.

Picture Album of All Sorts. With Full-page Illustrations.
The Chit-Chat Album. Illustrated throughout.

"Wanted—a King" Series. Illustrated. 3s. 6d. each.
    Great Grandmamma and Elsie. By Georgina M. Synge.
    Robin's Ride. By Miss E. Davenport Adams.
    Wanted—a King; or, How Merle set the Nursery Rhymes to Rights.
       By Maggie Browne. With Original Designs by Harry Furniss.

The World's Workers. A Series of New and Original Volumes.
    With Portraits printed on a tint as Frontispiece. 1s. each.

Dr. Arnold of Rugby. By Rose E. Selfe.

The Earl of Shaftesbury. By Henry Frith.

Sarah Robinson, Agnes Weston, and Mrs. Meredith. By E. M. Tomkinson.

Thomas A. Edison and Samuel F. B. Morse. By Dr. Denslow and J. Marsh Parker.

Mrs. Somerville and Mary Carpenter. By Phyllis Browne.

General Gordon. By the Rev. S. A. Swaine.

Charles Dickens. By his Eldest Daughter.

Sir Titus Salt and George Moore. By J. Burnley.

David Livingstone. By Robert Smiles.

Florence Nightingale, Catherine Marsh, Frances Ridley Havergal, Mrs. Ranyard ("L. N. R."). By Lizzie Alldridge.

Dr. Guthrie, Father Mathew, Elihu Burritt, George Livesey. By John W. Kirton, LL.D.

Sir Henry Havelock and Colin Campbell Lord Clyde. By E. C. Phillips.

Abraham Lincoln. By Ernest Foster.

George Müller and Andrew Reed. By E. R. Pitman.

Richard Cobden. By R. Gowing.

Benjamin Franklin. By E. M. Tomkinson.

Handel. By Eliza Clarke. [Swaine.

Turner the Artist. By the Rev. S. A.

George and Robert Stephenson. By C. L. Matéaux.

** *The above Works (excluding* RICHARD COBDEN*) can also be had Three in One Vol., cloth, gilt edges,* 3s.

Library of Wonders. Illustrated Gift-books for Boys. Paper, 1s.; cloth, 1s. 6d.
    Wonderful Adventures.
    Wonders of Animal Instinct.
    Wonderful Balloon Ascents.
    Wonders of Bodily Strength and Skill.
    Wonderful Escapes.

Cassell's Eighteenpenny Story Books. Illustrated.

Wee Willie Winkie.

Ups and Downs of a Donkey's Life.

Three Wee Ulster Lassies.

Up the Ladder.

Dick's Hero; and other Stories.

The Chip Boy.

Raggles, Baggles, and the Emperor.

Roses from Thorns.

Faith's Father.

By Land and Sea.

The Young Berringtons.

Jeff and Leff.

Tom Morris's Error.

Worth more than Gold.

"Through Flood—Through Fire;" and other Stories.

The Girl with the Golden Locks.

Stories of the Olden Time.

Gift Books for Young People. By Popular Authors. With Four Original Illustrations in each. Cloth gilt, 1s. 6d. each.

The Boy Hunters of Kentucky. By Edward S. Ellis.

Red Feather: a Tale of the American Frontier. By Edward S. Ellis.

Seeking a City.

Rhoda's Reward; or, "If Wishes were Horses."

Jack Marston's Anchor.

Frank's Life-Battle; or, The Three Friends.

Fritters. By Sarah Pitt.

The Two Hardcastles. By Madeline Bonavia Hunt.

Major Monk's Motto. By the Rev. F. Langbridge.

Trixy. By Maggie Symington.

Rags and Rainbows: A Story of Thanksgiving.

Uncle William's Charges; or, The Broken Trust.

Pretty Pink's Purpose; or, The Little Street Merchants.

Tim Thomson's Trial. By George Weatherly.

Ursula's Stumbling-Block. By Julia Goddard.

Ruth's Life-Work. By the Rev. Joseph Johnson.

Cassell's Two-Shilling Story Books. Illustrated.

Stories of the Tower.

Mr. Burke's Nieces.

May Cunningham's Trial.

The Top of the Ladder: How to Reach it. [Reach it.

Little Flotsam.

Madge and Her Friends.

The Children of the Court.

A Moonbeam Tangle.

Maid Marjory.

Peggy, and other Tales.

The Four Cats of the Tippertons.

Marion's Two Homes.

Little Folks' Sunday Book.

Two Fourpenny Bits.

Poor Nelly.

Tom Heriot.

Through Peril to Fortune.

Aunt Tabitha's Waifs.

In Mischief Again.

School Girls.

Cheap Editions of Popular Volumes for Young People. Bound in cloth, gilt edges, 2s. 6d. each.

For Queen and King. | Three Homes.
Esther West. | Working to Win.
Perils Afloat and Brigands Ashore.

The "Deerfoot" Series. By EDWARD S. ELLIS. With Four full-page Illustrations in each Book. Cloth, bevelled boards, 2s. 6d. each.

The Hunters of the Ozark. | The Camp in the Mountains.
The Last War Trail.

The "Log Cabin" Series. By EDWARD S. ELLIS. With Four Full-page Illustrations in each. Crown 8vo, cloth, 2s. 6d. each.

The Lost Trail. | Camp-Fire and Wigwam.
Footprints in the Forest.

The "Great River" Series. By EDWARD S. ELLIS. Illustrated. Crown 8vo, cloth, bevelled boards, 2s. 6d. each.

Down the Mississippi. | Lost in the Wilds.
Up the Tapajos; or, Adventures in Brazil.

The "Boy Pioneer" Series. By EDWARD S. ELLIS. With Four Full-page Illustrations in each Book. Crown 8vo, cloth, 2s. 6d. each.

Ned in the Woods. A Tale of | Ned on the River. A Tale of Indian
Early Days in the West. | River Warfare.
Ned in the Block House. A Story of Pioneer Life in Kentucky.

The "World in Pictures." Illustrated throughout. 2s. 6d. each.

A Ramble Round France. | The Eastern Wonderland (Japan).
All the Russias. | Glimpses of South America.
Chats about Germany. | Round Africa.
The Land of the Pyramids | The Land of Temples (India).
(Egypt). | The Isles of the Pacific.
Peeps into China.

Half-Crown Story Books.

Little Hinges. | Soldier and Patriot (George Wash-
Margaret's Enemy. | ington).
Pen's Perplexities. | The Young Man in the Battle of
Notable Shipwrecks. | Life. By the Rev. Dr. Landels.
Golden Days. | The True Glory of Woman. By the
Wonders of Common Things. | Rev. Dr. Landels.
Truth will Out. | At the South Pole.

Three-and-Sixpenny Library of Standard Tales, &c. All Illustrated and bound in cloth gilt. Crown 8vo. 3s. 6d. each.

The Half Sisters. | Krilof and his Fables. By W. R. S.
Peggy Oglivie's Inheritance. | Ralston, M.A.
The Family Honour. | Fairy Tales. By Prof. Morley.

Books for the Little Ones.

Rhymes for the Young Folk. | The Old Fairy Tales. With Original
By William Allingham. Beautifully | Illustrations. Boards, 1s.; cl., 1s. 6d.
Illustrated. 3s. 6d. | My Diary. With 12 Coloured Plates
The Pilgrim's Progress. With | and 366 Woodcuts. 1s.
Coloured Illustrations. 2s. 6d. |
The History Scrap Book. With | The Sunday Scrap Book. With
nearly 1,000 Engravings. 5s.; | One Thousand Scripture Pictures.
cloth, 7s. 6d. | Boards, 5s.; cloth, 7s. 6d.

Cassell & Company's Complete Catalogue *will be sent post free on application to*

CASSELL & COMPANY, LIMITED, *Ludgate Hill, London.*

information can be obtained at www.ICGtesting.com
'e USA
'120313

'9011B/547/P

9 781175 098368